OUR STORIES, OUR LIVES

A Collection of Twenty-Three Transcribed
Interviews with Elders of the Cook Inlet Region

By
A.J. McClanahan

General Introduction
By
Ron Scollon

About the Cover: *Storyknives:* Yaaruin (Yupik)

Stories serve as a way of providing instruction and as a meaningful way to pass on Native legends and myths.

Storyknives were used by young girls to draw pictures in the mud or snow to illustrate their stories. They were made by the young girl's father out of ivory, antler or wood.

Through the story telling process a child would learn moral values and the traditions of their society. Through the words and pictures pass the legends, lives, dramas and deeds of a culture that will never die so long as there is a memory with voices to make the words and hands to draw upon the earth.

Kathy Kiefer

Photography — Douglas Van Reeth, Kathy Kiefer, B. Agnes Brown, Michael Ross, Arlene Reiser, Doug Wilson, page 106 and Anchorage Times, page 92.

Cover Design — Kathy Kiefer

Review Committee — Clare Swan (Kenai), John Monfor (Kenai), Emil McCord, Sr. (Tyonek), Leo Stephan (Anchorage), Dr. Nancy Yaw Davis (Anchorage), Dr. William Workman (Anchorage) and Karen Workman (Anchorage).

Graphic Design, and Typesetting — Alaska Media Productions

Publication of *Our Stories, Our Lives* is funded by a generous grant from ALASCOM, Inc. and by grants from the Alaska Humanities Forum and The CIRI Foundation.

Table of Contents

Forward

The statements and private remembrances in this book are exercises in what might be called the collective memory of a people. They are reminders of the extraordinary pace of change for Native people in Alaska, and particularly for the shareholders in Cook Inlet Region, Inc. — over 6,300 Alaska Eskimos, Indians and Aleuts. Probably more has occurred in the last one or two generations to change their world than had occurred in the preceding one hundred generations. It is startling to see the accommodations that have taken place, accommodations that have been eased in some instances and aggravated in others by the passage of the Alaska Native Claims Settlement Act in 1971.

The pace of change itself is reason enough to invest in the task of remembering. Without overt effort, without the kind of nourishing of the past that this book represents, the next generations will have an even remoter sense of their foundations. It is well that The CIRI Foundation has undertaken this project, supplementing other efforts to help strengthen the heritage of the Natives of the Cook Inlet region.

This is a book, not only for Alaska Natives, but for all who are concerned about the role of memory, of consciousness of the past and of cultural tradition in the building of personality and community. Our gratitude should be to the participants in the book and those whom they represent, for taking the time and undergoing the reflective pain in helping the rest of us understand whence we come and our contribution to this land.

Roy M. Huhndorf, President
Cook Inlet Region, Inc.

Preface

The following stories of 23 Alaska Native shareholders of Cook Inlet Region, Inc. speak for themselves.

Many of the people are incredibly candid. Their stories are the stories of human beings who have endured painful things in their lives. And yet, they are the stories of people who have overcome difficulties with both grace and humor.

Because these people come from such different geographical and cultural backgrounds it is difficult to pinpoint specific themes that are a common thread in their stories.

But perhaps the one common focus throughout their lives has been their goal of living with dignity. They are not complainers. Although many have had to do without in their lives — without education, without luxuries and sometimes even without food — they don't tell a tale of woe.

Many of these people have migrated into the Cook Inlet region from distant corners of Alaska, and they have brought with them diverse cultural backgrounds.

Specifically, however, some themes show up. Alcohol abuse has been a problem for some of the people and most of their lives have been affected in one way or another by it.

Food — and its gathering — often has been a major focus of family life. Illness — particularly the deadly flu epidemics in early years, tuberculosis and infant mortality — has taken its toll.

In addition, several of the people said they are happy with today's amenities, although there is a distinct longing for the past in some stories.

The shareholders interviewed for this project in 1985 generally have been somewhat reticent to discuss their private lives. They guard their privacy, and frequently they go to great pains to avoid the limelight.

Generally they agreed to participate because of their desire to communicate a bit of their view of the world to young people.

The shareholders selected for this book were chosen in an effort to represent all of Alaska's major Native groups. They were selected from among the corporation's shareholders who are at least 55 years old.

Most of these stories came from one taped interview with each person, lasting up to two or three hours or more. Although I generally asked people the same questions — such as what food they ate, what their homes were like, whether church was important to them and how they felt about being Native in a predominately white world — the answers ranged from deeply personal events in their lives to funny anecdotes.

I have edited the tape transcripts to the extent of rearranging some material. Occasionally words have been changed for purposes of clarification, such as spelling out an abbreviation.

In most cases I have simply sought to put the information in a somewhat chronological order. I also have deleted much material in an effort to keep the project manageable.

I am indebted to these people for their patience. I also am grateful to my husband, John T. Shively, for his understanding throughout this project, and my CIRI Foundation supervisor, Lydia Hays, for her gentle guidance.

Alexandra J. McClanahan

Our Villages In Alaska

Wiseman ●

● Candle

Bethel
Tyonek ● Talkeetna
Old Iliamna ●

Enlarged
Area

Sitka

Unalaska
● Unga

Metlakatla

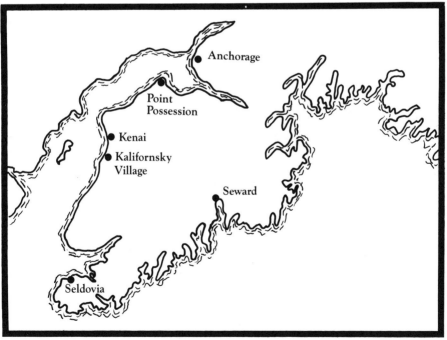

● Anchorage

Point
Possession

● Kenai

● Kalifornsky
Village

Seward

Seldovia

9

General Introduction

A laska is a state of newcomers. Very few of us remember Anchorage when it was a few buildings along a single mud street now called Fourth Avenue. There are not even many who remember Fourth Avenue before the buildings on the north side of the street dropped one story in the Good Friday earthquake of 1964. A large number of Alaskans were not here at the time of the Alaska Native Claims Settlement Act in 1971.

Most of our parents and grandparents live elsewhere. We cannot go to them to learn what life was like here in Alaska before we came, before the settlement act and the pipeline, before statehood, or before the Second World War. We cannot ask them what effects these events have had on the people who lived here then and what effects they have had upon the land.

For this knowledge we turn to the true elders of Alaska, the people whose land it is — the ones who were born and raised here. They can help us know our past and give us guidance for our future.

Here in this book we have the thoughts and reflections of 23 of our elders. The oldest among them was born before the turn of the century. The youngest was born during the Depression. In their lives these 23 elders have seen two world wars, the terrible flu epidemic of 1917 and 1918, widespread death, disability, and dislocation from tuberculosis and more recently the tremendous impacts of statehood, oil development and the settlement act.

These elders have experienced the introduction of education and laws made elsewhere for other people. In their lifetimes they have seen Alaska tugged and pulled by worldwide social, political and economic forces. Many of them are children of those who, while living in their own land, have experienced the culture shock of shifting languages and cultural values that we normally think of as happening only to immigrants. In many ways they have become like immigrants in their own land.

These 23 elders speak with eloquence, dignity and good humor about significant historical events, events that parallel the history of North America. It was Columbus who first brought North America to the attention of Europe in 1492, just about 500 years ago. From that time on Europeans have seen North America as a place of resources and riches for Europeans, first by exporting those resources and then by inhabiting the lands themselves.

Nevertheless, it took Europeans some 250 years to reach Alaska. It was a Danish sailor in the employ of Russia sailing East out of Kamchatka with a Russian party who arrived first. At the time of Vitus Berings's sailing, Alaska was indeed a rich land, not that the Russians ever saw much of it. The vast area which is now called Alaska was home for people who spoke some 20 languages as different from each other in some cases as any in the world. It was a country larger than Europe with greater internal cultural, geographic, and climatic diversity — far too rich and varied a land to be comprehended with a single name.

Yet much in the same way that all of the lands of the Western Hemisphere came to be called "America" and the original inhabitants "Indians," all of the land on the Alaska Peninsula east of Russia was called "Alaska" and its inhabitants "Aleuts." In time the name "Alaska" came to be extended to the entire contiguous land mass. Modern Alaska had taken its first step toward statehood by a definition brought to it from outside.

The "Russian Period," from 1741 when Bering came to 1867 when Alaska was purchased by the United States, is well known for the exploitation of ocean fur-bearing animals, principally the sea otter, and for a number of incidents of brutality perpetrated on the Native people. The Russians are not so well known, however, for their schools and the literacy they brought to Alaska. The priest Veniaminov, later to become St. Innocent, missionized widely along the coastal region of the land from Unalaska to Sitka. Schools were established, and some Alaska Natives in those regions became literate participants in the church. In at least one case an Aleut became a navigator in the Russian Navy. In addition to literacy in Russian, many became literate in their Native language as well.

While Vitus Bering was sailing east to locate North America, the 13 British Colonies perched on the eastern shore of North America were making their first moves toward independence. From 1976 with the Bicentennial of the Declaration of Independence to 1986 with the Bicentennial of the Constitution of the United States of America we are commemorating not just the independence and nationhood but also a bold experiment in establishing a nation on the basis of a written document. While the Russian missionaries in Alaska were busy seeking to establish literacy and the Orthodox faith among Alaska Natives of the coastal region, Thomas Jefferson, James Madison and Alexander Hamilton were busy establishing a nation based on literacy.

It is no wonder then that by the time Western Europe had come to meet Eastern Europe here in Alaska, literacy and education were at the heart of nearly every issue. It is no less a wonder that the history of Alaska is so often based on paper milestones. Three examples are the Alaska purchase in 1867 (based on a deed of sale), statehood in 1959 (based on a written law), and the settlement act in 1971 (based on a written law).

This literate understanding of events and of people is so much a part of European thinking that with the exception of anthropologists and others specialized in the field we tend to dismiss oral testimony as "hearsay." We tend to ignore the events of the past which do not conform easily to our written descriptions.

Common Themes

The 23 stories in this collection are oral histories. This is not the history you would get from a professional historian. This is the personal history of the lives of 23 people from the turn of the century to the present. The histories were guided by the questions of the interviewer and so show a certain amount of consistency in addressing some themes. At the same time these elders have chosen to speak about issues of importance from their own experience as well.

Certain themes come out again and again in these histories. There are major events mentioned by all or most of the 23 elders. The wars, statehood, and the settlement act are all there and that is not surprising. But the reader is struck by the terrible losses of the flu epidemic of 1917 and 1918. Whole villages died out; other villages were devastated. To stay free of contamination many people were forced to relocate either their own families or their whole villages. If we remember that in some cases a village would constitute the bulk of the population for an entire dialect group, surely the flu epidemic must be seen as a major factor in creating the sense of cultural loss and cultural shock widely spoken of by present Alaska Natives.

Tuberculosis and other respiratory diseases were epidemic. And while they were never so suddenly devastating as the flu epidemic, they also had the effect of widespread debilitation and dislocation. The age-old pattern of family care of the ill was broken when people were placed in sanitoriums. Among those who were removed from their families by illness an appalling number died or were permanently enfeebled. Those who were able to return often felt that they were strangers at home when they returned after so many years.

Another theme that comes up frequently is the mixed ethnicity of many of these elders. Many of them had European fathers or grandfathers, the great majority of whom were Russian or Scandinavian. While some of their fathers were miners or traders, there is among them a surprising number who left Europe to resist or protest the spread of World War I throughout Europe. Alaska was apparently enough like their homes in Russia, or Sweden, or Norway that they could easily adapt to the weather, to fishing our waters, and to the subsistence life. It was also far enough from Europe to be safe from prosecution.

In spite of their mixed ethnicity, or perhaps because of it, there is little in these histories about discrimination. While many Alaska Natives have felt acute discrimination against their culture and language in schools, on the whole these elders felt they have lived their lives freely without being treated negatively by others.

Multilingualism is the natural linguistic climate of virtually all of these elders. While many of them were not themselves bilinguals, they frequently refer to bilingualism in their homes and their communities. The influence of the Orthodox faith on many of them can be seen as it is in one case where a Swedish-speaking father and an Athabaskan-speaking mother used Russian as the language of the home. The restriction to speaking English came about with schooling under the American system, and other languages were suppressed in the process.

Most of these 23 elders from the coastal region of the state tell of their Russian Orthodox faith. For some it is a deeply and consciously held faith to this day. For others it is so much taken for granted that they hardly think of it. Others have rejected it. Several of these elders mention retaining their childhood faith even after other missionaries or other experiences have tried to separate them from it.

All of these elders speak warmly of the places they were raised. They speak with great affection about their early life in the forests, around the lakes, or on the ocean without disguising the hardships and difficulties of that early life. They speak of the yearly cycles. The most frequent cycle they mention is spending the winter in town for school and the summer out preparing the winter food and wood. It is clear from the way they speak that for them town life was only a temporary stop in a life lived on the land.

This is not to say they do not speak with fondness of the towns as well. The fellowship of Fourth Avenue in the early days when that was all there was to Anchorage is not surprising, maybe, but some of them speak of the continued sense of fellowship on Fourth Avenue in today's Anchorage in direct contrast to the more widely held perceptions of degradation.

Of course, the main reason these elders were in town was for education. Some of their parents had a deep belief in the importance of education. Some of their schools were places that the elders remember with great warmth and respect. They often speak of a teacher who befriended them and became a guiding image for the rest of their lives.

For others schools were odious, stifling prisons. There is one story of the escape one of these elders made from a boarding school. It should be remembered that these are people who were expected to be mature, productive people much earlier in life than we now expect. One man speaks of helping to support himself and his family by trapping by the time he was 10 years old. Another mentions the captain of the boat he worked on was only 17. Most of the women were married and beginning their families by age 15. A prolonged education removed from the realities of day to day work and life must have seemed a foreign activity and required difficult adjustments.

The central theme of all these histories is change. Maybe it is not the events themselves which are the most interesting but the attitude of these elders toward change. It reflects their overall attitude toward life. They all emphasize their ability to respond and adapt to conditions rather than attempting to control them. Again and again, they speak of the importance of preparation, of getting oneself ready for what comes along rather than trying themselves to take control of events.

And while all of these elders have shown their great capacity to adapt to conditions and technologies that did not exist when they were children, they all warn us that our present comforts and our present technologies are only temporary. These elders who have seen so much change warn us to prepare ourselves for change. They point out how useless money is in the woods when you need to get in your food, water and wood. They warn us how we have gotten out of the habit of using our bodies and now seem to rely entirely on using our minds. They tell us that the best investment is to prepare for the natural but difficult conditions of the subsistence life.

Not that any of them at their age would choose to return to the difficult life of their childhood. They have the sane dignity to point out how much they appreciate the comforts they now have in older age. They all agree that the hard life is good for younger people but awfully hard for older ones.

Perhaps the key to understanding these histories is their diversity. These people are all different from each other and glad they are. For instance, one of them states quite strongly that different languages and different cultures as well as different life experiences are the key to avoiding the conflict we see in the world today. He believes that too much of the same experiences, the same language, the same goals, produces conflict, and that our path to both interpersonal and international peace is by maintaining diversity in people.

These people have lived rich, full and varied lives. They have taken care of themselves and others by hunting. They have worked at many jobs. They have worked on the railroad, on boats, for hotels, canneries, the military and especially on construction projects. Again and again, they have shown themselves to be capable of finding a new job, learning it and doing it well. This is the life experience that gives them in their older age the confidence that they have known life and that they can adjust to what comes to them.

The theme that unites these oral histories, however, is the theme of respect and leadership. It starts with the reluctance of these elders to talk much about themselves.

15

They do not want to set themselves up as experts. They are almost shy in speaking of their own lives. As you read you will see none of the ego of the usual literate autobiography. You will read of the important people who preceded these elders. You will hear of their own elders, the ones they respected as children — the ones they still hold out as examples today. You will hear them say, "We do this because this is what our grandmothers did." You will read of children in school who are thought to be shy or unresponsive but who are quiet out of deep respect for their teachers. Finally, you will read of great leaders such as Chief Chickalusian who was always looking for a way to help someone in need. This is an important concept of leadership from which we can all learn.

Indirectly these elders have told us their own status. They have taken the time and effort to help us by telling us about their own elders and their own lives and experiences. There is much for all of us to learn from the lives of these elders.

A Note on Transcription

The role of the transcriber in oral history is difficult. In written histories the historian decides what research to do, the historian makes the judgments about which facts to include or which to leave out, and finally the historian sets the tone of the history by careful choice of written style and format.

In an oral history these tasks are divided normally between the oral historian, the project director, and the transcriber. A.J. McClanahan, the project director and transcriber, has achieved a successful balance of preparation with questions, selection of responses, style and format. Although she prepared the interviews with questions that covered a range of subjects from the elders' views on education to their views on the settlement act, she urged them to speak freely about subjects of their own choice. This had the effect of encouraging them to address issues that in her judgment were important but yet allowed the introduction of issues that might otherwise have been missed and shifts in emphasis on points important to the elders.

The biggest problem of oral histories is style. It is usually recognized that written style and spoken style are very different from each other. We are accustomed to seeing only written style in print. As a result, a direct transcription from a tape-recorded spoken interview can often look unprepared or awkward, especially when one or two-line paragraphs are used.

In writing we use paragraph breaks, variation in sentence structure and choice of words to show our emphasis and our attitudes toward what we are saying and toward our readers. In speaking we depend heavily on our tone of voice, our pacing, the feedback we are getting from our listeners and facial and body gestures to express our attitudes and more subtle meanings.

This means that writing down just the words will miss all of these subtle aspects of communication and leave the transcription open to the possibility of misunderstanding. It also may contribute to making the speaker appear naive when, in fact, this is not necessarily the case. The dilemma faced by the transcriber is whether to write the actual words of the speaker even through the tone of the voice and gesture are missing or to try to capture the subtle meanings through a change of the actual words, the sentences or the word order and emphasis.

McClanahan has achieved a careful balance among these difficulties by making minor adjustments of the original speaker's text to ensure that the spoken word will not be misunderstood when it appears in print. She has made some rearrangements of material and has made some editorial choices about what material to include. Overall the result is a set of oral histories that is very faithful to the original but which can be read in print. These edited transcriptions retain the style and character of the original oral histories she recorded.

People and Languages

McClanahan has grouped the oral histories into five general categories according to the indigenous language of the areas in which the elders were born or spent most of their lives: Cook Inlet, Southeast Alaska, the Aleutian Crescent, Western Alaska, and Northern Alaska. The Cook Inlet region itself has been divided into Lower Cook Inlet East, Lower Cook Inlet West, and Upper Cook Inlet, reflecting a greater number of Dena'ina among the contributors.

Most of the people of the Cook Inlet region are the Dena'ina (sometimes written 'Tanaina'). The Dena'ina language has been classified as one of the Athabaskan languages. This large language family extends from Holy Cross on the lower Yukon River in Alaska (Ingalik language) to Fort Churchill on Hudson Bay in Canada (Chipewyan language) and as far south as the Stikine River in British Columbia (Tahltan language). Other members of the Athabaskan family of languages are found in Oregon and Northern California as well as in New Mexico and Arizona. The best known languages in this family are Navajo with the greatest number of speakers and Apache.

The Dena'ina live from Kachemak Bay (Homer) on the east side of lower Cook Inlet around to Pedro Bay on Lake Iliamna on the west side of Cook Inlet as well as the Upper Inlet area. They extend inland including Lake Clark to the town of Stony River on the river of the same name. Their area extends north to encompass the southern face of the Alaska Range, the Cantwell area and the Susitna River area.

Many of the Dena'ina have moved throughout this region from one side of Cook Inlet to the other or from the Susitna River area to the lower Inlet region and from all over the region into Anchorage. While there has been a considerable amount of dialect variation within this large region, Dena'ina has been considered to be a distinct language. The Russian Orthodox faith was established in this region with the arrival of the first priest at Kenai in 1844. To this day many Dena'ina people continue to hold this faith. As a result many Dena'ina people spoke Dena'ina and Russian as well as English.

The Tsimshian people are not indigenous to their present region in Alaska. They came from Canada to Annette Island just outside of Ketchikan in 1887 led by their strong Anglican missionary, William Duncan. The other Tsimshian people still live in a large region surrounding Prince Rupert in British Columbia. Tsimshian is not related to any other Alaska Native language.

The Tlingit people live in the large region from Ketchikan to Mount St. Elias along the southeast coast of Alaska. In the north their region extends into the interior to encompass the Atlin area of British Columbia and Teslin in Yukon Territory of Canada. Their language is distinct from any other Alaska Native language.

The City of Sitka in Tlingit territory was the Russian capital of Alaska when the capital was moved there from Kodiak in the early 1800's. At that time it was named New Archangel. More recently it became the home of the Sheldon Jackson school which later became a college. Sitka has also been home to many Alaska Native youths because of their extended residences there in boarding schools at Mt. Edgecumbe and Sheldon Jackson.

In the Aleutian Crescent there is a considerable amount of confusion about languages and people. The Russian name "Aleut" has come to be applied to all of the people living in the region from Prince William Sound east of the Kenai Peninsula, extending along the south side of the Kenai Peninsula including Kodiak Island and the Alaska Peninsula, all the way out the Aleutian Chain. All these people commonly refer to themselves as Aleuts to distinguish themselves from the "raw fish eating" people to the north who were not Russian Orthodox. The great majority have Russian names, and to a great extent, at least in the older generation, they are bilingual in Russian and their Native language.

As to the Native languages of these people the picture is somewhat different. From Prince William Sound down the Alaska Peninsula to Perryville and Ivanoff Bay the language spoken is called Alutiiq. Some sources call it Suqpiaq. In English it is usually called Aleut. While criteria for determining whether a language is a distinct language or a dialect of another language vary from linguist to linguist, Alutiiq is considered to be a distinct language but fairly closely related to Central Yupik to the north and west.

The language spoken on the Aleutian Chain and the Pribilof Islands is also called Aleut. This language, however, is quite distinct from either Alutiiq or Central Yupik. Some linguists have classified it as forming a distinct group from the Yupik-Alutiiq-Inupiaq or Eskimo group. Like the speakers of Alutiiq, the Aleuts were strongly influenced by the Russian Orthodox faith and the Russian language. Many became literate in Russian as well as in Aleut.

There are three other languages in the Eskimo language family in addition to Alutiiq, two of which are represented in these oral histories. Central Yupik and Inupiaq are different from each other but, of course, bear many resemblances as members of same language family.

Bethel is at the heart of the Central Yupik region. This extends from Lake Iliamna in the southeast west to include Bristol Bay, the Kuskokwim River and Nunivak Island, as far as the Kuskokwim River at Stony River, up the Yukon River to Holy Cross and north on the west side to Unalakleet.

From Unalakleet the Inupiaq language extends all across the northern region of Alaska and Canada and includes Greenland. The elders from Wiseman and Candle refer to their language as Eskimo. In this case Eskimo means Inupiaq. The Russian influence was relatively strong in the Central Yupik area but virtually non-existent in the Inupiaq areas of Alaska.

These 23 oral histories represent all of the major language families of Alaska.

Ron Scollon
Haines, Alaska

Lower Cook Inlet East

Feodoria Kallander Pennington is part Athabascan and part Danish.

She is a retired cook, who today lives in Anchorage, but spends as much of her time as possible at Point Possession, the tiny village where she grew up. Alaska's largest city is a far cry from her home community that once existed southwest of Anchorage, just across Cook Inlet's Turnagain Arm.

Mrs. Pennington was born on April 5, 1921, and she takes great pride in her background. She believes it is very important to maintain her subsistence skills and to teach them to her children and grandchildren.

She spoke in her home, taking time after the interview to show photographs of her large family.

Feodoria Kallander Pennington

". . . I am proud to be a Native because that's what I am and that's what I'm going to be. It's my life."

My name is Feodoria Pennington. And I was born at Point Possession, Alaska, on April 5th, 1921. I have three sisters that were also born at Point Possession.

My grandfather was the Native Chief at the time I was born. He was called Chief Nicoli. My mother told me many things about the people during my grandparents' time and of her time at the village of Point Possession.

As far back as I could remember the people of the village trapped, hunted, fished and raised vegetable gardens.

The people trapped many kinds of animals, such as muskrat, mink, weasel, fox, lynx, beaver and rabbits. The villagers trapped in the winter and fished in the summer. Most of the fish were sold commercially, and my dad also had a fishtrap.

The trapping and fishing was the village's and my family's main livelihood. My dad sometimes cut pilings and ties for the Alaska Railroad. And he had the pilings and ties barged across the Inlet to the vicinity of Anchorage.

We raised potatoes, lettuce, radishes turnips, cabbage and onions. There were wild berries from which we made jellies and jams.

The womenfolk, during the fishing season, smoked salmon and salted down salmon in barrels. Some meat was canned and some of the meat was salted down and preserved in barrels.

They also made moose jerky and smoked some of the meat. The moose fat was rendered into lard for use as cooking grease. None of the moose was wasted, and even the hide and horns were utilized.

23

The men subsistence hunted only. Besides moose, they hunted rabbits, porcupines, ducks and geese. The men occasionally went ice-fishing in the wintertime and brought back many fish.

The women snared rabbits, some for food and the rest for their hides. We were not able to buy the fancy food which we now sometimes eat, such as TV dinners.

Before Cook Inlet froze up we all went to Anchorage or Kenai on one of the large cannery boats to get our winter supplies, mostly staple goods. The women went shopping for beads, yard goods and thread.

I used to sit alongside my grandmother and help her thread needles, which she used for hand-sewing comforters, blankets, parkas, moccasins, winter hats and other articles of clothing.

We didn't have electricity so we worked by oil or kerosene lamps. My grandmothers and my mother did their sewing in the wintertime. They made beaded gloves and trimmed them with beaver trim. They also made beaded moccasins and beaded hats for the men and boys.

We also tanned seal skin, beaver and rabbits. Nothing was wasted. All the scraps and remnants were saved and the young girls made clothes and moccasins out of them for their dolls.

In the earlier days at Point Possession they used dog teams for transportation to Kenai. I remember my grandmother hitching up her team of dogs and traveling to Kenai to get a midwife to assist with the birth of my sister.

The dog teams were also used for hauling wood to the houses. The men sawed up big blocks of snow and melted it in a big tub for washing clothes.

A lot of the fish that were caught in the summer and fall were smoked and dried for use as dogfood. I remember helping my mother and grandmother pick up the dry driftwood off the beach and packing it up the hill to the smokehouse.

I used to help my mother and grandmother tan moosehides. We would go into the woods and look for a certain kind of wood or bark to smoke and tan the hide, so as to make them kind of an orange tan.

In those days everything was plentiful. Everyone was happy and no one had the aches and pains that are so common now. Our traditions were different. The younger respected the elder. When the older persons were talking, the young were quiet and listened to what they had to say.

I can remember in the back of my mind what the village of Point Possession was like. The people lived off the land. My dad also had a mink farm.

I had four uncles that lived at Point Possession who also trapped and fished.

Practically all the old village is gone, either rotted away or fallen in to Cook Inlet, due to erosion of the bluff. The 1964 earthquake took a lot more of the bluff and more houses along with it, and also some of the cemetery.

In 1917 or 1918 a flu epidemic hit the village and wiped out most of the people living there. Most of the people that died from the flu were buried in the cemetery.

The population at Point Possession at one time was about 50. And then they said it started to decline down to just my grandmother's and my mother's side of the family.

Everybody else moved to different villages. They moved or died. Now, it's just me and my family.

Among the houses that are still standing is my grandmother's, although portions of it have rotted away. My grandmother's house had a roof made of wood shingles, and the sides were wood-frame siding.

She had a great big strawberry garden on one side and a rhubarb patch in the corner of her fence and another area where she grew only potatoes. The rest of her garden was a variety of vegetables. The original village was close to the bluff, and it was sloughing. Our house, which was a big old log house, was one of those houses near the bluff. So my dad and his friends decided to build us a new house. They put up a nice house for us. It had a big front room, a big kitchen, a bedroom and a big loft where the children slept.

They also built a large smokehouse, which was attached to the house. When they were not using it as a smokehouse it was used as a place to store our supplies.

We also had a kind of pantry where we kept our butter, eggs and other perishables.

There were at least eight houses in the village. When the flu epidemic struck the village it wiped out practically everyone. A few of the adults survived, and they took it upon themselves to take care of the young.

My grandmother was one of the survivors. She took in a small boy and treated him like her own son. His name was Mike Nicoli, and she raised him until manhood.

There were nine of us altogether in the family. And the first four of us were girls. They wanted boys in those days. Dad was mad. We worked like boys. We sawed wood and chopped wood and kindling.

We were just regular little tomboys when we were growing up. I am the oldest.

I was seven years old, and my dad and mom said, "Well, you have to go to school. You and your sisters, Annie and Mary."

So we had to move to Anchorage to go to school. That was back in 1927 that we moved to Anchorage so we could go to school.

I didn't know a word of English. I could only speak in my Native tongue. It took me almost two years to learn English in the White Man's way.

The style of living — at that time — in Anchorage was different to me, coming out of the woods, you know. Moving into Anchorage was hard for me to understand.

I didn't know what recesses were. I thought it was time to go home. Mom, finding me home, said, "What are you doing home?"

And I would say, "Well, they let me out. And I came home."

It was kind of hard for me. I cried because I wanted to go home. I didn't like it in Anchorage.

My grandmother got sick one summer at Point Possession. So we had to bring her in. She was sick for a long time and died with TB.

In those days, they didn't have doctors available. We took her to a doctor and he kept her in the hospital a week. And the doctor said she'd need bed rest at home.

And then my grandmother died. Mother had to take care of her, and feed her and bathe her up to the end. Then Mother got the same thing. She died with TB because she was taking care of Grandmother.

At the time, she was carrying her last child, the youngest child, Julius Kallander Junior.

What happened was my grandmother was taking care of her son, Johnny Nicoli Junior, and he died with TB. She got it from him. It was contagious, and we just lived in that one-family house.

Mother was sent to a sanatorium in Palmer, and then the hospital burnt. They sent her to Seward Sanatorium. She died in Seward Sanatorium. And, also my uncle, Gus, died in Seward

Sanatorium of TB.

Mother died in 1944, I believe it was.

Our Russian Orthodox priest was from Kenai and came to Point Possession in the falltime. He would have four or five babies to baptize, and then have Communion. And then he would go to Anchorage and hold service for three days to baptize the children that needed to be baptized.

They had Holy water, and then they had candles lit all the time. Everybody prayed — morning and at night-time before we went to bed.

I remember Grandmother with her little handkerchief over her head, kneeling down and praying every day. You didn't have to have a church to know how to pray.

The reason I got away from the Russian Orthodox Church is that we didn't understand the Russian. We didn't speak Russian. You just sit there. We're all wriggling around, trying to get out of church because we didn't understand one word the priest is saying.

So we just got away from it. We just started going to a regular church — Episcopalian. And then we finally ended up in a Salvation Army chapel.

My grandmother and my mother used to make trips to Anchorage, even before I was seven years old. They had a cannery tender that came and picked up our fish. And that was our transportation to Anchorage.

Even when I was a little baby they were transporting me to Anchorage. They had things to do in Anchorage, buy their supplies in the summertime, and then return back to the village in the fish boat and wait for winter.

We had to move to Anchorage, like I said, when I was seven years old. I and my sister, Annie — she was six — had to go to school. When school was out we'd return to Point Possession to do our fishing. We would come back to Anchorage as soon as school started. We did all our drying fish and canning in the summer before school started.

We had bad times. They called us names, all kinds of bad names. And they threw rocks. I had a rough time going to school. We just walked away and didn't say anything. We weren't brought up that way.

We had a lot of girls as friends. We made friends, but it was the boys we had trouble with. We seemed to get along good with the girls.

I was proud to be a Native because that's what I am and that's what I'm going to be. It's my life. I would get so mad sometimes at those white kids.

I said, "You don't know what it is to be a Native."

What they had was mean parents, and the kids were so mean. I said to myself, "If grandmother caught me doing that she'd whip me!"

I was timid, shy. And I just couldn't understand why kids were that way because I wasn't brought up that way.

But after that, it was easy. We didn't have problems in school. After we got older we made many friends. But the first and third grade was bad.

The school was located across the street from the Egan building on Fifth. It's kind of a vacant lot now.

The school had first through eighth grades. We had nice teachers. They were very nice to us.

My dad was born in Copenhagen, Denmark. He spoke Danish and English. We were teaching him how to speak Native!

He moved to Anchorage when we had to go to school. He moved into Spenard where he had a little cabin. He stayed out there and cut wood. He sold wood by the cord to the people in Anchorage.

That was his livelihood in the wintertime. He just couldn't hack the city life. He couldn't stay in Anchorage, too crowded. So he moved out to Spenard and lived in the woods.

They (family members) told us all kinds of different stories. One of them is, for instance, about Captain Cook, when Captain Cook landed on Cook Inlet. Grandmother told Mom, and then Mom told us that Captain Cook buried treasure at Point Possession. She said it was a map in a jar. So when big boats went by they dumped the garbage in the Inlet and there'd be some jars floating around.

If we saw a jar floating around by the beach when we were playing and the tide was coming in and going out we'd grab a long stick and try to push the jar onto the beach. We would run up the hill to the village with the jar.

We'd say, "Mama, is this it? Is this it?"

And she would say, "It's just an empty jar, nothing in it!"

To this day they still tease me about buried treasure: "Are you still going down there every summer to look for that buried treasure?"

Anyway, I understand that's why they call it Point Possession. Originally, it was Nicoli Village.

When Captain Cook dropped anchor, he took possession of the land. And that's why they call it Point Possession. That's the story that people in those days told — that Captain Cook dropped anchor there and the Indians came out to meet him.

The Indians had their own boats, their own spears and they lived there before Grandmother. They were her ancestors. Some Natives migrated over from Tyonek.

Like I said, we're all related one way or another in Tyonek, Eklutna. Our bloodline is all over.

Grandmother used to tell us crow stories. Just like I tell the story of these new TV stories that you see. They're pertaining to these birds, just like a real-life story.

It's just more like a cartoon. The way they tell it in their own Native tongue it's so different than just talking about it in English. It's so funny in Native and more fun talking about it in the Native tongue. They just sat around and talked. They just laughed their heads off.

Explaining it in English — it's hard. You won't understand it.

After Mom died I worked in the canneries. Then I went down and helped Dad fish. I cooked for him when he was fishing. When I came back to town in the fall I got a job working on the Alaska Railroad. I worked five years with the Alaska Railroad.

The ANS (federal Alaska Native health agency) hospital was built in 1950, and I went to work in the kitchen with a dietitian, as a food service worker. I learned a lot in the hospital. I went up pretty fast in my rating. They said I was a good worker and fast learning.

I worked different departments in the hospital. I quit and went into a restaurant work. My career was cooking in a restaurant for 17 years. I retired from the Captain Cook Hotel.

I worked in between the times at the hospital and Captain Cook Hotel in different restaurants. I put four or five years in a place and I got tired of it. So I moved on. But my career was in the Captain Cook.

(Mrs. Pennington talks about the alcohol problem.)

As time went on and they were making their own stuff, I guess, they started drinking more. The drinking caused a lot of problems. I saw a lot of that when I was growing up. I still do.

But we didn't have too much of that problem at Point Possession because they didn't have a liquor store. Grandmother wouldn't allow it because she was strict! They had to sneak it in.

(She discusses the Alaska Native Claims Settlement Act of 1971.)

The way I'm thinking about it now: It's kind of bad in a way. It's not right. It could have been better. It happened so fast. And people didn't know what they were really getting in to. Just like overnight. I think they could have done better for the Native people.

I don't have any problem (with discrimination). And all my children — going to school — they didn't have that problem. On the street — at one time when they had the signs saying, "No dogs allowed." The signs were changed and said, "No Natives allowed in the bars."

That sign was put in the bars back in the early '40s, I believe it was.

When I was working for the Alaska Railroad, I and my friend were partners, working there. She's the best friend I ever had.

Anyway, she and I were working together in coaches and we would hear people talking. Some of the people would say, "Oh, give Alaska back to the Natives."

They would talk like that — "Give the land back to the Indians" — right in front of us, you know. We didn't say anything. We just kept on working.

All my children are married, except two. I have eight children, five boys and three girls.

My brothers and I taught the kids survival. I said, "If anything happens to Anchorage — if you had a big earthquake or something happened that Anchorage got wiped out — you know how to survive off the land. Because we

taught you how. That's why you know how to pack water. You know how to cut wood. You know how to clean fish and put it up when the time comes. And you know how to preserve your food.

"Know your berries and your different kinds of greens that's growing. And you watch the birds — what they're eating. So you know what to eat when you're out in the woods, and you get lost. Just watch what the birds and animals are eating. Then you know what's good to eat."

That's what I taught the kids.

Like, for instance, we took one white child to Point Possession. They wanted to take him out of Anchorage and get him away from the street, you know, so he wouldn't get messed up.

We kept him down there all summer. We taught him how to fish. He was so green he didn't know how to build a fire or anything. He said, "What you doing?"

And the kids told him, "We're going to build a fire."

"How come you're doing that?" All these questions. A kid from a big city doesn't know how to survive off the land. So we were teaching him.

"That's how we used to live," we told him. "In my grandmother's time, this is how we lived."

And he couldn't get used to no water, no flushing toilet, no nothing. He had to go to the outhouse — outdoor outhouse — and no running water.

When my kids go out to pack water,

I told them to hand him a bucket. We taught him all that. And toward the end of the season he said, "You know, I like that. That's fun."

But anyway, that's what we taught our children. And now we're teaching all my grandkids. And so, if anything happens, even right here in Anchorage, they know how to survive.

Just because you live in a city doesn't mean that you can't survive. You know how to survive off the land. Disaster hits, you know what to do. That's what my mother taught me, too, when I was growing up. We used to go out in the woods, she'd say, "Don't dig that up. That's bad. This root is no good. This is good."

Two identical plants — and which one is bad. Which one is good. There's a lot of plants in the woods that you got to learn. There's two kinds that look almost alike, but they're different. One's poison and one isn't.

That's why they used to tell us, "Watch the birds and the animals eating. You know what's good and what's bad. The ones that they're eating are good."

My advice for them (young people) is to go to school and learn. They have a better chance than we did — going to school and learning.

I'd like to see all these children take advantage of it. That's what I told my children, "When I was going to school, we didn't have anything. You kids, nowadays, have everything in the world and still are not satisfied."

I don't know what they want. Everything's right in front of them. They should be proud of what they have. I said, "When I was a little girl I had to iron my uncle's shirt and socks and his handkerchief just to make a quarter!"

I still go to Point Possession each summer to put up smoked salmon and also put up salt salmon in barrels and canned salmon.

I applied for a Native allotment in 1954 and was awarded the allotment after the government checked out my claim to the area. My husband and I hope that sometime in the near future we can make Point Possession our retirement home.

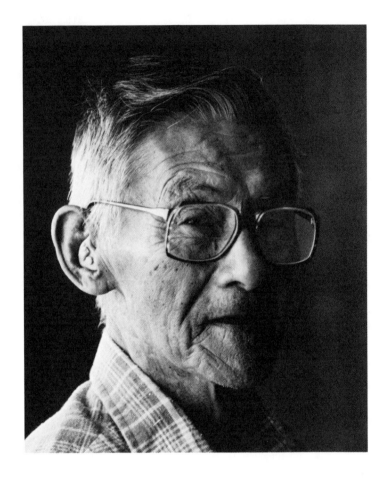

Peter Kalifornsky is a man of slight build with commanding dignity. He speaks quietly, but with authority. It is obvious that although his formal education has been severely limited he has spent much time studying his Native culture.

Mr. Kalifornsky is an Athabascan and was born on October 12, 1911 at Kalifornsky Village on the Kenai Peninsula.

He has worked for hours on end in recent years on his Native language and is helping officials of the University of Alaska-Fairbanks to preserve the language.

Speaking in his small and neatly arranged apartment in a Kenai retirement home, Mr. Kalifornsky frequently asked that the tape recorder be turned off so that he could speak informally and also to offer his interviewer coffee.

He keeps a date book, listing birth dates of family, friends and new acquaintances so that on any date listed in the book he can say a prayer for that person.

Peter Kalifornsky

". . . I take my believing the way I see it — for the betterment of your own life."

My name is Peter Kalifornsky. I was born down at Kalifornsky Village, couple miles from Kasilof River, on up. I don't remember my mom. Because my mom died when I was a baby. So my aunties took care of me until my uncle, Theodore Chickalusion, got married. And then he took me.

And he took me across the Inlet. He had a contract, cutting pilings for the Alaska Packers. A year-round contract. And there was no people around there until about 1920.

Then that Snug Harbor cannery started canning some clams. So he was hiring people from all over — Kodiak, Iliamna, Kenai, Ninilchik, Seldovia and up around Anchorage. And those people would be over at Polly Creek. That's where my uncle had a camp there. I was just — I don't know how old I was.

I was just a young boy then. Then there was old people over there. The old people, they would all go away from the other crowds. And they would gather in one tent. And they would tell stories. And they would invite me over to listen to them when they're telling stories.

And right now, in this Native language, I'm writing those stories. That's when I hear those stories and those songs — 1921. Then my dad remarried. Then my uncle sent me home to go to school.

And then (the step-mother) didn't live with us very long. She died 1925. And down in Kalifornsky Village my grandpa and Nick Ornocutt, my grandpa Alex Kalifornsky, the last grandpa of mine, and his partner Nick Ornocutt, they died shortly, one after another.

And the survivals were Nick Ornocutt's boys and one old man, Filipino there. He was there for a long time. They moved to Kenai. And that Kalifonsky Village was abandoned. And no one lived there.

So around 1974, maybe, then I started taking a notice to my old village there and try to locate it. And I did. And with CINA (Cook Inlet Native Association), our tribal help, I had a grave part cleared. And got fence put around it. And the church part there, got a fence put around it.

My parents were all Natives. There might have been some little other mixture in them. Mostly Russian, I think. So I don't know. Well, I consider myself full-blooded Indian. Athabascan, yes.

I went up to fifth grade. That's all. And I wish I had a chance, gone to school. I liked school. But then, I didn't have a chance.

With my Native language writing here. Sometimes I have a little problem. But then, I get it straightened out, one way or the other. (Laughs.)

That English is the hardest thing to learn. And that is for me right now. It still is a puzzle.

I learned to speak English when I was sent home to my dad to go to school — 1921, '22, '23, '24, '25. And after my stepmother died, everybody took off. She had a lot of boys. It was a big family. And they all took off for all different places.

So I was left alone in the house. So I took off for the woods. The only way

I knew how to survive. And after everybody moved out, I had to go someplace.

To learn how to survive in the woods, my uncle raised me out in the woods. And I have learned from my uncle. He was a hunter, Native style of a life. You know, the kind of food to eat and how to prepare it. There was no freezer. No stores. But out in the country, by yourself, with just a family there. My uncle and his wife, they had one girl, born 1915 or '16. That's when my uncle took me, around 1915 or '16. I don't remember.

The things to eat: my uncle would get a whole winter's supply of groceries from Alaska Packers. And he would have that stored away to last for winter. And the Native way of eating is another thing. You had fish. They put up the fish — dried fish, salt fish.

And there was always a lot of ways of fixing it for a meal. And there was always fresh meat to be gotten. Every time you want fresh meat you could go out. There was a lot of black bears, porcupines, rabbits, beavers. There was no moose on that side. But this is the kind of food that I was raised on.

Seal in the fall. He would get three or four seals. And that was prepared for the winter, some dried and salted. And beluga meat and the blubber of it were fixed and put in oil. Put away for the winter. That's the kind of food I was raised on.

I can't say it's better (that life). And I can't say it's better today. You got to consider looking at it on both sides. I was raised that way, so it's better for me. This life is kinda little hard for me sometimes. I get hungry for my Native foods sometimes. (Laughs.)

I miss my dried fish. I do get salt fish. And I do put up a little canned fish. And then there's other things. Like beaver, seal meat, porcupine. There's three things you cannot get today. So I crave for it sometimes.

There wasn't much sickness going around. A person would probably get a little cold. But then they had some herb medicine that they always stored away for the winter. Like wild celery roots and like those. I don't know what they would call that. They called it "peleen" — that they used inside the steam bath. And some other herb medicines that they used.

So there wasn't much sickness going around. Except after I got back to Kenai here — must be along 1926 or '27 — there was some kind of a sickness that was going around. I don't know what it was — some skin disease and things like that. But then the Hygiene boat come along and everybody was getting some shots and getting treatments.

And then following that then, this — they called TB — broke out. There was a lot of people got TB. Before that there was no sign of TB. That is according to the Native stories that's been handed down to me.

In 1956 I landed up in the hospital — with TB. It wasn't really infection of TB. But it was infection into my artery, down into my liver. But then,

through my X-rays and things there, there's a spot on my lung there, about pencil point. They don't know how far back that TB struck me. But it was cured before it got into sickness. So it left a scar there.

My family? My father, Nick Kalifornsky, and my sister, Mary. Her second name by marriage was Nisson, Mary Nisson. There was only two of us, Mary and I. So that family is like my own real brothers and sisters. When my mother died my sister was taken. One of our aunties, they took care of her.

(He tells a story from when white people first came to the area.)

This is a story about the big eater, Queljaq'i. It's a kind of a funny story about Denai. It says what happened long time ago, when the first whites come to these Denais. And they wanted to make trades with their skins. Even trade and so forth.

The chief ordered the people to start piling their skins to make an even trade with whatever they want to get. (Piling the skins as high as what they wanted to buy.)

But one person took a rifle to it. He was looking. He said that was not right. So he told them to take all them skins back. And he went up to this white man to make even trade. He agreed.

So he went back to the skin pile there. And he looked at what was going to be traded for. He took one skin and he hold it up the length of it. And it was longer than what they were trying to make trade for. But anyway, he agreed with him. What's left over, that skin, he fold it over. And he said, "We'll make an even trade." (Laughs.) So the white man agreed.

And then after that, then they want to use money. The whites want to use money, buying things from the Natives. So the Natives didn't have any money. They didn't know what money was. So they teached them the nickels, dimes, quarters, and thirty-five cents, forty cents, fifty cents, seventy-five cents and a dollar. And all in different changes. And they learned that pattern on their own language. (Names the Native words for each denomination.)

So they were making trades. And they had a cannery up there or something, canning fish. And then they were to leave. And then this sailboat was anchored out there. So they loaded everything on that big boat. And the Natives didn't know what that big sailboat out there was like.

It was fascinating to them. They load everything on there. And they went and they sailed away. And after that, they made that into joke. Queljaq'i. Big eater. He was going along and he was eating everything up. And then he came to two belugas, laying on the beach there. He put that on his tongue. And he swallowed it down like a jelly.

That means they had a barge or something there that was transporting whatever had to be loaded on that sailboat. So that's what they mean by two belugas laying on the beach there!

(Laughs.) They had to load that with barges out and take it out to the sailboat. And they would unload it.

Activities? They had songs. They sing. They have dinner party. The villagers, they were always getting together. Tell stories. They sing, and they dance. And then, for the younger people, they would do a lot of exercising. Jumping rope. Things like that. Run.

Another thing. They take a long pole, and two persons, they would push that pole from one on each end. They would push each other with that pole. And then jumping high. They rig up a height there. They would jump over the pole. They were always on the move. Doing something.

There was some sickness here. They claimed there was a lot of people that died on it. But I did not see that. It was around 1919. And then, after that, along in '20s there was some kind of a flu. But that didn't affect us too much. There were a lot of people died that winter. But some of us, didn't affect us much.

But before that they claimed there was some kind of a flu, striking the Native people, that took a lot of lives away. It was before my time. Nikiski, up Nikiski there. There was a big village there. They said some kind of a flu struck them. And then that village was wiped out. And these few people — there were survivors from Nikiski. (Names some of the survivors.) And they moved to Kenai after that. And then that Nikiski village died out.

The people drank. But it was not transported. Some people make their own — what they have learned from the Russians' time. I don't know. They called it Potato Hooch. (Laughs.)

But then they didn't do much drinking, day after day, like the way things go on with some. Once in a great while some family would have a little batch. Maybe five gallons, worked out. And they would have a little drink. And when that's gone, well, that's it. They didn't drink anymore.

And then when the country went dry, then the people didn't drink too much, either. I know I didn't. And the boys that were growed up with me, they didn't do that. Maybe would take a drink in the evening. Or at a dance or something. But the next morning, bright and early, six, seven o'clock, we're on the trail with our dog team. Haul wood. Or go out the trapline or some place. Or do whatever we had to do. We were always on our duty, what we have to do for the day.

The church is started from the first time when the Russians come, I guess. That story I don't know too much about. But then, even before my time, all the Native people they were strong Orthodox. And I am, too. And I follow that up.

This religion, believing — in the Native way, or English way or any other way, that was not handed to me. But I take my believing the way I see it — for betterment of your own life. I look at it this way: it's up to you if you want

to be in a religion. I do go to church. Set up candles. The same pattern what my parents been doing.

My grandfather had a church down in Kalifornsky Village. I think that it's a pretty strong way of life to believe. I know I do a lot of things wrong, that I am not supposed to be doing. Or talk about something. And that is not right, one way or the other. And I still do.

But I still go to church. And I still set up candles. I pray for myself, my relatives that's gone, and the ones that's living, and my friends and everybody. I pray for good health for them and myself.

On this settlement act of Alaska, that goes way far back from the Columbus time and how these Alaska Natives been affected from their lifestyle by the whites. Their way of life, and they have lived out in the country. There was no work. But they had a good, strong life, way of living. There weren't much sicknesses.

But, at the same time, this new way of life would come that cannot be overlooked. Or can't help from getting into it. It goes from that time until the Russians' time. Change a way of life and language and their heritage. And the Gold Rush time.

And then comes along statehood and all this. That all been affected to the Native way of life. But then, it had to be done, one way or the other, in order to make a go of it. Get into the new way of life.

So today, right now, I'm still working

on my Native language. Trying to preserve that's been disappeared. I'm the
only one left that's in here that can
preserve it.

And this is just what I'm doing.

Victor Antone Jr. is an Athabascan who lives in Kenai. He is a retired trapper and fisherman. His formal education has been severely limited. It ended when he hopped on the back of a garbage truck and ran away from Sheldon Jackson school at Sitka in Southeast Alaska.

Mr. Antone was born August 9, 1923, in Kenai, on the Kenai Peninsula.

He has great difficulty hearing and spoke with the assistance of a relative who offered to help bridge the communication gap where necessary.

Victor Antone Jr.

". . . they used to teach us how to respect older people. . . If older people come over there, we'd get up, give them the chairs. We'd go sit on the floor . . ."

When I was small? I growed up in Kenai area. I growed up mostly out in the woods. Out trapping. I didn't go to school till I was about three years old, I guess. I used to skip school — two grades every year, until I made it up to the ninth.

Went down to Sheldon Jackson school. I ran away.

The reason I wanted to leave Sheldon Jackson? They were too darn strict. Just like they are in the Army. You had to get up at six o'clock in the morning and stand by your bed. If there's a little wrinkle in your bed, they'll mess it up and make you do it over again.

And you had to go to school from eight to twelve and one to five. And from six to nine. Right after school, you go right to bed till six o'clock next morning again. They were strict. Any kid do anything wrong, we get all restricted in school. They wouldn't let us go no place. You had to stay right in that yard.

One day I sneaks out on a garbage truck. Six of us, we ran away. He (the driver) got us on the back of the garbage truck, and he hid us with our suitcase. Got us into town and turn us loose. And all of us went in different directions.

I had to work my way back to Kenai. (Laughs.) Took me a little while. I got on a mail boat.

I worked for awhile for him — captain, he was only about 17 years old. He made me a first mate on the boat between Seward and Anchorage all the time, carrying mail and freight. We used to make a trip about once a month, I guess. I used to take a boat from Kenai

41

on to Anchorage, and bring it back down. The captain, he used to take it way down to Seward. We used to take turns.

And after I was about 16, I went to work in a cannery. Get about a couple dollars a day, is all. I used to go to work, get through at the cannery, go out up to Anchorage along the railroad. Worked on a steamer for awhile. About six months, I guess. Worked down on Aleutian Islands. Down Attu during the War. We used to get bombed every night when I was down there. Japanese used to come down and give themself up.

I used to talk Native all the time until I went to school, came back to Kenai. Been talking English. Beginning to forget some of the language. I can't speak it, but I can understand everybody talking.

Take me a little while to think over it, try to say a word. I had it all mixed up with Tyonek, Susitna language and around Knik.

When I went to school I didn't talk my language very much. When I came back to Kenai, I mean. When I was out in the woods, my dad and them, they used to talk Native language. I understand it pretty good, until I got back to Kenai and went to school. Started talking English. And I been talking English ever since.

My mom was born right in Kenai here. My dad was born up in Knik.

I'm the oldest one out of the whole bunch. My sister was just one year younger than I am. I had three-four sisters, a couple of brothers. I'm the only one that's left right now. I got a lot of cousins in town.

It (home) was just a log cabin, two-room house. Not very much room. Had to burn wood all the time.

When I was going to school we used to have — on Saturdays and Sundays — a bunch of us kids used to help each other. And we'd saw wood all day. Enough to last all week. Any time we get through, we'd go play. They wouldn't turn us loose until we get all the wood and water packed.

Used to be way different a long time ago. Everybody used to walk around Kenai knew each other. Right now you go to Kenai there, you wouldn't even know nobody.

When we was growing up, they used to teach us how to respect older people. Sitting by a table. If older people come over there, we'd get up, give them the chairs. We'd go sit on the floor or any place.

(He discusses his reaction to Alaska gaining statehood.)

I don't like that statehood. I liked it the way it was before. Since it turned State, too many guys moving in. I liked it the way it was before — better than now.

I belong to Russian Orthodox Church. Only church I go to. Getting a little older, I'm still going to church.

They (missionaries) used to come around. Try to convert us to go to their church. Try to get us away from our own church.

We went out trapping. I started out when I was only about 10 years old. Doing pretty good now.

How to catch wolves, how to catch beavers and mink — I learned that from dad when I was only about 10 years old. I used to have my own line.

One time I went trapping, muskrat trapping. My dad found a lake, and I started trapping it. And I got fifteen hundred muskrats out of this one little lake!

I used to go around with a dog team. Night-time come I'd pull my traps. Morning-time I'd set 'em back out again. That's a lot of muskrats — fifteen hundred.

My mom used to get mad at me. She didn't like to skin! (Laughs.) I didn't know how to skin. I tried it, and I got it all cut up (laughs).

One time I was out trapping. I was only about 10 years old. I was way out in the woods. I heard dogs barking. I started looking around. I didn't think there was a wolf around there. But I guess must be about 10 or 15 of 'em. They made a circle around me.

What I did, I just sat in the middle. My dad used to tell me, any time a wolf come around, make a little fire and just sit by it. That's what I did until my dad heard those wolves and came and rescued me. (Laughs.) I didn't get scared. I didn't know how to get scared, I guess.

Right now, it would take a little while for me to get scared. I had a bear jump right over me — brown bear. I never get scared until I get home. (Laughs.)

I try to tell you what my dad used to tell me. Make a little camp, catch rabbits and stuff like that. Those days didn't have no tea. Get Hudson's Bay Tea (Labrador tea, leaves of an evergreen shrub — ledum plustre or ledum groenlandicum) and make that for your tea to drink. Hudson's Bay Tea is: you used to find these little green leaves. You could find it, and you could boil that in water. You could use that for a tea. Some old people used to use that for medicine. For colds and things.

Kill grouse and stuff. My dad used to try to find me. I'd go out for about four or five days at a time, by myself.

My dad would get worried. I'd be sitting by a camp fire, drinking something or eating. (Laughs.) My dad used to get mad at me. But he knew I could take care of myself. He'd teach me all about that when I was real small. I used to go out with him. I was only about four or five years old.

Dad used to go out hunting, and I used to tag along right behind him. If I get tired, he'll pack me on his back and bring me home. I was too small.

When I was small I had to build my own (toys) out of bark and stuff. See an airplane go by. That evening I'll be sitting down and building that airplane. I could memorize how it will look. I can still do that. I can look at a boat and build it.

Dad used to make 15 or 20 pairs (snowshoes) every winter just before Christmas. When we got back to Kenai, he'd buy all this stuff for us. Buy little toys for me. He used to work pretty hard on those snowshoes.

My mom used to help him. Webbing and all that. Dad used to go out, get a moosehide. Bring it home. Take all the fur off. Clean it. And cut it for webs and stuff. I don't know how he used to do it. But it's just like a little string when he cut it off. All even, too. I don't know how he used to do it. Fingernail or sharp knife.

Dad used to go out fishing. I used to out with him. Be on a boat all the time. Help him. Sometimes we used to work all week. Get about a half hour's sleep. Go right back out and start working again.

Sometimes we used to get so darn tired we'd just fall down and go right to sleep. We used to fish from Monday till Saturday. Just steady going. Our fingers used to be so blistered up, we couldn't even bend our fingers. Have to soak it in water before you could do anything.

(Mr. Antone talks about World War II.)

I was working. I was rated as master sergeant. Got big master sergeant's stripes! But I was a civilian, making good pay.

Working for the engineers that time. We used to be working down at Attu there. Bullets used to fly over our heads. And bombs. Sometimes bombs dropped down alongside of us. We could see our buddies getting killed right alongside of us and everything like that. Step over

a Japanese, American. In mud way up to your knees. We had to stay in a little tent.

Army flew us out there. I was rated as master sergeant in Army Engineers. Fix all the airstrips, build houses. I had to sign a year's contract. I couldn't get out till my year was up. I stayed out there a whole year.

That was quite a rain there. You could take a bucket — sideways — and fill it up. The wind blows, you can't walk around. You got to walk on all four to get around.

(He says discrimination was not a problem.)

No. We didn't feel any. We been treated all the same anyway — soldiers and civilians. Anybody was treated all the same. Live right together and work together. We didn't bother them. And they didn't bother us.

They didn't care if we were black or white or Indian or Eskimo or anything. Everybody was treated about the same — getting the same kind of pay like the next guy.

Drinking seemed like it used to be biggest problem around here. I started drinking when I was about 17, I guess. Drinking ever since I got older. Now I don't think I took a drink for seven years now. Going on seven. It don't bother me any. I feel good. Eat good.

Before when I was drinking, I used to go to a doctor all of the time. About every week, sometimes twice a week go to the doctor. Now I don't ever go any more. I feel pretty good. That's all.

Elsie Sanders Cresswell is part Athabascan and part Swedish. She was born on March 2, 1927, in Kenai.

She has a determined no-nonsense air about her, and although she has faced some grave disappointments in life — such as her family not being able to afford to send her to Sheldon Jackson school at Sitka in Southeast Alaska for high school — she shows no bitterness.

Mrs. Cresswell today lives in Kenai and spoke from her home there, which is comfortably cluttered with her possessions.

She lived Outside briefly in the 1940s, but returned to Alaska when she was divorced from her first husband, a soldier stationed in Kenai during part of World War II.

Church is very important to Mrs. Cresswell, as are traditional Native values, such as honoring one's elders. She is also a good cook and readily offers a vistor home-cooked food, as well as recipes.

Elsie Sanders Cresswell

". . . We listened to our mother and dad. You know, respect the elders. Listen to what they say. That's all you have to do — have faith in God and have faith in your elders."

My name is Elsie Cresswell. I was born and raised in Kenai. I went to the Kenai Territorial School, as far as eighth grade. There was no high school here. So that's my education.

My mother was Native, and my dad was from Sweden. Thirteen children in our family. I was the fifth child.

My father was just a sailor. Came to the States (New York). Then he came on a ship from San Francisco to Alaska. Right from Sweden. By himself.

(She says she is not sure why her father left Sweden.)

I don't know. He never did tell us. (Laughs.) He was a fisherman. He had fishing locations on Salamatof Beach. He worked at Libby McNeill — Libby Cannery. He fished for them, you know, all those years.

Him and my mother got married in 1921. He was born 1881. She was born 1901. So she would have been 20 years old.

Our house was a one-room log house my dad built. It was just a small one. The building is at Fort Kenai now. I donated it to the city. They wanted old houses out of logs for Fort Kenai.

There was just about seven of us that's alive today that was raised in the house, you know. The (others) were babies when they died. I helped raised 'em. All of them. I raised them, helped my mother. And my brother, he helped around the house, chop wood, pump water, stuff like that.

(She describes the food she ate when she was younger.)

Moose meat, salmon, berries, and we put up all our own — raise garden.

Perok. Meat perok. Made out of moose-meat and rice and baked between two crusts.

Put up all our salmon during the summer, and then wintertime, my dad would go out and get a moose. We'd put that up. We had no refrigerators, no deep freezes. So we just salted it, dried it, jarred it, you know. That's the way we preserved our food.

In the garden we raised vegetables — potatoes, rutabagas, carrots, cabbage, stuff like that.

The first thing I cooked for my dad when he worked for the Three C's (the Civilian Conservation Corps) in Kenai — corn beef soup and raisin pie. (Laughs.) That's the first thing I ever cooked. He used to work for them here. Gave them jobs, you know. There was nothing here. So that's what they worked. They done cut brush and stuff like that.

We had dogs. We put up fishing racks for them, dried 'em (fish) in the summertime. Then we bundle 'em up, put them in the attic for winter for their food. We used them to haul wood in from the woods for our woodstove. And hunting — when we went hunting they took the dog team.

We had lots of food. You know, my dad if he cleared $800 a season from Libby's for fishing, we got all our winter clothes for seven children, all our groceries. And still had money left over to go have a good time with! (Laughs.) I got my dad's receipts yet from Libby-McNeill, and they paid 50 cents a king and three cents a red. I got the receipts!

I'd rather have that life than the life we got today. Because it had more than the life we got today. We may have everything modern. But in them days people enjoyed themselves.

We listened to our mother and dad. You know, respect the elders. Listen to what they say. That's all you have to do — have faith in God and have faith in your elders. Because they'll lead you the right way. They won't lead you astray. I know that. I found that out for sure.

That's the best advice for children is to listen ... And we meet our priest in the stores or anything, we say, "Hello, Father," and all that. See, that's respect. We respect him.

They shared everything with one another. If somebody got a king salmon — first king — everybody in town got a chunk. They got a moose, they'd give meat to the other people. And nowadays you don't see nothing of it.

We helped a lot of Kenai people out there. There was one woman from Tyonek there. She had TB, and they put her in a tent by herself. So my mother used to — she was the only one — go in there and feed her, you know, and bathe her and stuff. Because everybody was scared of TB. But my mother, she went and done it because she wasn't scared. She just went. Friend of hers from Tyonek.

The people from Tyonek used to always come in the summer here, you know. And like this elderly lady. She had a bad leg. She was crippled.

They (other people) fixed her food, sure. But they wouldn't go and take care of her in the tent. They were afraid of TB. Because that was a big deal, you know, in them days. TB was a killer, you know, kill lots of people. Here in Kenai. All over Alaska, it was. They get it even in their bone, you know. TB gets in their bone, and they die from it.

She finally died from it. They couldn't save her. There was no doctors. No nothing. Just a midwife was here.

No children that I know of that had TB. Well, by that time it started diminishing, you know. This USS Hygiene ship came in here, and they were giving tests to the whole village that wanted to take the test. So everybody took X-rays and the test.

And there was a lot of them that, you know, never had it. But there was a few that did. And they sent them to a sanatorium in Seward. They had a place there for them. I still got those cards from that USS Hygiene. That ship, when we took the tests. I can't recall the year.

(She explains that she went to school as far as the eighth grade.)

Eighth grade. I liked to go to school. They taught us a lot in school. We had a sewing class, you know, to show us how to sew. Then the seventh and eighth graders, they had a class on touring Alaska. And we built a big boat.

And we toured Alaska from Point Barrow, clear around Alaska. And then we write, you know, history of Alaska,

about all these villages that we stopped off at.

And all of us — the class — we built all the staterooms. You know the girls made the curtains, the boys made bathroom fixtures out of plaster of Paris. That was beautiful boat we built!

All winter it took to build the boat. About six feet, eight feet long. That was built in the old Territorial School.

We had real nice teachers there that did come. They really liked children in Kenai. They really taught those children. They didn't fool around. They weren't cruel or mean or anything. But they gave you a lesson and they wanted you to do that lesson. And you did.

We were brought up and raised that we respect our elders and we listen to what they tell us. So that's how come school was, you know, no problem for us. Because a lot of us that listened, we learned. But a lot of them didn't, see. They just played around — here, there. They didn't care about school.

But me, I wanted an education. And I wanted to even go to Sitka, to Sheldon Jackson High. But that year fishing was poor. We didn't have the money, so my dad couldn't afford the tuition for that year. But I really wanted to go to school because I liked school.

So then after I was through with the eighth grade I went to work, helped the family out. I worked at Anchorage Laundry in Anchorage. I stayed up there with some people. And then I worked for the big shots — the bankers, their wives and the lawyers — doing housework. Fifty cents an hour! (Laughs.)

I was 16 when I first went out on my own.

We were in Anchorage before. When my mom got sick we took her in a boat to hospital. She had pleurisy real bad. So my dad took me and my other sister. We went to Anchorage to the hospital on the boat. That was when the boats were still running then. It must have been '39, '40.

There was nothing in Anchorage, just Fourth Avenue. And just Fort Richardson. And where Spenard is — that was all woods. There wasn't no Spenard at that time during World War II. There was just shacks in there, you know. That's all there was.

(She talks about the languages spoken at home.)

My mother and grandmother spoke Indian and Russian. My dad, he spoke English. He never spoke nothing else. They spoke English and Russian, Indian and Russian. About the same.

Well, I picked up a few things in Russian and Indian from my grandmother and mother. I can understand quite a bit, you know, what they talk about. But to come and talk it, I can't hardly. Few words, I could say here and there.

She (Grandmother) used to stay with me at our house, you know, after Grandpa died. They were about the same, like we done. They put up fish. Berry picking. They had those potlatches, things like that.

School — that was all American. All American school. When my mother was — her time. She went to that school — the Russian school. Used to be by our church where Fort Kenai is now. And lots of others here that's still alive went with her to that school.

And I went up in our church — Holy Assumption Orthodox Church — upstairs there in the attic. I found all them old books of them girls. My mother, all them when they went to school. Their books was laying up there. I don't know if they're still there or not. I haven't been up there for a long time.

The kids were half and half. Most of Kenai: what they were — they were all half white, half Indian, half Russian. Because their dads were all white men. Filipinos, white men, you know. That's all there was here.

We were like one big happy family in Kenai: That's the way it used to be — one big happy family. Somebody got sick, everybody'd go to their house to see what they could do to help them out. That's the way it was in Kenai.

There was problems all the time when they drank, you know. But what you expect? That's all they had to do. There was nothing else here — no recreation of any kind.

Kenai Joe (John Consiel Sr.), he came in. He put a building up '35. And he made a dancehall out of it. And he used it for children for roller skating. That's the only big building was here for things like that. I know. I was married to him in 1947. We had two sons.

When I went to work for him as a

waitress in his roadhouse, that's when I met him. You see, I went to the States in 1944. My mother passed away in '45, and I was in San Francisco. So I couldn't make it home. So then I came home in '46 from the States.

See, I was married to a soldier before, a GI. So then I came back here in '46, and I went to work for Kenai Joe. And I been here ever since. (Laughs.)

(The soldier) — Paul Karaffa — was a sergeant in the Army. I went to the States to his family out there — to Chicago. And my baby was six months old when we went out, under Army. Everything was Army then. So I went to San Francisco. He was stationed there. So I worked there for a few months, you know, got enough money. And then I came home.

In '43 the Coast Artillery came. The 75th Coast Artillery came to Kenai. They had their barracks over by the Russian Orthodox Church. Paul Karaffa was the sergeant in charge. I met him at the dancehall — Kenai Joe's dancehall. We used to always Saturday nights have dances.

People were scared of the Japanese. They had blackouts here in Kenai. And my dad used to be one of those men, worked at night, you know, to make sure all the windows were black. That's when the Japs were supposed to been 20 miles out of Kodiak that year.

And then there was really a scare here. All the men, soldiers was on alert. They had the trucks ready to evacuate the people. I was running around with

the sergeant. And he used to tell me all the things about it. So they had blackouts in the windows. Well, we only had kerosene lamps. So there wasn't much light that could show anyhow! (Laughs.)

We didn't have rationing here, nothing. We always got food and cigarettes. Booze, whatever you wanted (laughs).

People were scared, you know. But they had to just go along with it. You know, you couldn't do nothing. They had battery-operated radios, you know, they listened to.

I didn't know nothing about the States, except what we read in the books. I wanted to be home. I didn't like it, have no part of it. I didn't like the States. Too many people. When you're from a village like Kenai was — two, three hundred people — you wouldn't like it. Too much, you know. I don't know.

Alaska is different. The people are different than in South 48. Down there they'll walk over you. And if you got a shopping bag in a bus or anything, they'll knock it off from your hand, you know. They don't care. But up here, the people, they respect one another.

There's a lot of Outsiders up here in Kenai, but they're really nice. I met lot of them. I been in bar business for 25 years, and I met lots of people from the South 48. And the compliments they gave us Native people — how we treated 'em were, oh, 100 percent. They said, "We never met such nice people."

Because they'd go out to have a drink

with a Native, and they'd feed them in their homes. We didn't have much. But whatever was their food, they ate with them and appreciated it.

April 17th, 1947, married to Kenai Joe. Then he passed away in 1970.

We opened the bar in 1947, first bar. And then we built the Kenai Hotel in 1948. October. Poured the basement. And then we had a Model A truck that hauled the building from Seward. It was Army barracks. And my husband, he bought it — the buildings and tore them down. And our Model A truck hauled all that material to build the Kenai Hotel. That's what it's built out of — Army barracks, if they want to know the truth today. (Laughs.)

(Mrs. Cresswell says that there was little discrimination in Kenai when she was younger.)

No. Those white men, they treat those Natives good, I tell you. They were wonderful to the Native people. Oh, yes. They didn't hurt them no way. Never cheated them on nothing. They helped them a lot.

'Cause a lot of them weren't married. See, they were bachelors. And families that really needed stuff, they'd help them out. Because it seemed like the white man always had a dollar in his pocket where the Natives didn't have it! (Laughs.)

There's a lot of them, though, even now — right now today — in Kenai that classifies a Native below them. You know, underneath them.

(She talks about her church.)

That church means a lot to me today yet. I was the president for the sisterhood for our Holy Assumption Orthodox Church for 10 years.

You see, my dad was a Lutheran. My mother was Orthodox. And he didn't object to none of us being baptized in that church. 'Cause that's the only church we had in Kenai.

And then the missionaries finally start, you know, coming in. But we always went to our church, regardless of what. We'd go to see the missionaries, sure. They'd read us a little of the Bible. Give us little pamphlets.

But our church was Orthodox, always. They couldn't change us regardless of what they promised us: How we should be saved again and all that stuff. And here we were baptized already, and you never take that away! Once you're baptized in the church, you're baptized. (Laughs.)

Orthodox always. I always will be until the day I die. And my three sons are baptized Orthodox. And my two grandchildren are baptized Orthodox.

(Mrs. Cresswell says the Alaska Native Claims Settlement Act of 1971 was good for Natives.)

We figure, boy, it's going to help the Natives. 'Cause a lot of them needed it. As far as I'm concerned, to me, it don't make no difference if it did or not in a way.

I'm not well off, but I mean I could take care of myself. Where a lot of them here can't, you know. They kind of depend on that for their checks every three months or you know.

We were all for it. We figured Natives was entitled to what they took away from them in Kenai. You know all our hunting grounds, where we camped, where we fished, where we got berries — that's been all taken away from the Kenai people. They have nothing.

Now they have to go and buy a piece of ground for $10,000. And it was ours from the start. I mean for nothing we had that. You know, that's wrong what they done to the people. They should never have done that.

And now we applied 10 years ago, almost 15 years, for some land through the Native deal. And we still got no land yet to this day. Native allotment. We're still working on it.

Now they put state parks in for that — the land we're supposed to got. So I don't know what they're doing. They're just trying to push Alaska people born and raised here out and let the whites take over everything, I guess. That's the way it looks to me.

Statehood was wrong. You know the people that was in Kenai — voted for that statehood — they're not here now. They're all back in South 48.

So we're left paying all the bills. (Laughs.) Nobody here — Kenai people I know — wanted statehood. They didn't want a city, either. But we got it. Well, they say progress you can't stop it.

Us Natives here in Kenai weren't happy because they restricted us a lot on our hunting, our fishing, our livelihood. But we still get our fish. We still get a moose, even if it's road kill. So it's not too bad, what's going on.

You know when this was a Territory, they obeyed what laws they had better than what they're doing today. I think today it's just for spite they're doing things. Because we only had the U.S. marshal here, and the commissioner. And there wasn't that much going on. No killings or stuff like there is today. No break-ins. Leave your doors wide open, never lock them at night or anything.

We used to fish on Salamatof Beach in summertime. We just put a wire around our doorknob and go down to our fishing site. We come back — nothing touched in your home. Nobody touched nothing in your homes. Never stole nothing out of your place. Or outside, nothing. You leave your ax, shovel, anything. Nowadays you can't. Can't even leave your newspaper outside. They'll steal that.

It's sure different. It's changed. I mean since I been going to school and what's today. I mean it's really changed something terrible.

Ralph Ulf Petterson is part Athabascan and part Swedish and Russian. He is a retired commercial fisherman and today lives in his mobile home in Kenai.

He was born on August 1, 1910, in Kenai, and has lived in the Kenai Peninsula community much of his life. He spent a number of years in Seattle, however, when he contracted tuberculosis almost 40 years ago.

Mr. Petterson's first marriage did not survive the separation his illness required, and his second wife died of cancer when the couple's daughter was nine and son was seven.

He's not a complainer, however. In fact, he found many reasons to laugh as he discussed his life.

The past looks good to Mr. Petterson, who recalls the early days of his youth fondly. But, he's a realist. He says at his age he prefers the modern world.

Ralph Ulf Petterson

". . . I had nothing when I come back. I had to start all over again."

My name is Ralph Petterson. I was born in Kenai in 1910. My mother was born in Kenai.

And my dad, he was born in Sweden. And he came across from Sweden when he was 18 years old. He left home. He went to New York. And then from there in '98 when the Gold Rush hit Nome, a bunch of them got together and they bought a boat — a sailboat — and came up to Alaska, mining.

And a storm blew him into Kachemak Bay. So they landed there and hauled their provisions across the Kenai Lake. And they were mining. And after about three years the company broke up.

So then he came to Kenai, and, of course, he met my mother. And then that's where their life started.

He left Sweden because Sweden was going into war, and he was the only son

to that family. And his mother didn't want him to go into war and lose him. So she sent him to America.

I guess she lost him anyway. He never did go back. But he always wrote to her. Mom was born in Kenai. Part of her parents, some of them came from Russia, years ago. I don't know, one of her relatives, anyway. Her name was Matronia Demidoff. That's the way we spelled it in school. But it's Demeidov, I guess the Russians spell it.

Her father was Russian and Indian, and so was my mother. Athabascan. They spoke Russian and a little Indian. But mostly Russian.

There was five in our family. I was next to the last. And they're all living but one who died from appendicitis years ago. Ruptured appendix. The youngest one, my brother, he's a year younger than I am. And my oldest sister, she's just hit 80. My sister, she's here in Kenai. She's 78.

What was Kenai like when I was growing up? (Laughs.) It was beautiful. 'Cause we just didn't know better. It was a good life — then. Course now I wouldn't go back to it if I was my age.

But if I was young, I'd like to go back to that because I could enjoy it. We did more than we do now. In other words, there's a little difference. We mixed together and played. And we used our body, running. Which nowadays, you sit around and use your head.

We always hauled our wood with dogs. We always had a big dog team — five dogs, that's a big team. Generally, you'd have three. And we all hauled our wood with them.

My dad was a fisherman. He was a miner. When he first came across he was a butler in New York. Boy, he could cook, too, I tell you. Make any kind of seafood you wanted. And then he came and, well, they were mining. And then he went fishing. Until the end, he kept on fishing, doing that work. All with fish, see? So it wasn't bad here.

House? It was a cold log house! We get a fire going when we went to bed, in the evening, you know, the fire was going real hot. Teakettle boiling on the stove. Everything's hot. Top of the stove, you could see red. It was hot.

Get up in the morning and even the teakettle was frozen on top of the stove! Six hours afterwards. (Laughs.) That's how they cool off fast. They were cold,

those log houses! I don't know, they just didn't have the right stuff to chink 'em with. They chinked 'em good enough and all, and the fire was burning and it was warm. But when the fire was out, it was gone. The heat was gone.

We had three bedrooms and a big living room and a big kitchen. Everything was big, you know, those days. So we had lots of room. And a lot of dogs, too, in the yard.

We was living about a block away from school. I liked school, specially those pretty teachers.

There was 110 (pupils) and two teachers. But that was in 1918 and '19. I went through eight grades. I didn't learn much. But I lived the rest of my life on it. It was enough.

World War I? Well, I know one thing. We had to hide our flour and stuff. Because my dad always had lots of groceries.

And we had a ceiling upstairs and floor on top. And we took these 50-pound sacks of flour and we stuck them in between the roof and the top so the people wouldn't come and search us and take it away and ration it off. Or give it to somebody else. Even in those days we were still short.

(In 1921) my dad was there working at the cannery, and he was a watchman. When he was working in the summer they had nobody to take care of the cattle. So he told the boss, "I got a boy at home that maybe could take care of these."

He said, "Okay, bring him over."

That's how I went over and took care of these cows. They had two cows, great big cows, too. And I could hardly pack the milk. Man, I had buckets! At least eight gallons of milk I'd have a day from those two cows.

I took care of them, and then they were going to get some moose — calves and bring over and take to California to start a herd there. And I took care of them and fed them, gave them a bottle.

They were really fighting for that milk. They liked their milk. And they took a bunch of them over to California. and I don't know whether that herd is still there or not. And I never went to California to find out, either.

When I was 11 I was big. I grew early, seemed like. And good thing I didn't keep on or I'd be a giant. 'Cause I grew pretty fast. I was 14 or 16 pounds when I was born, and I just kept on being big. When I was 12 years old I was six foot tall and I weighed 164 pounds. I had no fat on me. And after that I only grew two inches. So I was just lucky! (Laughs.)

Food? Well, our food was seasonable. In the summer we ate a lot of fish. Start fishing, and we ate fish. And we ate fish late in the fall. And then they'd put up fish. They'd salt it. They dried it.

And then meat start coming and we'd have meat. Those years it was caribou and moose. Eat a lot of beans and rice, you know. And cheese. They bought it in great big rounds, twenty-five pounds. We'd have four or five of them for the winter.

We used to have big root cellars. They took the vegetables, and they put them in the cellar. Had bins with sand in them. And you put your carrots, turnips, rutabagas in that sand. Cover them up with that sand.

And in the wintertime, they was just as fresh as like digging out of the garden. And we used to have to go down in the wintertime, oh, once or twice a week. Bring in a bunch of stuff from down below.

Cover it up! We had big stacks of hay. You got this long hay you see growing like that here and there along fences and wherever — turns yellow just like straw. Cut it down, make a bundle about that big and tie the middle up. And then use that and lay it all over the floor. And just pile it up there and over the hatch, the deep hatch down about that deep.

Fill that up full, more boards and more hay on top so no air could can go in. Nothing would freeze. Just kept nice and cool. I bet you that temperature down in those root cellars never varied more than one or two degrees — the whole year, not just in winter.

So it was good living.

We used to have apples for Christmas. Up here no boat, nothing traveling, and yet, we'd have apples. Put 'em in a corner in the house, somewhere where it's cool. But you didn't put apples down in the cellar. They'd taste that mold or something from the cellar or whatever it was, that cellar taste.

And we had cattle. They had a few

cows. Always somebody had two, three cows, so we had milk. And in the summertime we had that clabbered milk. Russians called it "prostokvasha." Boy, I liked that. That much of the cream on top you know. Sprinkle sugar, little cinnamon on it. That was good.

Then we had potatoes. All had gardens, everyone. We had cabbage, lettuce — anything you want — turnips, rutabagas. Instead of eatin' apples and oranges, like in the summertime, we were raiding the gardens. And we take that turnip, especially that turnip like when it's small like that. You cut it in half and take a spoon and just scrape it. It is delicious when you get used to it.

But you take something at the store here, like a turnip. I tried to do it. And well, it tastes a little bit like a turnip, but that's all. But when you get one out of the garden like that, there's so many different flavors in it, seemed like. It just tastes delicious.

And then the cabbage, they'd take and tie a bunch a cabbage up in the attic. Hang it up there and let it dry. Then in the wintertime they made soup. So we had our vegetable that way. We had a lot of vegetable. More vegetable, I guess, than we have now. 'Cause at that time we had so much we could just use it.

Nowadays it's too expensive. They can't buy it. (Laughs.) They got it, but they can't eat it! Too expensive.

(Mr. Petterson talks about his father's activities.)

In the wintertime he used to be out trapping. He'd go trapping. And in the summertime he was working at the canneries. Then he was a watchman there, too. He'd stay all winter. He wasn't home too much.

We grew up pretty much by ourselves. We hauled our own wood ... We had to go pack water. We had to take a sled and barrels. And we had to put them on the sled and go after water. Fill every one full, come back about half empty. It's splashed out of the sled.

Specially when they were going to wash clothes, that was terrible hard work. Haul that water for washing clothes. That took a lot of water.

They all worked to a certain extent. They worked hard, I guess. But not too bad. They were used to it. But they always kept our clothes clean. I don't see how they could.

When I first started fishing — when I left home — I had to wash my own clothes in the summer. I always rubbed the skin off my knuckles on the washboard. You ever try a washboard? You'll use your knuckle skins quick, I tell you. In about 5 minutes. (Laughs.) You got to know how to hold the cloth. Otherwise, you just rub your knuckles right off.

At home, (the language was) Russian. My folks spoke Russian all the time. Then when we started school they wouldn't let us speak anything but English there. We had to talk English so that's how we lost everything — our Indian language.

I can get myself in trouble, but I can't

get myself out of it in Russian! (Laughs.) I understand most everything in Russian. I mean, the common language, not the big words. Like around the house, anything around the house.

That all kind of disappeared because they stopped us from it. And now they want us to go back to it. Oh, the hell with that! (Laughs.)

Mother asked him, she said, "Carl, why don't you talk Swedish to the boys. Talk Swede."

He says, "Oh, no, they're talking Russian now. They'll mix that up with English, and we'll never understand them if we put Swede in it."

And the best part, when they got married neither one could understand the other. (Laughs.)

They was there for quite awhile. And my mother was getting lonesome to go home. And they were only living block away, maybe, from her home. Something like that. And she wanted to go home. And she was afraid to go, I guess. Not supposed to, you know.

So she told my dad — she finally learned a few words — and the first words she ever told him in English: "Carl, me, you go Mama."

And he jumped up, and he said, "You bet we go!"

He took her over there, and after that he took her all the time. That was her first words. (Laughs.)

He never thought of taking her over for a visit. Of course, to him it didn't matter. He was a stranger. But he forgot she was lonesome. Boy, after that, then he keep on taking her. But he was a real good husband.

In those days, when they spark a girl — you know, they see somebody they liked — the outsiders would come over, and they'd see somebody in the family. So they'd go to the parents and they'd ask — that they'd want to marry this girl. And they didn't even know who they were. And the parents would say okay if they thought they was a nice man or something. So they'd marry.

My aunts got married that way. My mother, she was about the same, too. And couple cousins, I guess, that way, too. And those that didn't get married that way, they had sweethearts. And they got married that way, you know. The new style, we say. They got divorced right away!

They were all good to their wives, those old-timers that got married that (the old) way. So I think that that's the best system. They should go back to it — take it or leave it.

We had Norway town and the Russian town. And kids would fight back and forth and throw rocks. Mother would say, "Well, let's go to Norway." It used to sound so funny.

All the white folks, they all liked the Indians, seemed like. They talked good of 'em all the time. They treated 'em decent ... Up here, anyway, they were gentle.

These people that come and settled here, they settled here to take the country as is. They weren't forced to do it. They weren't bad like some people think they might have been.

Course you hear about some of the stories down around Sitka and Kodiak when the first Russians come in and fought the Indians. Well, they were coming in more like, like thieves you could say — taking something away from the other person.

But these guys that came up here and settled, they come for a different purpose. They come to have a home and to live, to build a family. That was different type of people that way.

It was late when they put the big bars in. Like now, you just go buy beer anytime you want. But in those days, they had bars. They got drunk and all, I guess. I remember a couple of the bars.

But seemed like nobody was over-drinking, except during their leisure time. But they didn't drink those days. They didn't have enough of it. I don't remember the saloons, but after the saloons there was no liquor around here. They'd make a barrel of beer. Everybody'd come around when the beer was ready. They all went and they had beer.

Maybe you got drunk. I doubt it'd last couple days because it didn't take a barrel long to empty. And then they sobered up until the next batch was ready. But there never was that steady drinking like they do now. They had time to recuperate and heal up ... There wasn't much drinking.

We played right together all the time, specially evenings. And then the old folks get together, talking stories and drinking tea. Of course, we was rough-housing in the next room.

Then later years as we grew up, well, then we started having card games in the wintertime. Russians had a game they called "Mariasha" (phonetic spelling). I don't know, I don't play that no more. Don't ever see it around. I even forget how to play it now.

We had fun. They were always talking stories. The Russians call it "skazkii," little stories.

I started fishing right away. I went fishing, and I been fishing every since. I retired about two years ago.

I got sick. I had to go to the hospital in Seattle. I was there during the War. Most of the time I was laying in bed completely knocked out. TB!

I had a guy working — I had a fish trap and he was working for me. And after he got through work in that fall, about two months, and he died. I picked the bug up from him. That's about 37 years ago.

I guess one of the happiest times for me was when I got married. I was married twice. I was married when I was 23. Had a double wedding in town. The priest's son and I got married together at a double wedding in church.

That was a pretty good wedding 'cause the priest's son was there, too, and he made a special ceremony out of it. It was good. That guy is still alive here.

(But) when I went to the hospital, she left me.

For one thing, I was in the hospital 23 months without stepping on the floor one time. And then the first time I stepped on the floor was after 23 months. I was in the hospital six years.

See I was convalescing, too. They asked me if I wanted to come back. They were going to send me back. I said I was satisfied. I didn't cost them nothing, just a little groceries. So I guess they were making money on me. So they just kept me there. State was paying for it! (Laughs.)

Nothing happened. I got well. Oh, I had the operation after that. I didn't need one, the doctor said, but I took it because I knew I couldn't sit still. And when I come out I went to work right away, building, doing carpenter work.

So I was really glad I did that, otherwise maybe I wouldn't be here right now.

It's kind of odd. There's no TB around now. Just like an epidemic it hits, I guess. Like a flu. I suppose maybe that's the way it works.

When I first came up when I come back I come in the wintertime. And there was snow here. In those days they had a lot of fences around town. All the fences are down now. Used to be wire fences.

I came back, and there was snow piled on the side of the road. And those fences was half broken down. It looked so terrible, I felt like going right back. But then after a couple days, then everything looked good again to me.

Even the moose meat didn't look good when I started eatin' it. It looked to me like it was just black. It didn't look right. But after a couple days it was delicious.

I had nothing when I come back. I had to start all over again. That was in '49. Fifty my first child was born. She (the second wife) followed me up. She died of cancer. Well, the girl was nine and the boy was seven. So I had to raise them all by myself.

And I did, too! My mother helped me for a little bit. She got sick, had a heart attack and cancer mixed. So she had to go the hospital. And I raised 'em myself. It was quite a job all right. But I did it.

(Mr. Petterson discusses the Alaska Native Claims Settlement Act of 1971.)

I kind of liked it. It was a great deal all right. I don't know. We deserved it. People up here worked hard. We didn't get the deal from the people in the States that you'd think a person should of.

They come and they took. But they didn't leave nothing. They'd come up here for working. They'd bring their own crews up here. They didn't hire much people here.

That (the settlement act) was good deal. It helps a lot. At least it takes the money and spends it where it should be — amongst the people, not just a few.

Church? Russian Orthodox. I still belong to it. I never changed. No reason of changing. One is as good as the other. Well, everybody went to church in those days.

But nowadays, I don't know. The bell rings, nobody goes. I don't know how come they don't do that ... That church used to be full. Almost everybody in town would go.

My family, they were connected with church all their lives. They was either readers, or they was way up in the church.

(Christmas), you'd have to see it to believe it. The service, there was good services. Then after church, they'd have big dinners. The tables were set. They'd have tables set right in the house. People would come there and just help themselves.

Of course, it was practically all family, you could say, the whole town. You go to the other place, same thing. You didn't even have to be invited, just go over there. They'll sit you down and feed you. You can walk around all day, and bust open.

And there was lots of it, too. You didn't see one pie on the table. There was 10, 12, 15. And big roasts. I don't know where they got that food ... They had everything, just everything you wanted they had. But now, I don't know. If you got the money you can eat. But you ain't got it, you can't eat.

They didn't have doctors, but they seemed to know what to do. They took good care of them. You'd be surprised at the medicine they used. Some of them is even used now. They seemed to get along good. Real bad sicknesses,

they might not. Otherwise the smaller ones, they knew what to do. They used herbs and stuff.

My grandmother was a midwife. She was a real good one. She used to go as far as almost to Anchorage there — Moose Point, down Ninilchik, and all around. Small outside places. They come and pick her up and take her over.

And she only lost one woman in all her years. And that was her own niece. I don't know what happened. Anyway, she lost her. But outside of that, they had no trouble.

She was kind of strict, too, grandmother was. Telling the people what not to eat and what not to do. And not only that, after they had babies she made them stay in bed nine days. My sister, too, they still stayed and laid in bed nine days. I don't know why they always stayed in bed so long. Now they have a baby and they send them home the same day.

My grandmother and them, they talked a lot about Kodiak and down there. Because Kodiak was affiliated with Kenai pretty close. Seemed like they went back and forth.

They talked about Kodiak more than they did about Russia itself. The people in Kodiak, seemed like they knew the people there. They went there — the sailors, years ago they went hunting for sea otter way down there, below Seldovia and towards Kodiak. There was a few people from Kodiak up here.

They had doctors there then. And

there was a few guys from Kenai went to California, they went to school down there. They got their education pretty well. They'd go down to Sitka and Kodiak and get educated there, too. So they weren't completely isolated.

(Mr. Petterson discusses modern fish and game issues.)

Seems to me like if you caught one or two fish you get the thrill and that's enough. Why sit there and fish day after day after day when you don't need them? Or even fishermen put them back in the creek. Like some say, "Oh, we put them back."

Well, some do and some don't. But every fish they put back, there's very few of them that are not hurt. Somehow they're hurt. I don't think it's good for the fish.

Not unless we wanted to eat, we never fished. We could fish all we wanted to. But we never fished just for fun. There's no sense to it. Who's going to sit there like a fool, fishing and throw them back in the river?

My dad and them was always after us: Don't hurt the birds' nests or anything like that. Don't hurt them.

They're young. We need them. They want to live just like we do. Which was right. They'll come in handy some day.

Fiocla Sacoloff Wilson was born in Kenai, but she grew up in Anchorage and Eklutna after her parents died when she was only nine years old. She is part Athabascan and part Russian.

Mrs. Wilson was born on June 30, 1916, and spoke about her life in her Kenai home, a well-furnished and comfortable house.

Faith is important to Mrs. Wilson, as are traditional values.

Mrs. Wilson laughs at the irony of being brought up in a federal Indian school, where pupils were punished for merely speaking a language other than English, and participating in a program aimed at preserving cultural heritage. She herself was forced to wash her mouth out with soap once when she was caught by a matron at the school who overheard her say something to a friend in Russian.

Because she lost her own mother at such a young age, Mrs. Wilson said it was very important to her to try and give as much as she could to her own children.

Fiocla Sacoloff Wilson

". . . I think we were happier because we worked a lot harder."

My name is Fiocla Wilson. And I was born here in Kenai, Alaska. I left when I was nine years old. I went to school in Anchorage and Eklutna Industrial School where I graduated.

My parents died when I was nine years old. So I was brought up in the school, Eklutna Industrial School. It was like a Bureau of Indian Affairs school.

I had sisters and brothers. But they were here in Kenai. I had three sisters and two brothers. But they've passed away since. I was the third to the youngest. My older sister kept my younger brother and sister.

My father was part Russian. And his name was Ephiem Sacoloff. And my mother's name was Eugenia Sacoloff. But her maiden name was Kassilovski.

I have no idea what she died of. I was too young.

I think we had a two-room house at the time — kitchen and bedroom. I remember it was very clean. I had a nice home life while she lived. But then after she passed away I was brought up in school. I'm real thankful that I was brought up in school because it did teach me a lot of things.

(She talks about food in the early years of her life.)

We lived on fish and moose meat and lot of berries and things like that.

One of the ways we preserved our berries was we used to put them in cold water and just put them down our cellars. Everybody had cellars, those days, to put their food and stuff in. And so if we wanted berries in the winter, they were just like fresh when we took

I remember we used to go up the river, where my mother used to put up her fish in the summer. You know? Like smoked salmon, stuff like that. We picked a lot of berries, and put up berries and things like that. Put up salt fish for wintertime. They put up certain kind of dried salmon for the dogs.

I believe we were healthier years back, where people had their own natural teeth. Now it seems like there's all that candy and all that fast food and stuff.

Like the Eskimos used their seal oil and all that stuff, and it was just like cod liver oil. I raised my kids on cod liver oil for vitamins.

I think we were healthier because we worked a lot harder. We had to do a lot of walking because we didn't have cars and stuff.

(In Kenai) We used to have to go to the American School and learn English from nine o'clock until 3:30 in the afternoon. Then, from 3:30 to 4:30 we had to go to the Russian school.

And we had to learn the Russian language an hour a day. That's how I remember some of my Russian. But after I left when I was nine, then of course, I had to pick up what I could when I came back here.

My parents spoke Russian and Indian. But our mother mostly spoke to us in Russian. So I really don't know much of the Indian language.

Being brought up in the school there we couldn't speak no other language but English language. Because if we got caught talking in either Russian or Indian, you know, we got punished for it — then.

There was another girl from Kenai, and I said something to her in Russian and the matron heard it. We both had to wash our mouth out with soap! I don't remember what I said. Wasn't anything bad or anything. It was just something that I said in the Russian language, 'cause the other girl spoke Russian, too.

And she made us both wash our mouth out with soap. So that's how strict they were. And that's why I can't understand now why everything's getting back so that they want us to talk our Native language.

At that time the government wouldn't allow us to talk in those languages. And now, they're giving funds to get back to our old heritage.

Being in that school at that time, they never let us do no Native culture. Every once in awhile there would be — like there was a person from Juneau, an Indian, Tlingit Indian, and she came and was showing us how they did their Chilkat blankets or something. But they were there just one day, so we just didn't learn anything.

I think it's getting back now. After the Native land claims, I think people are going to try to go back to their heritage. Why, I think it's good.

I'm real sorry that I never ever taught my grandchildren. I could never speak to them in Indian because I was brought up in school where I never learned it. I teach them a little Russian because

I remembered Russian a lot more than Indian.

My sister spoke real good Indian. I mean when I came back, they were teasing my husband. They would talk back and forth in Indian. And I would go somewhere and cry, because I'd think they were making fun of me. Or they were talking about me. (Laughs.)

The Russian Orthodox Church was where we all went to church there. Saturday night and Sunday morning, we had to be in church. I liked church.

The real old people spoke in Russian and in Indian. But I also remember going to Russian church. And all those people had the most beautiful voices.

Like the Russian and Native women all knew the Russian langugage, so they would sing in Russian. The women had high soprano voices. The men had the deep tenor and bass. And, I mean, the singing was beautiful back then, compared to now. And everything, those days, was just in Russian. But now when I go to the Russian church when there's a funeral or something, the priest has it in English.

Then after I went to school, then I went to a Protestant church. I think it was a Presbyterian church. And I'd gone to that until I came back here when I was 17. Then I started going to Russian Orthodox church again because that was the only church.

Then when the missionaries came in and had a church, I went to that. And I still go to the same church, to the Kenai Bible Church.

(Mrs. Wilson describes the Eklutna Industrial School.)

It was a really a nice school. There was 150 boys and girls. They were all part Natives, you know, part Indians. So I got along pretty well with all of them. Got along good with the staff members.

At the time when I was there it was up to the eighth grade only. And you had a choice of going to some other school. It isn't there anymore. They moved it to Mt. Edgecumbe.

There was kids from all over. There was none from the Eklutna Village itself. There was a village about maybe a mile away from the school. But these were kids from all over — up North and the Aleutians and places like that.

I thought we had good teachers. Being a teenager, of course, I thought they were strict. But now I'm thankful that they were. They taught us everything.

I mean besides going to the regular school I would take a half a day — go to school in the mornings. Then in the afternoons I would work in a kitchen or something. Learn how to cook suppers and stuff. Then the next month our next detail would be like working in a laundry. And one month, taking up sewing. That would be like home ec, you know. And maybe one month of being a waitress for the staff members. So they had us pretty well organized to do different things.

I had a teacher that always told me never be ashamed of your nationality.

And it wasn't your nationality that counted as much as your character and your personality. And she always told me that I would go a long ways if I would just be the way I was with my personality and my character. Because she said I had an awful sweet personality.

Our home ec teacher, and she was our cook also. And she's the one that told me that our nationality didn't count as much as our personality and character. She was really good to me, and I really liked her.

I just remember her telling me that, that nationality didn't count as much. It was nice to have nationality, but she said it was our character and personality that would take us a long ways. And she always said that I had a personality that would take me a long ways. And so I always remembered.

And then another thing she used to always tell us: if we try, not to say we can't do it. You know, like try, try again. Something like that. Something to that effect.

So that's what I always believed in. So even when I came back here to Kenai, and that's where — when I was 17 and came back here — that's when I found out that, like the Russian people were sort of, you know, kind of made fun of the Native people and stuff. Where they thought they were better or something.

And that's the first time I ever knew that there was a racial problem. But I fitted in with everybody.

My husband was in love with a Russian girl (earlier). And her parents didn't want her to go around with my husband because he was part Native. But what makes it funny is now those very same people all say they're part Indian. And now they all get along fine!

When I came back to Kenai, he came to our house and told me he would show me Kenai. 'Cause I left here when I was nine, so, of course, when I was 17 Kenai had changed so much.

He wanted to show me the different things. So that's how we met. I stayed with my sister. This was just a small village then, and everybody knew everybody. He was only four years older than I was. I was 17. He was 21 when we got married that fall.

Kenai is a lot bigger today. It's a lot more modern. When I was a kid we had to pack our water. There was no electricity. I mean we used kerosene and gas lanterns for lights. And everybody used wood. There was no other means of heat. We used wood stoves.

When I was a child they used to have masquerade balls. People would dress up in masquerade clothes, and they would go to each house. And we'd try to guess who they are. And some of them would really dance around. And I used to think that was fun.

And even when I got married, they used to have masquerade balls, and everybody would dress in costumes. And I thought that was fun.

It was a close community. And when

the Russian church would have their Lent — for the whole seven weeks — even the Caucasians, the white people, would go with the Russian people and not have dancehalls open or anything like that for the seven weeks of Lent.

And then when Lent was over on Easter Sunday, and right the next night then they would open up the dancehalls so we could have dances.

(She talks about the effect of World War II.)

We had to darken up our houses and have no lights showing. To be on the safe side, when it got dark we had to have either something like black shades or shutters from the outside so there'd be no kind of light to show. In case the enemy flew over and could see a light, they could bomb or something.

In the States I remember they rationed gas and sugar and everything. But the canneries up here brought all the sugar and all the gasoline we needed. So in the fall that was the only way we could get our winter supply was from the cannery. We'd get sugar by hundred pounds. A lot of flour and rice and our staple goods like beans. And our canned vegetables and canned fruits and stuff, we all got from the cannery.

That would last for the whole winter, till spring when the boats would come back again. We did have a grocery store here. My husband fished for the cannery, so he would get all his staple goods right from the cannery to last.

Seemed like we weren't rationed up here because I remember even people would say they couldn't get silk stockings and stuff. And we would order to Montgomery or Sears, and we would get them. Where the people in the States, it would be in the papers where sugar was rationed and gasoline and anything that was silk.

We used to commercial fish. I enjoyed that, taking the kids out on the beach. Live in tents. And it was just like a vacation for my children. They really enjoyed that. Living on the beach and living in a tent. Camping. It was fun for them.

Our fish site was just below Wildwood Station, out on the bluff. We had our fish sites there. And we fished there from 1934 until the early '60s. And then my husband went to drift fishing. Got himself a boat and started drifting. And then, of course, we weren't on the beach anymore because he sold the beach sites to get a drift boat.

We'd go out around May 30th and stayed there until August the eighth. Then we'd come in on the weekends. I did a lot of the laundry on the beach, but we'd come home and I would wash clothes in my washing machine.

We didn't have electricity, but my husband got a gas washing machine. And I would wash clothes and bake my bread and stuff at home. So then, go to church on Sunday, go back early Monday morning, back to our fish sites.

We had six children. We had eight altogether, but we lost two.

It was just like having a picnic or something. Didn't have a big house to take care of. We had two tents — one for cooking and the other for our bedrooms. He had them up on a platform, so I had wooden floors and everything.

He used to have a window put in so I could watch him while he fished. He had a little water pump for me, so I just pumped my water from the porch. So it was nice. I didn't have all that housecleaning to do at home. (Laughs.) I had to do my cooking, three meals a day. We had to go according to the tides.

My children were all small. We had two children; then after six years we had six more, one after the other. (Laughs.)

In the summertime, only meat we could get was from the cannery. The only way to preserve food in the olden days — we didn't have no freezers or anything — so we had to can all our meat and can our fish and dry our fish and salt our fish. Have things like that.

There was no doctor here at all. I mean, in the summer the cannery brought their own doctor. If anybody was really sick, the doctor would come and look at them and tell us what to do. We didn't have doctors here way back then.

I had all my children at home by a midwife. Didn't cost money compared to what it does now (laughs) if you had to go to a hospital!

There used to be some TB cases. You know they used to say it was TB cases. But now when I think of it, I often wonder if it was like cancer, and nobody knew of it. Because if you think — if

it was TB, everybody would have TB because they said it was contagious.

I do know that when I used to have a sore throat, after I was even married, my uncle used to bring some kind of roots. I would have to soak it in water and gargle my throat with it and things. And I know my mother-in-law used to pick some kind of tea. I think they call it Hudson Bay Tea (ledum palustre or ledum groenlandicum). It was something that grew wild in the woods.

And when we'd have real bad colds she would boil that and let us drink that. And she said that would cure our cold. I think people used it that had TB or something, too. Used to drink that tea.

And if we had real cuts or something like that or people would have boils or whatever, they would pick pitch off the trees. You know, the pitch off the spruce trees? And they would make a poultice with brown sugar and stuff and put it on whatever it was. And that would draw out the poison.

(She talks about the different values people had then.)

People always shared. Like if someone got their first king salmon in the spring, they would give a little piece to everybody. You know, share? The same with moosemeat. If someone got their moose in the fall they would give a piece to everybody.

And people really shared. And nowadays it isn't that close-knit feeling. I guess because people are scattered or what. But it isn't like that any more.

Seemed like everybody just shared. I mean we were either all poor or we were just in-between. Because everybody helped one another. Even after I was married, I always tried to help people. I still do.

(She discusses whether the Alaska Native Claims Settlement Act of 1971 was good for Alaska Natives.)

My husband really didn't think so. 'Cause he always said that money would go sometime, and then we wouldn't have no more. And then for the ANS

(Alaska Native Service, the federal health agency), as far as having ANS help, he said in time we wouldn't have that, either. That was his feeling about it. Now, I don't know myself.

I think he was right when he said it. He said he didn't think it was that great of a thing.

I think in your territorial days we got more. It seemed like our kids, when they went to school, they didn't have to buy their papers and pens and stuff like that. The Territory furnished every-thing.

Then when it got to be statehood my children had to pay for everything they got in school. But, of course, statehood brought a lot of modern things. And we can't complain if we want everything that's modern. We can't say, "We'll go back to the old ways." 'Cause it was a harder life.

Speaking of a religious life, my mother died when I was nine years old, and maybe the Lord had a purpose in it. I always told my husband, "Well, if I have my children I would always make the best mother and try and do everything I could that they would be proud of me."

Because I didn't have a mother. My mother died when I was only nine years old.

And I was brought up in the school. I'm real happy that I did go to school, cause I don't know what my life would have been if I was raised here in Kenai without a mother.

Lower Cook Inlet West

Frederick T. Bismark Sr. is an Athabascan who was born on April 6, 1923, in Anchorage.
He has lived most of his life in Tyonek, where he lives today. His family moved to the village
during the Depression when times were particularly tough for those in Anchorage who were unable
to practice a subsistence lifestyle.

Mr. Bismark spoke openly and candidly — offering many wry explanations of his views —
at the village community center in Tyonek.

He has a strong sense of family and community ties, and he was instrumental in building much
of the modern village.

Mr. Bismark speaks often about having worked hard all his life, raising his 11 children. He
points out that it was a feat made more difficult because of his lack of formal education. He
managed to overcome that lack, however, even to the point of becoming a pilot.

Frederick T. Bismark Sr.

"I traveled Cook Inlet when I was seven days old. I've been on it ever since."

Well, I was born in Anchorage April 6th, 1923. I lived in Anchorage till I was about ten years old ... During the Depression, we moved down here to Tyonek.

My dad used to build fish traps all over Cook Inlet here. And the last fish trap Dad built, why, we stayed here and fished it ... There was so much fish we got 125,000 fish that year with a fish trap. And after that, why, he went to commercial fishing — set-netting.

I traveled Cook Inlet when I was seven days old. I've been on it ever since.

During the Depression, life was so tough in Anchorage, we had to move out here where we could live off the country.

It was really tough when we first moved out here because there was no

buildings of any kind. They had the village down here about three or four miles below Tyonek.

We moved up here when they started building the new village. We worked. And I mean we worked hard all our lives. First thing they done was build a school. Build a school here in Tyonek. Then they put a big sawmill in, a steam-engine sawmill. And we went to work for the federal government here — what they call the Civilian Conservation Corps.

Dad and I both worked. We worked eight hours a day. We got 25 cents an hour. And we made 61 dollars a month. I hauled all the logs for the sawmill from the airstrip up here. We didn't have any power of any kind. All we were using was axes, hand saws.

We were using block-and-tackle to

pull the trees down — pull all the trees down, stump and all. And the good green logs — I was hauling it out with a dog team. And that's where we got all our church lumber from. We built our church from rough lumber, from the timber here that was pulled out on the airstrip here.

After we got the church built, then the people that were able to kept cutting logs. You cut the logs and they sawed it up in the sawmill. You got half of the lumber. And the village got the other half. We worked that way for years and years.

And we worked on the airstrip for a good many years — Civilian Conservation Corps.

But at those times we were only getting two cents for fish, for every fish we caught. Went from two to five and from five to seven and from seven to 14, 19, and I think it got about as high as 70 cents per fish when they went into poundage.

My wife and I — I married my wife when she was only 15. And she's 16 years younger than I am. But her and I, we worked hard all our lives ... We raised five boys, six girls, two grandchildren. Never in our life have we been on welfare or food stamps. We worked hard all our lives.

We used to fish down at West Foreland. We used to fish the kings and the reds and silvers. We had 16 shackles of gear between my wife and I. We got caught in a storm down there and we lost everything we owned! We lost our

boat. We lost our motors. When we got through we didn't have nothing.

That was about 27 years ago. And then I used to be the U.S. postmaster. But I couldn't make enough money to support my family because I was only getting 55 dollars a month at the time. I finally quit my job, and I let my wife take over. She was postmaster here. And she's been postmaster for close to 30 years now.

After I lost everything, then I went to work on a cannery tender. I worked about five years, I think. Then after that, I skippered a boat on Cook Inlet here for about five years.

Then, the family was getting bigger. Kids were started to grow up and my wife couldn't handle them no more. So she says, "You either come home or either get a divorce." So, I quit the boat, and I came home. I bought some other fishing sites. And I bought more fishing gear and stuff. And I've been fishing ever since.

When I first come into this country, there was no moose in this country. The moose didn't come in here until the '40s. And I guess it was the Lord's way of taking care of us. Before the moose ever come in here, there was a lot of grouse. There was millions of grouse, millions of ptarmigans and millions of porcupines, beavers.

And after the moose come in here in the '40s, then all the small game disappeared. There's no more grouse, no more ptarmigans, no more porcupines, no more beavers.

I always go back and think about those days.

I've testified time and time again at the (Alaska Department of) Fish and Game hearings that I have no idea where the moose come from. The game biologists have no idea where they come from, either. And today, they still don't have any idea where they came from.

And then in the '40s to the '50s, nobody used to hunt in this area. And there was so much moose that you could go down to the river — by boat — and you climb up on the bank and pick out the moose you want. But now, there's so many hunters in the area. You spend 30 days down there, you're lucky if you see one or two moose now.

I think within the next ten years we're gunna have another moose crash. I'll bet money on it. Because, just like it happened, they just came right in, and you have no idea where the come from.

And I think they're going to disappear the same way again.

You know, I've worked so hard all my life. I trained my boys. I have five boys. The youngest one is 16. I've trained them to preserve food. My boys — alone — can go down to that beach, down to the fish camp, and all five boys can get to work.

And they can smoke fish. They can salt fish. They can can fish. They know how to hunt. They know how to take care of their game. They know how to bring it home and preserve it. They can

do all that. I don't have to be out there. I don't have to show them no more.

And the reason I make them preserve a lot of food? Well, like last summer, I had 40 cases of salmon. And the kids get mad because sometimes we're working too hard, putting up too much fish. Pretty soon one of the boys says, "Dad, how come we put up so much fish? How come we can so much fish?"

I said, "Do you really want to know?" They said, "Yeah." I said, "Well, what if the Japs or somebody come over and bomb all our industrial areas? And they bomb all our ... farms and everything."

I told them, "I don't care if you got a million dollars in your hand. You're not going to be able to buy anything. If you got 10 million dollars in your hand, you're gunna starve to death." I say, "All that hard work you put in this, you can use that for two or three years. Even if you can't buy nothing. You'll survive."

And the funniest part of all this is I never had any education ... I used to belong to the 302 Operating Engineers. I operate heavy equipment. I operate cats and graders, loaders, cranes. I was a sea captain for five years. I owned my own business. I used to own a tug and barge. Got out of that.

Got into the airplane business. I used to own three airplanes. I used to have an air taxi. And without an education, I'll tell you, it's the toughest thing in the world to do — try to learn an airplane. That's the toughest thing in the world to do without education!

And I keep pushing my kids — 11 kids. And I had a meeting last year with my kids. I told my kids, "You kids are a lot smarter than I am. You kids should be able to do things for yourself. I'm the dumbest one in the family. I don't have any education."

But my oldest daughter got up, and she said, "Dad, you're smarter than all of us put together." And she had one year of college. And I couldn't say anything.

Well, Anchorage is a lot different from what it was when I left 50 years ago. Fifty years ago, you know every businessman on Fourth Avenue. You go down to somebody's store, you go in there to buy something, and there's nobody around. Nobody around, and you holler and holler. And nobody answer you.

You go next door. The manager or the owner, he's next door talkin' with the barber or somebody. And all the stores were that way on Fourth Avenue … They didn't even lock their doors. They didn't even lock their cash registers. 'Cause everybody knew each other on the Avenue there.

But, no. Nowadays, you can't do that no more. There's a lot of change. People start comin' in. Like one time, I heard a remark when I was in Seattle … Somebody was talkin' about the Arctic Slope.

And the other guy said, "Aw, the Arctic Slope is just a big block of ice. Just let the Eskimos have it. We don't want it."

Well, after they struck oil up there in Prudhoe Bay, they want to run the Eskimos off now.

That's the same thing that happened to Tyonek. We got gas on the reservation here. We got a lot of natural gas. Never struck any oil. But we leased most of our property to the oil companies for drilling rights. They struck gas. I don't know how many gas wells we have on the village property.

After we got our money here, I was the president, and then I became chairman of the finance committee. Instead of giving each individual money, we made a deal with the people — take it or leave it. We give each individual five thousand dollars. Now, if you want to take your five thousand dollars and go to Anchorage, go ahead. That's all you get.

But the deal we made with the people here — for the single housing or $18,000 homes — if you take your five thousand dollars and put it in a home, we'll pay the rest off. And you can have a one-bedroom home. Five people got $25,000 … And that's how everybody in the village got a home. And I thought that was real good idea.

Before we got into spending money, they sent me on a tour. I've been all over the country. I've been to New Mexico, Old Mexico, Arizona, Colorado, Oklahoma, California, Washington, Kansas, District of Columbia, Cleveland, Chicago.

I think I covered just about all the states, looking at all the Indian reservations to see where they made their mistakes and see where they made good investments.

Like the Ute Tribe in Colorado. Those people didn't have anything. But they went into business. They started a herd of cattle — the Indians themselves. They get a calf or cow or steer or something, they put it in the pool. They kept doing that for years and years. They had the best stock of cattle in all of the world. They built their cattle herd up to 24,000 head of cattle.

Well, they got into some money. And they just give the money to the people. And the people would buy a brand new cadillac. They'd run out of gas on the road, they'd sell the car for a bottle of booze. And just walk away from it.

Well, they kept giving the money, and the people won't go back to work. And their cattle start going down. They start peddling their cattle for a bottle of booze. Pretty soon they quit giving them money. They said no more money.

And those Indian cowboys went back to work on their herd of cattle. They had it almost depleted — completely depleted. And the year I was out there, they had the cattle built back up to 18,000 head of cattle again.

So if you give the people the money, it don't do any good in my opinion. Just that one thing there, I thought they were pretty smart when they cut the money off.

But in Arizona it was different — the Navajos. The Navajos have over a hundred million bucks ... and I went

to their council. They were braggin' how good it was. They had their own schools. They had their own police force. They had all this. They had all that.

But their poor people were still living in hogans, in burlap tipis. You go out and drive along the roads and highways, and you see burlap tipis there. And they're braggin' about how good their schools are, their own police force and everything else.

But they weren't taking care of their people. I don't know. I didn't think much of that. That was the most important part.

Our late attorney, Stan McCutcheon — he won our lands claims for us here. We had 26,000 acres. And when we won our land claims, our late president, Al Kaloa Jr., died in a hotel fire in Anchorage.

At the time I was the vice president in the village council. Well, when he died in the fire I had to take over.

So that's how the land claims got started. And Tyonek never got any credit for it. The first time the AFN (Alaska Federation of Natives) meeting was put together, Tyonek paid the transportation from all over Alaska for Native leaders to attend the first AFN meeting.

Emil Notti was the president. And at the meeting, Emil Notti stated that AFN didn't have any money. They had two dollars in their account.

So our attorney got up. He said, "The president, before he died, made a state

79

ment that we're gunna help the others."

He said, "I have the vice president with me here from Tyonek. We'll loan the AFN $100,000 cash."

And I just about jumped out of my shoes because I didn't expect anything like that. But I had to sign a $100,000 check over to AFN.

And we paid for transportation for all the people — all their expenses in Anchorage. It cost us $150,000 for the first AFN meeting. On top, we loaned them $100,000. A quarter of a million dollars into AFN to get the land claims started.

And, actually, Tyonek never got any credit for it. I bring it up at meetings and stuff like that, there's people say, "Yeah, I know. I know." But nobody'll ever come out and testify that Tyonek was the instigator of the land claims.

And, it hurt me sometimes. And there was a big AFN convention in Anchorage when my good friend Stan McCutcheon died. And there was a funeral. And it really hurt me. AFN didn't stop the meeting long enough for people to go to the funeral or nothin'. I left the meeting, and I went to his funeral.

Stan was such a good friend of mine. He was my attorney and the village attorney all the time. Never charged nothin'. Never charged the village. Never charged me. I was so proud to have him for an attorney.

I was at a meeting in Fairbanks. One of my boys was born while I was at that meeting in Fairbanks. Stan was so proud to hear that, he announced it at the meeting. And when my turn came, I told the people at the meeting that I named the boy after my attorney, Stanley J.

I really enjoyed that land claims fight. I spent about two months in Washington, D.C. I flatfooted 435 congressmen and senators and their aides. I put my point through to all the senators. They get a different version from other people, you know.

They don't know the truth. They don't know the truth about Alaska. And once you sit down and tell them, explain it to them, they put it down in writing. And they remember it.

I kind of hate the land claims, right now, as it is. The reason I say I hate it — there's only so many people benefittin' from the land claims. Everybody's fightin' for power. Power. Power.

And I don't like that. I don't like to see it. All they want is power. Now look what's happening to the North Slope Borough. It's something I don't like to see. It's something I don't like to talk about.

But it's happened. And if the people keep fightin' for power that's what's going to happen to all the other corporations. And I don't like it. There's no way in the world I like it. But what can you do about it?

Like 1991. How many of the kids are going to hold their stock? Not very many. After 1991, I'd like somebody to tell me — and I don't care who it is — how many Indians are going to own land after 1991? I'd like to know that.

How many's going to be able to pay taxes on their property after 1991? Five percent? Then 95 percent is going to lose their land. I don't see no land claims. I don't see any land claims because they're going to lose all their land.

And the reason I fought for land claims is I thought we were going to get a piece of land. It's gunna be ours, and we're not going to be able to lose it. Or we'd utilize it the way we want it. But no. Today, it's not. It's altogether different. You're talking about culture. In my own opinion, I don't think I'm any better than anybody else. I don't think anybody is any better than I am. Because the Lord put us here. And I think we should be all equal if we abide by the Bible, like we should.

You know the Lord gave us different languages, and he sent us in different directions. He sent us in different directions with different languages so if we meet each other we wouldn't be fightin' each other. We wouldn't be cussin' other.

I don't like the idea of sending our students over for foreign exchange. Because they're learnin' our language, and we're learnin' their language.

The Lord didn't plan it that way ... The Lord gave us different languages, sent us in different directions so we won't understand each other. We won't fight each other. And, so, for that purpose, I don't think we're any better than any other.

I read the Bible quite a bit, once in awhile. My wife and I, we both have a Bible. If you're a believer, it really helps. I mean it helps.

I had a tug and barge. They loaded the barge with two bulldozers and they brought it down here to the village. On the way back to Anchorage they sunk the landing craft. That was about eight o'clock at night in August and pitch dark! I mean pitch dark.

It was blowing about 60 to 70 miles an hour out there and they had about 15 to 20 foot sea out there. And I had a radio in my house — a marine radio — and they called "mayday."

I answered them, I said, "What happened?" They said they were sinking. The landing craft was all steel. But the house was wood. And when the boat was sinking, the waves were hitting the house so hard, it broke the house off. And the house was just floating level with the water in 15 to 20 foot sea out there.

And the two crew members they hung on to the house, with just their heads stickin' out of the water.

Well, when they called mayday and said they were sinking, I told my wife and my kids, I said, "Come on. Get in front of the Holy Picture — icon."

I said, "Get on your hands and knees and pray for the crew. Pray for the two crew members. Ask God to save them."

They were in the water for about 40 minutes. There was helicopters come about 40 to 50 miles up the Inlet here.

And right today I wonder. Pitch dark,

and all they had was search lights off the helicopter. They spotted those two men, hangin' on to that house with just their heads stickin' out of the water — 15 to 20 foot sea. Now how did they ever find them?

I always wondered. Did the Lord answer our prayer? They were in the water only 40 minutes, and the helicopter picked them up and took them to Anchorage.

And I believed. All my life I've believed in the Lord. I've never gone hungry. My kids has never gone hungry. My wife has never gone hungry. We all had plenty to eat.

But it takes a lot of hard work. A lot of hard work ... I really believe there is a Lord. If you ask Him for help when you're in trouble, I think you're gunna get help.

You know, all the years since as far as I could remember — our folks teach us the Orthodox Church. And that's kind of dying out, too. Because everything is in English. The younger generation probably like it. But I don't. Because I love that Slavonic singin'. I really love it.

I've tried for years and years to get somebody here to teach the kids to keep the Slavonic singin' up in church. And nobody seem to want to teach the kids how to do it. I got two girls — one is living in Anchorage and one is in Savannah, Georgia, now. They never had any training, but they both go to church all the time. They learned to sing in Slavonic. And they're both good Slavonic singers in church.

The church, to me, is of great value because we worked hard to build it. We didn't have the money to build it. Everything was volunteer work, donations. At those times, you know, we only put a quarter in the plate. But that was big money in those days. It's like when I first come here, we were getting two cents for fish.

We're losin' our ways here. People don't talk the Native language any more. When I first come to Tyonek I didn't know not one Indian word. I learned how to talk it.

My wife was born and raised here. She can't even talk it. She can understand it, but she don't know how to talk it. It wasn't too hard for me to pick up. But when I lived in Anchorage, I wasn't around no Indian people. I didn't have no need to learn it. But after I come here I had to. Because in the Olden Time, that's the only language they talked — Indian language. Max Chickalusion — when I first met him — he didn't know the English language. The only thing he knew was Indian language.

It's a pretty hard language to learn. But once you start learning, then it's not too hard. The people here don't use the Native language no more.

They teach bilingual in school. But I don't like that, either. I really hate that. What they do in the school when they teach bilingual — they take about three or four different languages from the area here.

Like Susitna is only about 50 to 60

miles from here. Kenai is about 50 to 60 miles. Nondalton is about 150 miles. Dillingham is probably a couple hundred miles. They take all the languages and just put them all together. And they teach that bilingual in school.

Well, my kids come home from school, they talk to me in Indian, and I don't understand them. I talk to them in my language, they don't understand me. They don't know what I'm talking about.

(Mr. Bismark discusses what he recalls of Indian medicine.)

I really don't know that much about the Indian medicine. When my mother was alive, I didn't pay that much attention to what she used to use.

But I know one thing. I was fishing one year when I was about 14 years old, and I was just a kid then. I was running the outboard motor, and I reached back and I touched the flywheel. The flywheel touched me here, and I got fish poison in my hand.

And, God Almighty, my hand swelled up about this thick, I guess. My mother took something that looked like spinach. I don't know what it's called, but she took it and put it in a wash basin.

It looked like spinach when you cook in it water. Take it and put it in boiling water and boil it and boil it. And the water just turns green ... My mother took it and pull it off the stove after it cooled off enough so she can put her hand in there. Then she took my hand and she put my hand in it. Then she took that stuff looked like spinach and wrap it all around my hand. Then she put it back on top of the stove.

And, God Almighty, you could almost bring it to a boiling point that way. She done that all day that day.

Next morning I got up and, God Almighty, my hand was just grey and green or something. And it started drawing that infection. My whole hand just about turned green and grey. So she took a razor and she hit it.

And, man, that hurt. I was hollering. She just squeezed it as hard as she could.

Next morning I got up and my hand was just like this — nothing wrong with it. That's about the only Indian medicine I know of.

I had a real tough life all my life. I don't have anybody. I lost my brother. And I lost my sister. And I lost my dad. I lost my mother. I lost my uncles, my aunties and my father-in-law. I lost my father-in-law to cancer. I lost my mother to cancer. I lost my uncle to cancer. And almost lost my wife to cancer, too.

Well, I can sit here and talk for two days and I'll never get done. I enjoyed talkin' here ... I try to do the best I can. And I think if somebody would make use of some of this knowledge, it'd be beneficial to the younger generation.

I sure do want to thank you.

Alexandra Kaloa is an Athabascan who was born on September 26, 1910, in Kenai. She lives in Anchorage today at the Anchorage Pioneers' Home.

Mrs. Kaloa spent much of her life in Tyonek. She moved there with her parents who wanted to find a place with fewer alcohol and racial problems than those they saw in Kenai.

Mrs. Kaloa is deaf. She spoke in her tiny apartment after reading questions that were written for her. Her daughter, Agnes Brown, assisted in communicating with her when the sense of the written question was unclear.

Having spent much of her life helping others as the wife of one of Tyonek's key leaders and as a midwife, Mrs. Kaloa has seen her share of hardship. But she speaks with great pride of the assistance she offered people in the village.

Alexandra Kaloa

". . . You have to do what you have to do, even if you're scared you have to try your best anyway."

We were very poor. And when I went to school, I went to American school and Russian school. I used to talk Russian, but I don't know anything now. And my mother used to put up dog salmon, and fish for dogs.

The mailman — my father and the mailman used to come from Kenai to Seward for mail. So you had to have lots of dog feed. I used to help my mother fish, cut fish, cut fish.

Kenai is on a high hill (bluff). I used to go down to the beach and then pack the fish up on my back. Three times a day. Night-time, my mother used to go with another old lady — together. But we had a hard time.

Boy, I used to be so hungry sometimes. We had lots of moose meat and fish, dried fish. We didn't have no supplies till spring-time. There wasn't no airplanes then, only boats, and very small boat that they delivered supplies from here to Kenai.

Whatever they were short of we got in the spring-time. But there was lots of beans, flour, sugar, lard — all the things that we needed ... We had two stores in Kenai then. So if one store was short of something we'd go to the other store. But we had to have so much a week. So much sugar, flour, milk and so forth.

I was a husky, strong girl then. I would get so hungry. Well, good thing I helped my neighbor. They had chickens, pigs, horses and milk cow and eggs. And my girlfriend, she baked fresh bread. She bring out fresh bread to me. I had all the cream I want. I would churn butter. She give us milk and cream and sour milk every day. And we give them fish and moose meat whenever they need some.

My father worked in the cannery in summertime. But they didn't earn very much. So we were very poor — just had enough to buy food. Not enough clothes. My mother was doing sewing. She make me moccasins and skin clothes and fur clothes. Now I think about it, I think of myself dressed as a very rich person.

But I thought I didn't dress very good. But I wish I had the clothes that I had then now. (Laughs.) Fur clothes. Fur coat, handmade. Handmade moccasins, even the skirt and shirt, all made out of hide and trimmed with porcupine quills, looked like beadwork. They dyed the porcupine quills, and then they sewed into the skin. It's like embroidery work.

I think we all had that kind of clothes. But things were pretty cheap in them days. You'd buy a pair of canvas shoes for 35 cents, a pair of cotton stockings for 25 cents.

Well, the old storekeeper was very nice to me. I used to go to his store. He had arthritis in his legs. So I helped him. I cleaned the store for him, put stuff on the shelves for him. And he give me discount on anything I want.

I used to like peanuts. Everyday, he'd give me about 10 pounds of peanuts. (Laughs.) I had to live mostly on peanuts, gum, and candy. Gum was only a nickel then. Peanuts were 10 cents a pound.

My father talked English and talked mostly Russian. My mother couldn't even talk English, talked Indian language, Athabascan. I went to school, and I teached her how to write her name.

My father was working in the cannery. I mean they work in the cannery every summer. And they earned a little money. But my mother did all that skin sewing. She made more money than my father, I think. (Laughs.) Gee, that's hard work. When I think about it — to tan all that hide, and have to make her own thread — sinew thread.

My mother? She just had three boys and me. I was the only girl. So I was a regular tomboy. (Laughs.) Fight? I learned how to wrestle and box.

I had to to be better than the boys. My brother Jacob was older, a little older than me. Just one year older, and I was his tail. Wherever he go, I was there, too. He was kind of sickly, so I had to do the fighting for him. (Laughs.)

I belong to the Russian Orthodox. We go to church every Sunday, Saturday and Sunday. I was going to the Russian school, so I used to sing. We practiced singing for one month before each holiday. Like now, we would start about a month before the ninth (of January). The ninth is big holiday. Christmas. Our Christmas, Russian Christmas.

So we practiced singing for about a month. So many girls and so many boys. And then, when the holiday come we go the church and sing, in the group. Boys and girls in one group. And the older people sing, and then we follow.

I learned how to sing and all that

different stuff. I was a girl, but I had a voice like a boy. So I had to be the leader in singing.

I still go to church. I go to the church here now. That's why I move here (Anchorage). 'Cause we haven't got any church in Palmer. The priest come to visit us, but he spent too much money going back and forth. So I move here, and it's closer to the hospital.

Oh, we were used to white people. There was a lot of white people living in Kenai. I mean some of them were married to the Russians. Mostly Norwegians. I was used to white people.

They help us, too. I was about nine years old. The First World War. I was helping nurses. I helped nurses pack water or melt snow. So I was used to white people all the time.

Oh, I didn't speak very good English. But when I went to school, I started talking better. But before that I talked like the old people, how they used to talk. Everything I said was funny. I mean it sounds funny now to me.

But I was talking pretty good by the time I was nine years old. I had to because I helped the nurses. Even then I was an interpreter. When the nurses go around, I had to go around with her. And I talked to the Indian. Then, I turned around and talked to her.

So I been an interpreter almost all my life. Even when I moved to Tyonek. They didn't talk English at all when I first come to Tyonek in 1925.

Even then (in Tyonek) I was helping nurses; and I'm a midwife, too. So I

interpret for the Natives, even for the chief because he couldn't hear. And he doesn't understand very good. So I have to interpret to him. It's hard to interpret. Especially in Indian. When we talk, we talk backwards. Instead of I say, "Do you want to have a cup of tea?" And I talk in my own language, I say, "A cup of tea, you like?" That's why, I said, we talked funny.

So I know how to talk English since before I went to school anyway. And then I talk Russian. But I forget it now. I don't even understand it any more. My father used to talk Russian to me all the time.

But I never talked to any Russians since I moved to Tyonek. Nobody talk Russian there.

I had an old grandfather. He used to come to our house. He was kind of blind. So he'd come to have lunch with us all the time. And after lunch he used to put me on his lap and tell me Indian stories. Oh, he used to talk for hours.

But I don't remember now. It's getting so it's hard for me to even talk my own language now because I don't talk to anybody for a long time. I mean since I moved over — more than 15 years ago. So it's hard for me to even talk my own language. And I didn't like it when someone would say they didn't even talk their own language. And now I'm gettin' so I kind of forget.

(Mrs. Kaloa discusses village medicine.)

(Being a midwife is) kind of scary. But, it's just like bein' a doctor. You have to do what you have to, even if you're scared you have to try your best anyway. I never get scared. I think of all the kids I delivered. I delivered about 123.

I only lost one, one child. It wasn't my fault. It was the mother's fault. She didn't take care of it.

It's not hard to be a midwife. You have to have a strong nerve, or whatever you call it. Some people get so scared they just shake.

And some ladies, even if there's only a little blood, they get so scared, they faint.

Oh, yes, we don't use medicine. We used plants. We used different kind of plants for different kinds of things. I'm forgetting how to use them. My mother, she taught me how to use plants for medicine. But I'm getting to forget now for 25 years now. I've been crippled that long now. My back.

My parents moved to Tyonek. I moved there with them. But my mother died a long time ago. My father died after my mother.

We had a boat to take us and move us to Tyonek. And they both stayed until they died. There's no bars, no nothing down there. So they liked it better over there.

Oh, my mother didn't like it in Kenai. There was too many white people. They started building bars and drinking and things like that. So she didn't want to stay there anymore. So we moved to Tyonek.

There was an old man, used to be school teacher. I worked for them, they were both old. I clean house and she teach me how to cook. I didn't know how to cook then very much. And the old man, he teached me during the evenings. So I at least passed the first year of high. But he died. So I didn't go to school any more. That's all.

When I moved to Tyonek, I teach the women cleanliness, how to wash their hands and sterilize things. There was a lot of TB then. There's quite a few people with TB. That's how come all the old-timers all died away so quick. Had TB. I took care of them, too.

This one lady I took care of — I saw her every day. When she was dying, she said, "You'll never get TB." I said, "How could that be?" And she said, "Anybody that's died, whatever they tell you will come true," she told me. My brothers all died with TB or something. I never got TB yet. And I'm 74 years old. So I think it's true.

Oh, my first husband, he was from Tyonek. But he died, too. He was with me only four years.

Then, after he died, my second husband, I meet him again. I knew him before in Kenai. Then ... the chief said, "Why don't you marry her? She's a good woman."

My mother and dad was alive when I had my children. I was all alone when she (Agnes Brown) was born. No doctors. No nurse. No nobody. I delivered her myself, on the Fourth of July. So everybody was celebrating. I didn't get scared.

The next day my mother came over. She said, "How are you?" I said, "I'm okay. I had my baby yesterday." Oh, she couldn't believe it. I get up in the morning, boil water, make tea for myself. Then they start coming to see me. I said I don't need nobody now.

The first village was on the beach. There was a creek running close to the bank, and then this land comes out like a peninsula. And Cook Inlet in front. So you can imagine when the Turnagain Arm wind and the creek got full, they both overflowed like that.

We were running, in the dory, from one house to another. Oh, the swells was about as high as this house when Turnagain Arm was blowing. So as soon as the tide went out, the old chief held a meeting. And he said, "We got to move. Whether we like it or not. We can't stay here. It's too dangerous."

So he hired my husband to move the village in '31, I think. I was pregnant then. I got pregnant before my first husband died. He never even saw his father. But my husband was working for the chief then. I mean my second husband was working for the chief then.

After he worked for the chief for quite awhile he moved the village from down there to the new village — to the present village. And then he asked him to marry me. So I had three children already and one on the way. So I got married to him, anyway.

But I still work for the village. I mean I work for the village — without pay. Now everybody get paid, whatever they do. Sometimes when I deliver a baby

they give me five or ten dollars because they wake me up. Sometimes twelve o'clock. It's the only time I saw money.

And they wanted him. My second husband was a good worker. The chief wanted my husband to be a foreman — in the village — teach the men how to do real work. They didn't know how to work then. All they knew is fishing.

So my husband, after he married me, then he moved to the village. But he was outsider. He was not supposed to move there. But the chief wanted him as a foreman to help with the work. So he stayed there.

He moved the old village ... everybody up. And then he helped build houses ... a sawmill. That's why the chief wanted him to stay there, to help work.

But still I helped in the village. I was a midwife ... I had doctor books. And doctors and nurses gave me lots of books to study. I helped the people that way. That's all.

(Mrs. Kaloa talks about her happiest time.)

Oh, I remember when I was a girl. My mother couldn't afford to buy me anything for Christmas. Boy, what the other girls were wearing! Most of the girls had patent leather shoes. White stockings. Organdy dress, and nice big white ribbon. We had long hair. We used to wear a ribbon in our hair.

And one night I went to the store to help the old man, fill his salt and things like that up. He said, "Alexandra! Go behind the counter. There's a box under the counter." He said, "That's for you."

Well, after I got done with my work. I put everything on the shelf that had to be. I went around the counter — a big box. Gee, I opened it up and there was nice patent leather shoes. White stockings. Organdy dress — a nice blue one with flowers on it. And nice big ribbon, wide ribbon and barrettes. Oh, my, I got so happy, I cried.

I think that's about the happiest moment I ever had. I mean when I was a girl. Well, as I grew up I had lots of happy times. But had more sorrowful things happen to me. Now I still feel bad I lost my husband. February. Last February (1984). I still feel lonely. I still miss him.

(She talks about Native values that should be preserved.)

Well, the way the Natives are. What I see today. The younger people doesn't respect the older people. In Indian way, you have to respect your elders. You have to listen to what they say, and always treat them with respect.

That's how they teach me, I mean my parents teach me that way. They tell me, "No matter how old you are, you have to respect people that's older than you. Treat them with respect." They told me. But some children doesn't even respect their own parents now.

I can't understand that.

Bill S. Pete is an Athabascan who today lives in Tyonek. He remains close to his elderly father, Shem Pete, who is a repository of Native culture.

Mr. Pete is a retired commercial fisherman. He was born on January 18, 1920, at Susitna Station, and spent much of his life in the Anchorage area.

As a child Mr. Pete moved to Tyonek with his father when flu took the lives of many Susitna Station people. Among his earliest memories of Tyonek is the man who became for him the quintessential Native leader, Chickalusion. What impressed Mr. Pete the most was that the Tyonek chief was always willing to lend a helping hand, whatever the need.

Mr. Pete was unable to obtain more than rudimentary formal education, but he says that has hurt him little in his endeavors. In most of his jobs he has been chosen as a foreman.

Bill S. Pete

". . . just about all the old people like me learned how to trap from the time they were about seven or eight years old."

We came from Susitna. Up at Susitna, there was a woman, used to stay in the roadhouse. And she taught us how to read and write.

Me and my dad — and I suppose everybody else — always had white man's grub. Ever since I could remember. Only thing that was different was we put up our fish. If we never put up any fish, I don't think I could get along. Moose meat and fish — well, any wild game, as far as that goes — I don't think I can get along without that.

(He recalls some of his happiest moments in Susitna.)

Swiping strawberries in white man's gardens. (Laughs.) And that's about all. Summertime we used to. There was a bunch of white people at Susitna, used to make a great big garden. About three or four acres.

And they used to plant lots of strawberries and stuff. Whole bunch of us kids used to sneak through the brush and swipe the strawberries. And I thought that was wonderful.

And when the mail boat used to come back up there — at least once a week — that was lots of fun to watch. Because that was something new!

Look, you're in a little village like Susitna Station. Why, anything — you see airplane land — whole bunch of us kids used to go there and look and wonder what's going on and stuff like that. Mail boat or anything.

Or else somebody come with a skiff or a dory or whatever you call it. We thought that was something new. And whole bunch of us kids used to go there and look. That was about the most fun we had was watching people come and

93

go, I guess.

And we got down here to Tyonek. And we fished that summer. Way down Granite Point, I believe it was.

After fishing, I went to school. I went to school for about three months. And then wintertime came, so we went back to Susitna. We trapped up there. Springtime we came back down here and fished again.

We used to fish here until about 1935. After I become 16, why, I left here and went to Anchorage. I went to work on the railroad. I been working for I don't know how many years. Since about '38, I guess.

And then I had cerebral hemorrhage. After that I started trapping and commercial fishing. I just kept right on commercial fishing. And then my back got so bad I couldn't do any commercial fishing. So I just retired, I guess. And here I am.

In World War II, why I was down to Whittier. I helped on that Whittier Tunnel ... Besides that, I used to be down at Seward. I used to work on the boats all the time down at Seward for quite a little while. And that's about all.

I spoke English all of my life, as far as I know. I was born among white people at Susitna Station. So I didn't have any problem with English. In fact, I had to come down here about ten years ago so I'd learn how to talk Indian. (Laughs.)

When I was about eleven years old my grandma used to talk Native all the time.

My only problem is when I want to talk Native I form whatever I need to say in English. Then I have to translate it into Indian language in my mind. And once in awhile I run into problems. And I don't know how to say some word.

Like animals — wolves and all those other animals — I don't know the names to them. There's lots of things I don't know the names to in Indian.

And as for me, when I left here in 1936, why I just stayed among white people. Ever since then until about five or six years ago I moved back down here.

Discrimination? Not that I know of. I don't know why — they regarded me as white man all my life. I worked among white people. Don't matter where I got a job, I generally got to be a straw boss or something. All my life.

If I went to work on the railroad, when I got on a gang, I just got to be straw boss or something. It don't matter what kind of job I was doing. I got to be straw boss. So I never did have any problem of this discrimination.

So I got along real good all my life with just about any people I ever worked with.

When we first come down here (to Tyonek) they had one great big old machine they call Model T, I guess it was. Tractor. And that's the only kind of machine I seen down here.

And when we used to work on CCC (Civilian Conservation Corps) — building this landing strip here — that was all done by hand power. They never did let them use that tractor. I think the strongest hand power we had was block and tackle. And, of course, they use ax and saw and picks and shovel. And that's about all they ever used! (Laughs.)

I'm a good carpenter, too. I learned that down here. It's hard to be carpenter.

Chickalusion was chief down here. Don't matter what it was. If you wanted cup of tea. Or, if you needed a hand. Or anything at all, he'll get right out there and help you. If you needed a home, why, he'll get bunch of people and help you. He'll boss the whole thing — how to build a house. He'll just walk around and tell everybody how to do things.

If somebody didn't know anything about how to do certain job, why he'd go and tell them how to do it. And they did it that way.

When I first seen him — long time ago — he was about five-foot-ten or something like that. The older he got, he got to be about as tall as my father. (Several inches shorter.) He must have been about 190 to 200 pound when I first seen him. He was a huge man.

Ever since I was a little boy, before we came down here, I used to go out and camp with my father. I knew how to trap. I guess just about all the old people like me just simply learned how to trap from the time they were about seven years or eight years old.

As long as they could walk with little snowshoes — little snowshoes about two or three feet long. As long as they could follow their father. They watched

them — how to cut wood and just about everything.

If I run up against it out in the woods: If it snows on me about one or two foot, I can just simply take my ax and hew out my snowshoes that they used to call banjoes. It only takes about couple hours to build those. As long as you got a rope of some sort, you can make yourself a pair of snowshoes with just an ax.

Just hew them out. Make it about this wide. You get four pieces about this wide. You split birch, alder or just about anything you get ahold of. You just hew them out, and make it about this thick. Or something like that. Put two cross pieces on there. Take your rope, and bend the front up like this. Just tie it up like that, and you fix it.

Don't matter how it is, you fix it. You put a rope or something where your foot is. Just about everybody in Alaska seen snowshoes, so they'll know what I mean. Just tie it on to your foot and go home. (Laughs.) And go home. And that's about all.

I been back and forth between Anchorage and Susitna ever since I was a six-month-old, I guess. So, in reality, I was almost raised in Anchorage. And I was raised among the white people in Anchorage — white kids — ever since I could remember.

There used to be a gang of us. About 14 of us used to play around. There was two colored people in Anchorage. And we thought they were white people (laughs), because they used to give us nickel and dime.

Every time we see them — every two or three days we used to see them. Whole bunch of us. They used to give us nickel or dime or pennies or some-thing — whatever they had. And here we thought they were white people until we were about ten years old, I guess. We didn't know they were colored people.

When I first seen Fourth Avenue — for the sidewalk they used to just have boards. And there was about three or four cars in Anchorage, I guess. They were old Model Ts.

(Mr. Pete describes his feelings about the Alaska Native Claims Settlement Act of 1971.)

Well, they just wrote it on paper. And they told me to sign this. So I signed it. I asked them what it was for, and they told me, "You're gunna get lots of money."

I never did get lots of money out of that, far as I know. At one time I guess they give us three thousand dollars. And that's the biggest one I seen. That was that dividend, they call it.

Just about all the Natives in Alaska get that ... They told us you sign this paper and you're going to get lots of money and lots of land. I never did see one square foot of land out of that deal, for myself.

I don't see anything wrong with that deal. In fact, when 1991 comes along, I'm not going to sell my stock. I'm going to keep it. And if lots of Natives keep their stock, the land's not going to get away from Alaskan people — Natives.

As far as I know there is nothing wrong with my education. (Laughs.) I went to school down here for three months. And that was my total educa-tion. I went to third grade.

In 1938 when I had a cerebral hemor-rhage, they were trying to find out if my brain got damaged. And they were giving me an IQ test. And they said my education was up to about two years of college. All my life I been readin' and studying.

Like I said little while ago: Don't matter where I went to work, I always got to be straw boss or something. Because I had a good education at the time.

(He offers advice for young people.)

Well, just stop drinking. That's about all. And don't use any dope. That's all.

Shem Pete is an Athabascan who was born on July 14, 1900, at Susitna Station, a tiny village that has virtually disappeared as a result of the ravages of the flu epidemic in 1918.

Mr. Pete has spent much of his life in Tyonek, where he lives today.

He is well known for his stories and his work on language and cultural heritage with the University of Alaska's James Kari. Mr. Pete likes to perform Native songs and is proud of his knowledge of his people's legends and stories.

At the same time, Mr. Pete has a sense of humor about himself and jokingly points out that Professor Kari sometimes seems to speak the Native language better than Mr. Pete does.

Shem Pete

"I know the old songs. Way back — 100 or more old songs."

Well, I born in Susitna Station. My father used to be chief. I remember when the oldest one — his boy, my brother — used to be chief ... My father was married to some young girls before. He got six boys. I'm the last one.

My brother, they make him chief. And they want to make me chief. But I give up. I don't want it. I told them, "The white man's good enough now."

But them days, them other days, why, the Natives they do their ways. Now, we got the judge and marshals. They told us the way they wanted it. But the way before was the way we wanted to live in.

But now, I don't want no chief, I told them. But they give me the chief clothes — dress, beads, feathers hat, rattle. Chickalusion give me that. The last man here. He was the boss for us here in Tyonek.

When the flu hit in 1918, Susitna was a lot of people. First week when the flu hits there we lose 36. Thirty-six we lose when the flu first hit there. Then, from there on we lose lots of people. We're only a few people left. I stayed there.

I got married in 1919. And I got a boy. Anyway, we stayed there for quite awhile. Tyonek was pretty small, not many here. So Chickalusion come up there, pick us up, brought us down here. And we stay here for a few years, and we lose him.

They give me all his clothes — beads on his clothes, feathers hat, the rattle, neck beads. They tell me, "You're the last one gunna be chief for us."

I told them ... "The white people do the place. They tell us: do that and do this. Not this way. Not this way ... I'm not going to be good chief. I won't go for that."

So they let me out.

My brothers take me up there (hunting north of Susitna) when ... I was young. And I killed a caribou. But I went out there fourth trip — I got 30.30. Oh, boy, I got something! I got little cannon, I thought. And I shoot the caribou, down they go.

When I used to be shooting with .22, they stagger around, and I just keep on shooting ... That time I was a man already, 14 or 15 year old. And, boy, I kill quite a few caribou. That's how we get the caribou.

We need the skin in them days. They dry them up nice, and they sell them two dollars per skin. Sometimes they get 100 or 200 caribou.

The last time I went up there — when I got 30.30 — we were nine men. We went up there ... We bring lots of caribou skin, and plenty caribou meat. Lots of moose up there. Like cattle, too, the moose ... we count over 100 moose.

... We seen so many fox up there. We hold our nose and walk around. When we go past ... lot of fox. When they kill the caribou, them old folks, they just take the hide. And them caribou was just piled all over. They don't kill no fox. They say black fox might be $100. But they want to be sure and catch the caribou that's two dollars a skin. They don't know any better, them old folks.

... Anyway, we take our meat down to Susitna Station — caribou meat,

moose meat. We put it in a cache — caribou hide, up top in the roof. And they pile them up upstairs. And the potlatch come — 100 skin, I guess or more they piled up in the middle. Blankets and money — oh, gee, over one thousand dollars it might be.

... Chickalusion come up there. He's so lonesome. Just a very few Tyonek people was here. He took us. We be eleven of us, brought us down.

Already my boys — Billy and (nephew) Sava Stephan, they do a lot of work, just like when I was a kid. They work for them old peoples around here. They hunt for them. They hunt the ducks, hunt all over. Sava little fella. They was only six hours different. Billy born first. And six hours later — her sister, older sister: Sava born, too.

... Boy, I'll tell you when we losed our boss (Chickalusion) we really thought Tyonek's no more. We don't know what to do. We're still here yet, after him. But I tell lots of stories. I know a lot of songs. I sing a song — every Tuesday I teach the whole village. The young generation — about ten years, twelve years old — they dance for me. And I sing.

... Lot of people think they're white people. And they don't want to talk to Native, hardly. And they don't go no place. They don't visit nobody. We used to go visit ... lot of fun. They quit that, too ... We just let them go. We used to have a lot of fun. We don't have not much fun no more.

I know the old songs. Way back —

100 or more old songs.

(Shem Pete, Sava Stephan and Bill Pete sing one of the songs.)

... There's another guy, fella named Jim Kari. I teach him four years, Native language. He from California, him and his wife. They come to Alaska, Cook Inlet. They know I know everything. So he follow me, and four years I been learn him the Native language, Native songs.

Now he got up in Fairbanks, about three or four stories. They got all the Native — how did they used to be ... how they make living, all that. And the singing, way back. I been teaching him four years.

... He just follow me, and I just tell him, tell him. And he write it down, write it down ... He got a lot people work for him, make good living ... So I teach him four years, story and Native language.

He talk Native better than us. Sometime he talk to me in Native, and I answer him in English!

Sava Stephan Sr. is an Athabascan who was born at Susitna Station on January 18, 1920, just six hours after his cousin Bill S. Pete was born.

Today he is a retired fisherman and lives in Tyonek.

Mr. Stephan is a shy man, but his strong interest in his Native culture and heritage becomes apparent even in a short conversation.

Mr. Stephan has little use for many of the modern world's technological advancements, especially since such things as "pressing a button" to light a lamp translate into hefty bills. He says he prefers the subsistence lifestyle of his past.

He spoke in the Tyonek community center, seated near Shem and Bill Pete. The trio at one point interrupted their narrative to perform a Native song.

Sava Stephan Sr.

". . . we never used to buy license . . . we kill moose any time we want. Now we have to buy license and everything."

We came down here (to Tyonek) since 1934, and I been here — I was used to be working on the church. I was working on the church committee for quite a long time.

Also, old man (Shem Pete), he been here quite awhile.

... I had a good life — all the way — ever since I came down here in the village. I think that's all I know.

Susitna? I was pretty small then. Used to have a church over there. I think I was about six years old when the church burned down. Old man was working, and our church burned. I barely remember that.

My parents was there — Anderson Stephan, my father's name. My mother's name is Inga. Used to be all my uncles is there. 'Thirty-four, I think they move us down here when everybody die off

from Susitna. Move us down here, and we still here yet.

... There was only us left there. I think that's why they move us down here.

... When I first came down here I was only twelve years old.

I was with my dad, all the time. I didn't go to school or nothing. Because he was takin' me out trapping. I think I was trapping since I was seven years old. I was traveling with him. All that time I was out trapping with him.

Until they brought us down here, we started fishing. Then I quit trapping, and my dad died down here, too. Since then I'm still in Tyonek, and that's all we can do — fishing. I never can go out trapping or nothing since my dad died.

So I don't see no one go out trapping over here, neither.

Then I got married and stay here, all that time. I have two boys left. One is a family boy and one stay right home with me at the house. And now I retire, and turn everything on to them two boys. My house, my fish grounds and my fish camp, everything turn over to them.

Now I'm here with this old man (Shem Pete) and Billy Pete. That's all.

I ain't got no brothers. My first cousin is Billy Pete, that's here.

All of us, we used to have good houses up there (at Susitna). Like a log house, better than this place here. Warm. All we used to use is woodstove in old-time way.

I don't care much — press the button and control the heat in the house now. We can't do nothing. We don't work or nothing. Press the button and light the lamp. Them days we used to use kerosene lamps. Burn kerosene. Now we do everything — with the chain saws and everything. Now we have to buy everything. Pay for water. Pay for the lights. Pay for the house. Everything.

We have the same food we used to have before. But we have to buy license. Before, we never used to buy license. We was out trapping. We kill moose any time we want. Now, we have to buy license and everything.

And all the moose over here: They cut all the trees back because Japanese was buying that timber over here. Everything is cut down and some roads all over now. We can hardly keep our moose. I never get my moose this year.

Two years now I never get my moose ... Someone had to kill a moose for us this year. We have meat to stay on with. But we put lots of fish up. That's all.

We used to have dog team. That's all. And then we used to fly from here to Susitna all the time. We used to pay out of our own pockets, them days. We never used to get welfare checks like today. Trapping, fishing and everything — all that money we used to make. Pay out of our own pocket.

... The first time we seen seal, we didn't know nothing about seal or beluga or stuff. (Laughs.) We seen seal on beach, dryin' in the sun.

... When we first came down here it was 1934. But I really moved here for good in 1936.

Our language is the same language as Tyonek. There was many, many Tyonek people down here. But all from all different cities, like Kenai ... Susitna ... Hardly any Tyonek Native here.

We been with white people so many years that we start speaking like that. I didn't ever been to school, but I start speaking English like this. Since I was with my dad, all the time.

I speak my own language, myself. But when the guys talking to me in English, I speak to them like that. Lots of guys ask me how did I learn to speak English. But I been with lots of white people. That's how come I speak English good. In the village they ask me that, but I must have been with white people many years.

... I got along with old Chief Chickalusion, chief in the village here. I got married to his daughter. He make me work on church there and everything else. After he died, my wife died, too.

... Albert Kaloa Junior, he was chief. He got burned up in a Anchorage fire. And there's no more chief after that. Only one we can call chief is Emil McCord, I think.

I don't remember when I first went out hunting. (Laughs.) I started walking with my dad when I was about five years old. I can hardly walk in snowshoes. But I been with him all the time after that since I started putting the snowshoes on. I been trapping with him all the time. Every year.

We used to make about one thousand dollars a year. Until they brought us down here. We quit trapping and stay down here, then.

... We used to eat good all the time. I don't remember, we don't run out of no food. The only time we run out of food is when we're out trapping back there. I had to come back about 50 miles with dog team to get groceries. That's the only time I remember. I was working

for old Chief Chickalusion then. He used to have a good dog team then.

... They used to have a lot of potlatches going on over here in Tyonek when the old fellows used to be. Now, the only one we got left is old man here (Shem Pete).

No potlatch going on. Nobody make potlatch. They call it potlatch. They make a party, and they call it a potlatch. Everybody come around from lot of cities — Kenai, Nondalton, Knik. They all come over here and have a party. They don't make no potlatch.

Potlatch they used to call — spread the money. They make about one thousand or fifteen hundred dollars. They make the potlatch with it. Give that all to the people, I guess. Blankets and everything like that. Rifles. They make potlatch like that.

... That's how they used to make potlatch. They don't do like that. No one knows in Tyonek. None of them, young generation, they don't know how to make potlatch. They know food and stuff — they call it a potlatch.

Parascovia Valun Rickteroff Roehl of Athabascan — Russian heritage was born on October 26, 1901, at Old Iliamna near the shores of Alaska's largest lake, Iliamna Lake.

Mrs. Roehl spoke at the Palmer Pioneer Home, aiming a number of her remarks at her grand-daughter, Ileen Sylvester. Mrs. Roehl is a natural storyteller, recalling entire conversations for her listeners.

The last surviving child in a family of 12 children, Mrs. Roehl has seen the death of many of her relatives. Nothing, however, prepared her for her husband's final painful days and death.

Parascovia Valun Rickteroff Roehl

". . . all the medicine — that Indian medicine — that's on earth, God put it on earth so the people can know about it."

You want me to start it now? Well, like that flu hit there in Bristol Bay first (after World War I). Then it didn't reach Old Iliamna Village where I was born. It didn't reach there. I know there was lots of people, whole Kvichak River, lots of people died from it, even the little babies, I think.

I think they said the little baby that they found was crawling around, nursing on his mother. His mother was dead. But he was around his mother, and he was nursing from her.

So the people that found that little child, they took him. I seen that man, too, when he grow up and get married. He came up to Iliamna Lake, he moved there with his family. So that's where he lived. That's how I met him.

That flu was really bad. I think if it came up to the village, it would have cleaned everybody out then. Because there wasn't very many up in Old Iliamna Village.

My mother had 12 kids. I'm the youngest one in the family. And I'm the only one that's living. Eleven kids, they're all dead, and my mother and dad, my sisters, all my uncles. I got nothing left, only me.

My mother's name was Mary Rickteroff. And my dad was, his Russian name was Wasillie Rickteroff. But they used to call him William, though, in American. Because they couldn't remember that Wasillie. So they changed it. (Laughs.) He was half Russian. My grandfather was real Russian. My dad was half because his mother was Indian.

My mother was Native. She came from Stony River. That's where my dad meet her. My dad and his dad was traveling after they moved to Iliamna Village and build home there.

Then they wanted to see how it looked like inside — inland. So they were traveling when they came up the Stony River. Then my dad meet my mother. And he wanted to marry her. She was willing to marry him, but she have to come back to Iliamna Village to get married. So he bring her back to the village. That's what my mother told me. Then they got married.

I wouldn't know how old she was. Because them days when we went to school our teacher never told us about things that we should know about our parents. They never did that. They just don't want us to talk about Native people.

But now, like I said, now when my kids are growing up, when they go to school, they want — the teacher ask them, "Who is your grandmother? What's your grandmother's name? What's your grandfather's name? Where are they from?" All those things.

I just went as far as third grade. Then my mother got sick, and I have to take care of my mother. Them days there was no hospital. There was no kind of medicine to get.

Only the teacher had little, like aspirin and things like that. Only thing — he comes up and see how they are and give them a little aspirin. It was tough, I'll tell you. When anybody got sick, they can't do nothing for them.

I must be around either 30 or 32 when my dad died. Me and Grandpa

wasn't married yet when my mother died. I must be around 13 or 14 years old then. I stay with my father and mother and brothers. I had two brothers still living yet then.

At home I speak white-man English. When my mother talk to me, then she talk to me in my own language. I understand her, and some words I answer her in her way.

I did. But now I'm forgetting, too, because I got nobody else to talk to. I got brother-in-law, he can understand. He's my husband's brother. Me and him used to talk together, you know. But now he's forgetting, too, because he got nobody else to talk to.

Only time my father used to talk (Russian) was when his sister was around him. Him and his sister used to talk lots. But they never explain it to us what it mean and things like that.

You know how kids are. We didn't pay any attention to it. I think if we asked him what it mean, I think he might tell us about it. Only word that I remember is how to say, "Sit down."

My dad's place — that was log house, big one, great big house. There was only one room.

Well, all my brothers ... nine of them was already gone. Just only two brothers and me was living, that's all. They get sick, but they don't know what kind of sickness they get sick from. They used to say they get TB. My sister, she die from TB, they claim.

When I was a girl, before I meet him (Charles Roehl Sr.), I had a cousin. Her name was Sophie, and her brother was Michael A. Well, the river was all froze. We used to fish through the ice. You have to go down the river about — oh, maybe 12 miles, maybe 10 — to fish. You can see all the way down.

One afternoon my cousin Sophie, she came down, she said, "Valun, let's go fishing down at Little Fish Village."

I said, "Okay." So I got my fishing line ready, got the bait. "You come down here. We'll start off from here."

So she did, and she came back down and then we walked down the river. We went around the corner where we can see. I said, "Sophie, who's that walkin' on the ice there? Two mens."

She said she don't know. She know, but she wouldn't tell me. She said she don't know. I can see good. I recognize them then. It was my cousin, Michael A., and my husband was down there. That was before I met him.

So we went down there and fish. They made a fish hole. Michael A. made fish hole for us.

So I was fishing, and he came around me and he talked to me. He said, "You think you folks will catch any trout?" I said, "I guess so."

He came around me. He said, "What you're doing today when you are home?"

"Oh, I was busy. I was just going to wash clothes when Sophie came down to tell me to go fishing with her, so I let my washing go until tomorrow."

"Oh," he say. Then we were talking and talking and talking. Then, after awhile, he said to me — Sophie and her brother was quite a ways from us — he said to me, "Can I ask you something?"

I said, "What is that? What you going to ask me?"

Well, him and his sister was going to Chemawa (a Bureau of Indian Affairs school in Salem, Oregon). I think they stayed there for 12 years. That fall they came back.

But I was on the mountain with my mother. I wasn't home. And his brother was telling him that, "We got friend, me and Sophie. She is not home. She is with her mother, up on the mountain, hunting squirrels. Boy, you know, if you're going to meet any girls, she's (laughs) the one to meet. She never smoke, she never drink."

And he told me, he said, "Can I ask you something?"

I said, "What is it?"

He said, "Can you be my girlfriend?"

"I don't know," I said. "How about the whole village of girls? What's wrong with them?"

"No," he said, "I can't."

"I don't know," I said. "Let me think first," I said. "We'll be friends. I don't know what you mean 'friend.' But I'll think about it." (Laughs.)

It took three years! He finally came out and told me that he would like to marry me. Well, my mother was still living yet when he was going around me. My mother know, too.

When my mother die, then I was alone with my dad and two brothers. He used to come up and visit me. I think we went for three years together.

He finally want to marry me.

One evening I was in bed already. My sister and her husband was with me. My dad was down the Fish Village. My brother went down to Nushagak because he hurt his leg. My other brother was already dead. I had only one brother left.

Somebody knock at the door. My brother-in-law say, "Come in." When somebody come in, he say, "Hello, Charlie."

I was thinking, "What did you come up here for this late?"

I hear him coming to me, and he come to me and he kiss me, and he say, "How are you?"

I say, "I'm fine. I wanted to go to bed early, so I went to bed nine o'clock."

Then he say to me, "You know why I come up for?" I said no.

"I wanted to ask you first, see what you think about it," he said. "I'm going to go home and ask my dad if I can marry you."

Then I didn't say anything for awhile.

"I'll tell you: I'll go home and ask him. If I don't come back then you'll know that he'll say no. If I come back up, then you'll know that he said yes."

"Well, he left. I don't know how long he stayed. He didn't stay very long. He came back. Somebody knock at the door. My brother-in-law say, "Come in." He call his name. And I was thinking, "Gee, I wonder." He came to me and he kiss me.

And then he said, "You know my dad say we can get married. So we're going to get married tomorrow."

My dad was down at Fish Village. He say, "I'm going to send for your dad. Me and your cousin going to go after him. And we'll bring him up so he can know, too."

So next morning, right after breakfast they went after my dad and they brought him back up. They came up around eleven o'clock, I think. Then afternoon, he came up to ask my dad. (Laughs.) My two cousins was with him, too. My dad say he wouldn't let me go until he hear from his dad.

He said, "No, he can't marry her because I don't hear nothing from his dad. Maybe he just want to marry her. His dad have to know about it."

Well, he told my cousins, "I'm going to go back down and tell my dad that he don't believe me." So he went back down, then he came back up with a letter. So he gave to my cousin. He read it to my dad. (Laughs.)

My dad wouldn't believe him! "You give to Michael A. Let Michael read it!" Well, Michael is my cousin, too. So he hand it to him, and they were standing by him. He was sitting on the bed. Michael read it to him same way.

"Okay. Well, just so long as his dad say he can marry her, they can get married."

(Laughs.) I think same afternoon we went down to marry. Teacher to marry us. So we get married September the tenth. I think it was 1923.

We was going to live in the village, Iliamna Village where I was born. Oh, that place was tough then, though — the people drinking, talk about one another. And it was too tough.

So he told me one time — we live there two years, I think — he finally told me, he said, "I wonder if you can ask your dad if we can move away from village, move down to Iliamna Lake somewhere. I can build home and raise our children down there. This village, I don't care for it much. Will you ask him?"

So I told Papa. I said, "You know what he is saying?" He say no. "He told me to ask you if we could move away from the village next fall, me and the kids. He pick out the place down Iliamna Lake where he want to build home. He say he don't like it up here. The people are talking too much."

"Well, I'll tell you," he said, "I'm not going to support you. I'm getting old, and I can't take care of you. He's the one that will take care of you. You go whatever he say. You go with him. If he want to build where he want to build home, you take them two kids and you go with him."

So I told my husband. He said, "I'm going to hire my brother-in-law and your sister's husband to chop some logs for me. And your brother know how to saw lumbers. I can help him, and we can saw all the lumber for the floor, for the ceiling, too."

So that fall we move. In October month we were living in a tent! (Laughs.) Ah, gee, that was tough. They built that home. They must have finished around before Christmas. Well, they just put the stuff in. They couldn't finish the ceiling. Well, he told his brother-in-law, he say, "That's good enough. We can pull through in here."

So he say we live in here just the same, just so long as we don't live in a tent.

Well, we didn't have no floor, no nothing. Mud floor. So I told myself, "I'm going to show him what kind of floor I can use." (Laughs.) So I went out. There was lots of little spruce trees not very far from my place. I chop some spruce tree branches and I bring it home. I went out, bring some more home.

He was chopping wood outside, and he didn't notice what I was doing, I think. Second time I came home, I think, he came in. He said, "What you going to do with them branches?"

I said, "Oh, I'll show you what I'm going to use it for. After awhile you'll see."

"Okay," he said. So he came in to drink water. So he drink water and he went back out to chop wood again.

Then I start putting them branches down. I know how to put it down, too, because that's the only kind of floor we used to use in the summertime in the tent. So I put it all over, as far as the stove.

So when he got through he came in. When he opened door, he said, "Oh, that's what you was doing! You made a floor out of it."

I said, "Well, we use it in the tent.

I don't know why we can't use it in the house (laughs) to keep the dust from flying when it dry!"

"Yeah," he say, "you're pretty smart for that."

We just live in there one winter, and then he put floor in there. Then he didn't like it up there, so next year, he say, "I'm going to tear down the house, and then we'll move to the mouth of Goose Bay."

That's the same bay, you know. Whole business is Goose Bay. Reason why, you see, Grandpa was going to stake that ground. He write out for it. But, you see, before we live there, about two years before that, there was reindeer herd came in from Outside. And there is a little creek running out. Head of it is a good place, timber and everything. That's why they lived with reindeer.

So they told him that he can't stake that ground on account of that. Then that next spring then he moved the house down to mouth of Goose Bay.

Grandpa Roehl (Charles' father) was German, you know, full German. And Grandma Roehl was Aleut. She was from Bristol Bay. That's where Grandpa was born, too, Bristol Bay. Auntie Marie, too.

I'm one person, I used to listen to my dad and mother when I was growing up. My mother used to tell me — the whole village used to drink. They make their own brews. They got drunk and everything.

When I'm old enough to know, then my mother used to tell me ... "Smok-ing is no good for you. Drinking is no good for you."

I think that's why I never did learn how to drink. I was against the drinking. I really didn't like the drinking.

Sophie was eight years old when we move away from Goose Bay. We moved down to that place where they call Iliamna now. Used to be roadhouse. We moved down there, on account of her so she can go to school — my youngest daughter. Then she have to walk three miles to go to school.

And then there's a friend and his wife was down there at the roadhouse. That winter (in the mid-1940s) he was talking to my husband. "You know, I'm going into Homer in November month."

He said, "What you going over there for?"

He said, "There's a house for sale. And I'd sure like to see how big it is and how far away from the school. If it's big enough for my family, and if it's not too far away from school then I'll buy it. Then, after fishing, then I'll move."

So he went that winter in November month. He came back. After he came back, next day I think, my husband went outside and I hear them talking out there by our place, outside of our front door. He stay out for quite awhile. I was doing my work, and get through. And he came back in.

"Hey, Mama!"

I said, "What?"

"You know Pete Nelson is going over to Homer. He going to buy a home over

there. They going to move next fall."
"Oh?"
So he went in November month. When he come back — that house that he was supposed to buy, it was right across the school house. But it was too small for his family — only one bedroom, living room and kitchen. He had a big family.

So there was another one. He look at that one. That one was big. It got upstairs and everything. So he took that one. Then he told this guy that he was buying house from, he said, "Can I take this picture home to show to my friend?"

"Yeah," he said.

"Then, we'll send it back to you."

So when he came home next day, my husband was outside and our friend came to him, show him that picture. So after they talk, then my husband come in. He had that picture. He showed it to me. "Hey," he said, "you know what I told Pete?"

"I said, "No."

He say, "I'm going to show it to my wife. I'm going to tell him that I'm going to go over and find out, see if I can pay down on it. And then this summer coming, we're all going to go down to the bay and work. When we come back then we'll move, too."

"Well, it's up to you," I say. "You're the one that's going to buy the house, not me." (Laughs.)

"So it's okay with you, huh?" he said.

I say, "Yeah. It's okay with me."

So that winter in November month, he went over and see it. It was right across the school house. So that spring we all went down to the bay, whole family. We all work. And that fall, next fall, after fishing we came back ... We came back.

"Hey," Pete Nelson said. "Are you going to go with us?"

"Yeah, we going to go if you folks are going."

"Well," he said, "the scow is coming in tomorrow. You better pack up tonight and we'll leave tomorrow." (Laughs.)

So we all packed up that night. We're rushing around. Two of my nephew hear about it. So the next morning, they came down early. All the sugar and flour and everything that's left over — we had a cache — it's all in the cache. He told my nephew, "You folks can have it. I'm not going to drag them things along when I can buy it over there."

Boy, they were glad to hear it. And then the next morning we took off up the lake.

(She describes her first night after arriving in Homer.)

Dark, no light! (Laughs.) And I told my husband, "How come there is no light?"

"Mama," he say, "You're not coming to city. This is just a little village. Just a little town."

"Oooooh," I said. "Well, like Anchorage when we come in, lots of lights, just like whole place was lit up. I thought it's going to be like that."

So we went to bed. Next morning we get up. I make coffee and we was having breakfast. Only two car went by. Then next time one went by. He say, "That's all you going to see is them three cars. That's all."

"My, how come?" I say.

"Like I'm telling you, this is not big town. This is just a little village!"

(Mrs. Roehl talks about what foods she ate when she was younger.)

Like fish and squirrels and rabbit, spruce hens and ptarmigans. In the spring-time, them days, there was no law for it. You can kill whatever you want. So when the ducks and geese come, then they get just enough to eat. We just live off of the country, them days.

Like my mama used to tell me: in the spring-time when it's getting no more snow, she said if you live on the salt-water side you wouldn't be hungry. Well, where we live there's nothing. Only thing you can catch is trout to eat. If you live on salt-water side you wouldn't be hungry there. There's lots of clam, lots of seal. All kinds of things that you can get.

You know, them fish heart and the stomach? She used to split them stomach and clean it all good and wash them. She even cook that.

You know, I don't know, maybe you hear about it, they talk about Indian rice (Chocolate Lily — Fritillaria Camschatcensis). I know what Indian rice is. They grow under the ground. Some of them is about this big. The root part, just like rice. The flower is dark, dark lavender color, real dark.

Only one flower, you know. They grow about this tall, the leaf part. One time, we stay in the Fish Village, we went up to Iliamna for something we need. When we're coming back my mother say to us, "We'll stop so I can get some Indian rice."

That's the first time I hear of it, too. "What is that, Mama, Indian rice?"

"Well," she said, "when I go and pick it I'll show it to you." So we all, me and my sister, we get out with her and we go a little up the hill. Then the stem is about this tall. The stem thin, I think it's maybe fat as my little finger, stem is. It just got flower on top, that's all.

So when she see that, she pull them all up, them stems. Then she start digging with a spoon, dig and dig until she get to that rice part.

When she pick them up, it's no different than rice, but they all in chunk, you know. Some of them is about this big in chunks. So she had a flour sack along, and she put it in there. She pick enough to cook. Well, when she pick enough, then we went back to the village.

We came home and then we went up to the tent. My papa was home. And then after my mother rest, and then after we eat and everything, then she start cleaning them rice, washing them. She washed them with the water, then she drain it out. Then she put fresh water and wash them real good.

Then I was watching her, then I say, "Mama, after you wash them, then what you going to do with it?"

"Well," she said, "then I have to cook it." When she cook it, then she would try to make it all loose. After she cook it — she know when it's done, but I didn't know. She boiled it. If she don't boil it, it can't get soft.

I don't know, them days, the old people never did like too much sugar. I don't know if she put any sugar or anything like that. I never did ask her. Then after she smash them and everything, whip them like, then she say, "You want to taste it?"

Then she take a teaspoon, and just a little bit on the end, and then she give to me and I put it in my mouth (laughs). I spit it out. I didn't like it. It's bitter.

Well, if you put sugar in it, maybe it'll be better. It's bitter, strong. I wouldn't eat it!

Wild celery is not strong. The skin is only strong. After you clean it good, inside, it's not too strong. But you can't swallow rice, Indian rice. If you tried, you wouldn't swallow it, I know, unless if you put sugar in it.

There's lots of stuff they used to get from the ground for medicine that I know of. Like, shucks, I even forgot the name. I know this stuff that I even forgot the name. If you cut yourself, you know, you can get it. I think it was the root part, you can use it for medicine.

Like this fireweed. If you got a boil, you got these fireweeds, and then you split it. After you split it, inside is soft. You can strip it out with teaspoon. If you do it right away, you'll have almost a teaspoonful.

Then where you got cut, put it on there. Put it right on your cut, and then rub it up. That'll help you. If you're in the woods and you got nothing, you can use that for cut.

There is lots of thing my mama used to tell me about things that you can get from the ground. But I can't remember it.

Like Uncle Eddie had TB when he was around 20, I think. There is a old lady in roadhouse — we moved down to roadhouse already — she come to me. She said, "Why don't you go in the woods in the spring-time — that's the only time you can get it."

You know, ... spruce tree branches? They grow right on the ground. I see them like that. They grow right on the ground all over. She say, "Why don't you go in the woods? There's lots of it in roadhouse here. Why don't you pick some? In the spring-time is the best, new shoots that are growing."

She say pick them quite a bit, then wash it and boil it, and then let him drink the juice like tea.

But I never did. Uncle Eddie went to hospital right away. So I never did went out and try it. She told me that it was good for TB. Well, long years ago old people, they got no medicine. They got no hospital. That was before the white people come to Alaska. They didn't know nothing about medicine. They just have to find things from the ground to use, you know.

Well, you know yourself that God put

them things on the earth for the people to use it. Nobody never put it on earth. Everything, what is growing, like spruce tree and all the birds that is growing, we never look after it. It live on and everything itself.

God put that on earth. We don't have to take care of it. God take care of it. So all the medicine — that Indian medicine — that's on earth, God put it on earth so the people can know about it.

I never went to hospital with all my kids. My sister is midwife for me. She deliver all my kids at home. I never went to hospital with none of my kids. I had seven kids. I had them all at home.

People used to share. If the people haven't got any stuff, like tea or flour or anything, if they can share some — if they got enough for themselves — they used to share with their own family. Well, the others, too. If they know that the other people haven't got anything, they share with them, too.

(Mrs. Roehl recalls a story her relative told her when she was young.)

They was telling me about this one time the Aleuts — I don't know which way they came in, maybe Bristol Bay way — they were coming up to the lake to finish all the people.

My grandpa and my grandmother, and there's part of village — Iliamna Village where I was born — the first place they would hit it is Pedro Bay. There used to be lots of Indian there, too. It was in the afternoon, I think they say. Or towards in the evening.

The boy was skating on the ice, you know. It could have been on the fall because he was skating on the ice. In the falltime when the ice freeze it's nice and smooth, you know.

And they had school there, Russian people living there, Pedro Bay. They got a fence around school and all the building. I think they expect that, that the Aleuts might sneak on them.

Well, they hear that Aleuts are coming to kill all the people in Pedro Bay. This boy was skating on the ice when they hear it. Well, lots of kids was playing, too, you know. But the older people rush and try to get all the kids in the gate, to get them in the gate so they can get them in the house.

And this boy took off for Iliamna, was skating. Ice must be smooth. You know he made it up to the village. Well, my grandfather was Russian. My grandmother was Indian. And my aunt was Russian, too. This boy come up there and notified them that Aleut is going to attack them, too. They're attacking Pedro Bay already.

Well, it's getting dark already. All the village, they got lights. They all came, the people that's related to my grandpa, they all came down to the store. Even my aunt, only aunt I had.

Grandpa had a store there. He had lots of gun and lots of shells. Everybody get in there to be ready to fight back if they attack. You know they can hear them when they were coming. You never see that old village, neither. The river run from the lake up the river.

Before you see the village, you come around the point. Then you can see the village.

Well, when Aleuts are coming, when they come around the point, they can hear them. The people coming up to kill all the people in the village, they know right away. They know because the lights is all lit up and everything.

I think maybe they didn't have enough shells, too, maybe. They got kind of scared. And they turned back. They didn't come right up to the village. If that boy didn't take off for there, Aleuts would have cleaned them off. They would have waited down below until they all went to bed. Then they would attack them, I think.

They would have killed everybody. I wouldn't be here, neither, then. (Laughs.)

(Mrs. Roehl talks about her parka, put into the Anchorage Historical and Fine Arts Museum.)

Museum? Do you ever been there? Did you see that beads parka? That used to be my grandmother's parka. But my mother changed the cloth. The beads is still on it yet. When my grandmother died, then my mama got it. Then when my mama got it, it was too small for her. So when my sisters are growing up, they all use it.

I'm the youngest one. I used to wear that to school, too. When I was growing up then she give to me. So I keep that parka till we moved to Homer.

Then I didn't want to keep it in the house. I was afraid it might get too hot in there. So when Grandpa built the cache to put our stuff in it, then I hang it in there. When Aunt Sophie get married, then she came down to let us know she got married.

After we had coffee and everything, and then we sit around talking, then Aunt Sophie say, "Mama?"

Then I say, "What?"

"What you done with your beads parka? You still got it?"

I say, "Yeah. I still got it, I hang it in the cache. I didn't want to keep it in the house because it's too dry."

"What you going to do with that parka?"

I said, "I don't know. When I'm going to die, I don't know what will going to happen to it."

She say, "Can I have it?"

"Go ahead. If you want it you can have it. You can take it."

"I'm going to take it right now because I got iron trunk at home. When I get home up there, then I'll put it in that iron trunk, and I'll keep it where it's cold."

"Yeah, go ahead and take it home," I say. So after awhile she went out in that cache and she brought it in. And we look at it good and everything. Then she put it in a bag. She took it home. So when she came home she put it in that trunk and put it away. I don't know how many days after. Then museum here got it.

(Mrs. Roehl talks about the custom of "dancing away" possessions of someone who died.)

They dance all their clothes, all the

things that belong to them. Now, if my mother didn't give me that parka, I wouldn't have nothing from my mother.

My mother used to have lots of dishes, little glass cup, tea cup. Oh, gee, I used to like it when she used to straighten up in the cache. I used to go in there with her. I want that cup real bad. And she told me, she say, "When I die, then you can get it. Your brother bought it for me, and I want to keep it till I die. Then you can have it."

Did I get it? No.

All the Nondalton people got everything that belongs to my mother. My mother had three trunk. Their cover is kind of high, high trunk. She had three of them. All her dresses in one box. All her underskirt that she uses for the church in one box. Shawl and handkerchief, silk handkerchief. Everything is in one box. Now when she die we didn't get nothing.

My mother had lots of relatives up that way (Nondalton). Like cousins. Not really close relation, but far apart. Well, they took everything, even trunk and everything. They even going to take the dish and pots and everything out of the house, too. But somebody spoke. I don't know who it was.

They say, "Leave everything in the house. Don't take nothing out of the house because they need it. If you folks take all the cups, plates and pots and teakettle out of the house what they going to cook in?"

Somebody in the village spoke up. If they didn't say anything, they would have cleaned our house out, too. Maybe they'll take our clothes. (Laughs.) Maybe they'll take the blankets and everything. Maybe.

Gee, when I think about it, if I know what I know now, they sure wouldn't get away with lots of things that belong to my mother.

Now when my husband get sick — well, he look after me. I can't see too good no more, and the doctor told me not to cook and do things like that and burn myself. So my husband told me, he say he'll take it over. He'll cook and things like that, but I can wash the dishes for him.

All this time, when we moved up to Palmer here, when we bought that house, I didn't know he was that sick.

He goes in the bathroom. I still can walk around yet with one cane then. I didn't use no chair yet. Sounds like he's vomiting to me. Second morning he's doing that, I was just ready to get up to go and see. I just get up, and I was just going to start walking to the bathroom when he come out. I said, "Papa, are you vomiting?"

He said, "No."

I said, "Sounded like you was vomiting."

"No," he said, "I'm not."

So that evening we had supper, and I washed the dishes for him. And I get everything done and he thank me. Then the next morning — I can't see the washing machine numbers, so he do all the washing — the clothes was piling up. And he wouldn't even wash the clothes.

So I told him, "Dial the phone for me, I want to talk to Nada." That's my daughter-in-law in Wasilla. I said, "Dial the phone number so I can call them so I can ask Naomi to come over and wash clothes for us."

He said, "Okay."

So he dialed the phone number for me, and I get on. She answered the phone, and I told her. She said, "Okay, I'll send her over right away. She's going now."

In no time she came. Well, when he hear the car coming, he went by the window and watched. So he was standing there, looking when Naomi come in. He say, "Naomi, how come you didn't take your mother's car?"

Then she say, "Grandpa, why?"

"I don't want you to wash clothes. But I want to go down to the hospital and see the doctor."

"Well," she said, "Norma Lee is over at Mama's place. She got a car. I can call her, and I can tell her to come over with the car."

Then he call Norma Lee. She says she is coming right away. So her grandpa told Noami, "You call the hospital and tell the hospital to come out with a stretcher. Because I can't walk. I can't walk all right to the hospital where they're going to have me."

She said, "Okay."

"So call them and tell them that you folks are taking me down. I'm real sick. And you tell them to bring the stretcher out before we come."

So Naomi did, and they answered, and they say they will.

Well, I went with them, too. And when we came to the hospital, nobody out there. No stretcher. Nothing. I told Naomi, I said, "Naomi, Grandpa can't walk. I think he is too weak. Go in and get wheelchair."

So she run in and get wheelchair and put her grandpa on. And she start wheeling him then. Then I told Norma Lee, "I'll sit in the car, and you follow them. And if there is anything wrong come after me right away."

So she ran in with them. And not even five minutes I see her coming, I think, "I hope there is nothing wrong."

So she came out, she was crying.

I said, "What you crying for, Norma Lee?" I say, "How's Grandpa?"

"Oh, Grandma, Grandpa is vomiting lots of blood."

"Well," I said, "did anybody come to meet him?"

"No. Uncle Eddie meet us, and he went back to rush the nurse to come out right away to meet him."

My son, Eddie, he was in hospital, too. When he hear his daddy was coming he know there was something wrong. So he walk down to meet him. Well, anyhow, they got him up there. And then after they get him in hospital and everything, then I went home. Then next morning I went down. I knew he was pretty sick.

That same evening at midnight, my son came up. I was staying in Anchorage with my daughter and her family so I can be close to the doctor in case they need me.

And then he say to me, "Mama, we gunna go see Papa right away. And I don't think I'll go back down to fishing right away. I'll stay up here, and we'll go down to see him every day."

So we went down and see him. We visit him for awhile, then we came home.

That next morning, at eight o'clock my son came. We just got through with the breakfast. We're ready to go down, phone ring. My granddaughter went in to answer the phone. Then she told her uncle, "That's for you."

Him and his wife went in there to answer the phone. When he's answering the phone, his wife start to cry. Now, his wife's dad was sick, too, in Nondalton. I was thinking, "Now, what happened?"

I wondered if her dad got worse.

Then my son talked for a little while, then he come out. He said, "Mama, they want us down in hospital. We're going down right away."

I said, "I'm ready. I'm ready to go."

So we get up and went out. Them days I still walk pretty good yet. We went out in the car and we went down to the hospital. We went down to the hospital, and we went upstairs where he was.

They put the chair by him, and I sit by him. And I took his hand. I notice right away that he wasn't going to pull through. So the nurse say, "Wait, Mrs. Roehl. If you want to kiss him I'll undo

all the machine first. Then you can come to him."

So I moved little bit, and she took all the machine off. And she said, "Okay, Mrs. Roehl, you can get close to your husband."

So I got close to him, and I kiss him. And that's it.

You know the time that he left me, I didn't shed a tear. My son, him and his wife took me back to the car and we went back to my daughter's place. We came in the house. My brother-in-law and his wife was there, waiting for us, too. I sit on the couch.

My daughter, she was sitting on the chair. She get up and she was going to come to me. She just got half way, and there she went. Her aunt jump up and just grab her like that, shaking her. She said, "Bertha, wake up! Wake up!"

Then she come to. She say, "Bertha, stop crying. Don't cry."

They sit her on the couch by me, and her sister and her husband was there, too, her youngest sister. Right away they sent for medicine.

We have party. They make party, and we have funeral and everything. All this time, I didn't shed a tear. Nothing.

But afterwards, maybe ten days afterward, then it hit me. I tell you, it's no good. When I wanted to cry, I couldn't shed the tears because my son and his wife and the kids was same room with me in the living room.

When I get up — when I started to head for my bedroom, my son know right away why I wanted to go in my bedroom. I just go in there. I just sit down, and I just start when he come behind me. He just sit by me. All of us break down — his wife comes. We all break down. That was tough thing.

I never think nothing of it before I lost my husband when anybody lose their husband or their wife. I never think. But I know what they go through.

I tell you, that's a hard thing to go through.

Upper Cook Inlet

Happy Nicoli is an Anchorage street person who divides his time between treatment in the Alaska Native Medical Center and the city's Fourth Avenue.

Mr. Nicoli is an Athabascan, and he was born on September 6, 1923, in Sunshine, a former village near Talkeetna.

Today Mr. Nicoli spends much of his time at Bean's Cafe, where free food is available, and when he is not in the hospital he generally stays overnight at the Brother Francis Shelter.

He spoke in an office at Bean's, where he is well known by other street people and the staff.

Alcohol has taken a heavy toll on Mr. Nicoli physically. Just getting around town is becoming increasingly difficult for him.

His fondest memories are of days spent alone — out in the woods.

124

Happy Nicoli

". . . I taught my dad and my mother how to read and write . . ."

My name is Happy Nicoli. I was born in Sunshine, Alaska. Went to school in Talkeetna, Alaska. Went to ninth grade out in the States.

Yes, I went fishing, trapping, moose hunting every year. Went out trapping all by myself. Sometimes they missed me. Sometimes I was missing. They thought I was dead out there. Sometimes they would search for me. Don Sheldon used to hunt for me with his airplane.

Then they find me, and they brought me back. I left all my traps up there. Never did went back.

I like it out in the woods. In Talkeetna and Sunshine, Montana Creek, Caswell, every place where my dad went. Done a lot of beaver trapping, went all the time by myself.

It's a lot of fun goin' fishing. Some-times you set a net out there, have a lot of fun dryin' the fish. Then you get a fish pole, catch a grayling, Dolly Varden, rainbow. It's a lot of fun fishing.

When I was about nine years old, she (mother) used to make me go trappin'. She used to trap. In those days, long time ago, boy, those mink, marten cost a lot of money. And the weasel cost about five dollars. Muskrat, beaver. That's what we lived — lived on the beaver.

Killing spruce hens, ptarmigans. When I got mink, marten, ermine, I skinned them, hang it up. Fox, wolf, coyotes — live out in the brush and have a lot of fun out there.

Nobody tell you what to do. If you want to sleep all day, you can sleep all day. If you don't want to eat, you don't have to. Then if you don't like the work,

125

you don't have to.

In the winter stay out there, go skiing. Sometime I use snowshoe. I like to chase moose in the wintertime, in the deep snow. I used to have a camera, used to take a picture of them.

(Good memories are) climbing a tree, act like a porcupine. Fall down off the tree. (Laughs.) That's when I first hurt myself right over here, too. I had broken ribs, broken back. Every time I'm walkin' along on the ice I always slip and sometimes I dislocate my back. Can't even get up. Now I got a brace back up in there now.

I'm the oldest one (in the family). There's only the four of 'em I got left. I'm just only the oldest one.

Yes, I went to church. I was baptized when I was young. Athabascan Church, Russian Orthodox. Then I went to Catholic Church.

I started drinking when I was nine years old. My dad used to make a home brew. I used to go down to the basement. My mom used to look for me. She know where I was at — drinking the beer. Home brew, with a sandwich.

It got me sick. Seems like I was going over. I had my head down. Seems like waves. Keep doing it over and over and then I got sick.

My mom used to spank me for it. And then I started smoking. I used to steal a cigarette from my mom and my dad. They used to chew tobacco. I used to steal that, too. Go out and hide in the brush. Sometimes they'd find me, about four days after they'd find me out in the brush.

I was doing all right in school. I taught my dad and my mother how to read and write, went to night school in Talkeetna. I was only about ten years old when I taught my dad and my mother to read and write. So they gave me credit for that.

I just translated what it means, and they understand all the handwriting.

I was over there in Talkeetna. I was only about seventh grade because I had TB, and they sent me out.

When I went to school. When they sent me out. And then I went back over there and I miss all my parents, staying with all the white mans.

And when I came back and tried to speak my own language, I don't know what it means. I don't even know what it means. (Laughs.)

But, after that, when I went to Seattle, I couldn't speak no more (Athabascan), no more.

Well, ever since I went to high school I don't even understand them any more. And I don't think about them any more, either.

White man's language. (Laughs.) That's the only one I understand anyway.

(Mr. Nicoli talks about World War II.)

I was working in Alaska Railroad. It was '40, '41 I went to work. I was only 16 years old when I went to work. When they bombed Pearl Harbor I cheated my age. I told 'em I was 18. So they just put me to work. I work about six months, and then I got drunk. Missed my job.

They fire me, and they throw me in Army. I spent four and a half years in the Army. Then when I got out and I got worse. My first payday come back, I got drunk again. And they fire me again. Go right back again. Until all the money's gone.

I was in Germany. Changed my name to Peter Nickholi. Changed my name, they throw me in the Army. And I was a paratrooper. Then I was missing all my life. When my mom died, they didn't send me back. They didn't notify me anywhere. And I was just missing person.

I was a paratrooper ... When I looked down to earth, I thought I was going to hit the ground. (Laughs.) Sometime if your parachute don't even open you might hit the ground.

So now I've changed my name again to Happy Nicoli. This is when I'll stick with it now.

(He talks about his years of treatment for tuberculosis.)

They kept me in there nine years, I think. I was over here six years, six years in the ANS (federal Alaska Native health agency), when it first opened up. I'm not sure what year it was, '51 I think when it opened up.

I been in there. Then they sent me out again. Then I went to Butte, Montana; North Dakota, a big Army hospital in Missouri where I got cured. Took about nine years, I think. After I got TB, and I got over it, I was not goin' drink any more. Then a whole bunch of friends over here, boy, they started me back.

Ever since that I can't stop. I been an alcoholic ever since. I been an alcoholic, went to the hospital, and I had my stomach all cramped, and were throwing up blood. Everything happened to me. I can't even eat.

When I go to the bathroom, nothing but blood. And then after that, oh, it was last year, my kidney gave out. Both of them. Got infected on both sides ... I told 'em over there in ANS, I told 'em, "I'm gunna die just like my dad. He died with drinkin'."

Yeah, I'm alright. They have to check me in there every two months. Keep me in there for three months.

(He talks about what he currently drinks.)

Vodka ... 100 proof ... Sometimes I drink about one fifth, and that's all. Then I don't want to drink any more. When I start getting my heartburn, then I quit. Right now I'm not eatin' at all.

I got a lot of friends. I got my own, what do you call it? Old age? Now somebody got a hold of my check last September (1984). And it's missing. Three hundred and thirty-one dollars and twenty-nine cents, and that's missing.

I'm missing about six checks.

And everybody wants money when I get a check. I loan them guys money and they don't pay me back ... They stole my money.

Sometimes I bum from some of them guys. They remember how much I loaned them money. I get it back.

Sometimes they just give me twenty dollars. I keep that twenty dollars for one week. I go half and half with my buddy, get a fifth all day, walk around. But two days ago he give me twenty dollars. I got about eight dollars left out of that.

I should have saved that for, oh, a can of juice. I can't drink orange juice. Tomato juice, I can't drink that. It give me heartburn, and then I start throwing up blood. They only one I can take is apple juice. I can't eat oranges. I can't eat lemons.

My dad died right over here in Anchorage. Drank himself to death. Without eatin'. Got so skinny when I went to see him. He said, "Son, this is last time I'm gonna to see you."

I put him to bed. I was going to church over there. They kept me in there, and early in the morning about five o'clock, they call me up, they said, "We can't tell you. Come to ANS right away."

And I went over there, and he said, "No. Can we give you a shot?" I said, "Yeah." So they gave me a shot. Then afterwards, when I got over it, boy, I felt bad ... He died over here, my dad. Right here in Anchorage. Took him home. Cost me nine hundred dollars to bury him. I thought, "Them Natives, they ain't supposed to pay for the grave. BIA's supposed to pay for it."

When my mom died over here in Anchorage, my dad paid for it, too. Cost him nineteen hundred dollars.

(He explains how he learned of the Alaska Native Claims Settlement Act.)

Oh, the BIA. I was in the hospital, and when I got out, they told me, "Did you ever put your name on that?" I said, "No. What kind? I don't know." (Laughs.) So when that BIA come, he said, "You got settlement act over here. You gotta sign up for it." So I did. And that's all.

(He talks about where he stayed before the Brother Francis Shelter opened.)

Down on Ship Creek. Ship Creek, across the bridge by ANS. Had a tent in there.

Cut a lot of wood (laughs). Keep the fire going all night. ... If it was during a snow like this, shovel snow. Sometimes little odd jobs. Buy food with it. And then buy a drink after that. Stayed out there for a long time.

I used to sleep out in the brush. Get a tent, and stay out there in the wintertime, too. Sometimes sixty below, and I'm still out there. Then I froze my foot, froze my hand, and my frozen ear. I been in the hospital for it.

I was married. I got two daughters. They're old enough. One of 'em is 18. One of 'em is 19. They're out in the States. I told them I can't even help them any more. They can help themselves.

My wife is gone. Down in her grave. She died about three years ago. They buried her in Eklutna.

(Mr. Nicoli talks about advice he would give to young people.)

I hope they don't drink. Drinkin's the worst one. That's how come I keep on drinking since I was a kid. Now, I'm an alcoholic now. I mean it's hard to stop. Best is not to drink. Just leave it alone. Turn your face the other way. Walk the other way.

If you like to be alone, go out in the brush someplace. Kill a moose. Hunt. Set trap out there. Go skiin'.

Katherine S. Nicolie is an Athabascan who was born in Talkeetna on October 15, 1914.

Today she lives in Anchorage in an apartment complex for the elderly. She has seen much hardship in her life and was not able to get enough education to learn how to read and write.

But Mrs. Nicolie is proud of her subsistence skills. And she says today she would be afraid to be in the woods only because of her uncertainty about people she might meet out there — not the wild animals.

She spoke in her home.

Katherine S. Nicolie

". . . I wish those days come back . . . I want to get back out of town. Now we lost the place where we been raised."

Oh, I'm Katherine Nicolie. I'm from Talkeetna. I don't remember my father. He died. And I wasn't raised in Talkeetna. Mom got married again and we moved to Kroto, and I been raised there.

And we had a hard time. No way to travel — with a dog team, that's all. And that's why we been raised out in the woods, and never been to school. And they have to travel, and kill moose — kill animal — to feed us, raise us.

And we been in Kroto until 1932. And then we start traveling ourself. We were big enough to travel.

I went to work in a cannery, till I met a boyfriend — got married. Year after that my stepfather got lost, and never did been found. Since then I had to take care of Mom. Mom was old. And I had a hard time with them. And the good thing is the railroad. My husband was fisherman and railroad worker.

And then I had three children. And Mom babysat, and I work once in awhile. Me and my husband split up. And we had a hard time. I lost Mom. I had to put kids to Lazy Mountain School. And that's as far as I want to tell you.

I'll start again. After we left Talkeetna, Mom really had a hard time. And she was married to the guy from Kroto. Had nothing.

I remember my stepfather's first baby. And his sister was staying there with Mom. And we don't even know what's wrong with Mom. She gets sick and we started to cry, and they chase us to one corner. And we heard a baby cry.

And the baby was born and we didn't even know where that come from! And that was Mama's baby. (Laughs.)

And after we been raised it was alright. And then we lost our stepfather. He teach us lot — how to live. We learn a lot from Mom and my stepfather.

So that's why I never could get stuck in the woods. I know how to hunt. I know how to take care of animals. And I can kill anything if I got a gun. That's how we used travel — with the dog team. And make our own money.

Us girls — my sister drowned and my brother drowned — now I'm only one left out of twelve. That's all.

Mom miscarried lots. And she said she had twelve. After she got married again, she had only two more. Must be ten from our father. But she miscarried. And she raised only two boys and two girls.

I'm grandma now. And I got a daughter in the hospital. Dying. They who been raised out in the woods, you know, that's what they do. Travel in the woods with us. And we lucky sometimes, we eat rice or beans.

Summertime, you know, come out in the Deshka River, we'll put up lots of fish. And we was pretty small when we learn how to cut fish, even, helpin' Mom.

We used to put up fish in summertime. And then in August month, the old man take us out to mountain, walk and canoe. And he had a hard time get a moose sometime. And they try. We travel till August. Till fall. Go way up the Kashwitna River, go down the canyon, by pack. Dog and all pack.

And they had to travel a long ways. And we'd come down the Kashwitna River. And the old man kill a moose — two or three of them. They dry them. And Mama cleaned the moose skin. And the old man know how to make a skin boat. And Mom sew them skin together. And then they make a boat out of it. And then they put in all that meat.

And then we'd drift back down to Deshka River. From there, after we'd come down. The ice come down, you know, and it would freeze up. And then they go trappin' then. He just takes my two brothers.

And then he make a little money. He either goes to Anchorage or Talkeetna, sell the fur. And then they break trail from Deshka River to Willow. It's 12 miles through the woods. Then they haul the groceries in. I don't know how many trips they makes in the winter before they get enough for summer ... We move up.

He had a big smokehouse. And he made a net himself — fishnet, by hand. We had a little skiff. I don't know where they found it. My brother and them, they go hunt a big rock. They use it for anchor out there. They put the net out and catch lots of king salmon. We was too small to help Mom. Mom was sittin' down the creek — all day to cut fish, cut fish.

And she filled all that smokehouse, all by herself.

Old man had a big cache out there

way up high so the bear or anything wouldn't get in. After they dry, drifted down with a canoe, filled that smokehouse up. Put all the sugar and flour upstairs. Then ready to hunt some more moose. Put up fish first.

Then we go back to Willow Mountain. And poor Mom. They were catchin' those ground squirrel. Make a coat for us. Make a blanket for us. Make a parka for her husband. They didn't have no shoepack or nothing. Mooseskin moccasin. That's all we used to wear. You get used to it — go in the water and it dries back up. Now you can't do it without gettin' pneumonia or something.

Well, we got to be smart. You know in the spring-time if you go too far out across the river or something. In morning-time it freezes, you know, in April month. You got to get back on the land. And sometime we stay up 'til two o'clock in the morning to get away from the place ... And when we come back they teach us some more. And they're glad when we come back.

Every summer. Same thing over. Falltime, go way out towards the mountain, go back up the canyon ... Those days was hardly any moose. Sometimes the old man travel, travel. He'd find a moose track and he'd have to camp behind to catch up with it. Only way he can get it easy is when there's deep snow. When there is no snow — like this — he can't get ahold of it.

You know, after we get big enough, told us to go put the trap for mink or

something. And then we don't know how to skin it. After Mom think we're old enough that we can try it. First, she told us to go try it. "You got to learn." So we tried to skin it and set it and we learned. And then we didn't need no help no more.

Me and my sister, those days we were tough girls. We get in a canoe only about this narrow, paddle, go on the river, go up the river and just about shoot all the beaver we want.

We make our own money. And the folks, oh, so proud of us. And we skinned the beaver ourself. We kill it. And, boy, it's good to be trained that way. But just that readin' and writin' — trouble I got.

I used to go take a tent after I lost my sister. Well, I had my own team, too, you know. Old man make snowshoes for us. Camp any place, all by myself. Trap. I don't think I can do it any more.

Well, I be scared. (Laughs.) Scared of people. I'm not scared of animal. (Laughs.)

We was doing pretty good, raised in the woods.

In Susitna River, from Deshka River, about 15 miles down on Little Susitna, there was a store there. One storekeeper there, that's all. One white man. Now it's full of white people (laughs). That's all we see is storekeeper.

(White people) scared them. And Mom was doing the same, you know. Every time they see white, you know, Mom always get the gun ready. And they notice it ... We see white people when she stay alone with us, she pull the gun on them all the time.

So they don't come near us. How could we learn (English)? She don't understand, neither. When the old man's home, and they talk to them, my brother answers for them.

Those years — they said there was school before the flu come. And long ago lot of people died. And they said there was school there. And some few went to school. And after flu, everybody went away. Everybody died off.

I think before we was born used to be Russian church. That burned down after no more school. After no more school the church was still there — I think about '21, and that burned down. That burned down and no more church.

I think it was about 1928. Me and my uncle's three daughters — about four of us — we used to go to store. And we can't even hardly say "gum" or anything. We point at anything to buy things. We finally listen to people talk English. We pick up some words from them.

And then, 1932, we learned a little more. Just to travel, you know. We were big enough to travel then, go back and forth to Talkeetna in summertime on the train. From Deshka River go up and canoe — paddle. And then walk six miles to get in the train. Get in the railroad track, and then put shoes on. And that's how we learned to talk English. Little at a time. Little at a time.

Since 1936, you know, I got married

to this guy from Point Possession. And everybody — all the Indian I know around here — they all talk English. I was gunna start learning from them.

I used to live near a woman married to a white in Talkeetna. She don't even talk English. Even her husband come home. She hardly say anything. She don't even talk. She didn't been to school, neither. She was just as bad as I am.

It's pretty hard for us. We don't see hardly any white people until 1928. Then we start travel on the trains by ourself, listen to people talkin'. When somebody say, "Hello." We say, "Hello." When somebody say, "How you?" We don't answer. Don't know how to answer! Poor kids. (Laughs.)

My brother went to school for seven weeks. And that's all. He was talkin' English good, though. Every time we say, "Talk English. Say something to us," we wouldn't even answer him. We don't know what he's talkin' about. (Laughs.)

And the old man get mad at him, "Talk Indian to them. How do they understand?" So he quit. He wouldn't say a word. No more. Maybe he wanted to teach us or something. But old man get after him.

Poor. Really poor. Sometimes I get mad. They should have raised us close to town, anyway.

(She describes the health of the people.)

No foolin', so many white people come from the States, that's why we get all the sickness, I think. Nobody get sick when we travel. Us kids in the water all of the time.

Now, you go out and it rains a little bit, you catch cold. I don't know. Those days, I never see anybody was sick. The sicknesses we had is toothache and earache ... Yeah, that's right, too, nobody get sick when we used to travel.

Now we get sick so easy. All kinds of sickness. Drink and smoke.

Those days when we were growin' up ... we were scared of our folks. Listen to them, just like they really going to club you ... My cousins ... when I come back to Talkeetna, they smoke.

Gee, that smells good. So I took a puff. And come back, and I sit along side of Mom. Mama smell it. She said, "Whyn't you bring it in here and smoke it?"

"What? I had nothing."

"I can smell it," she said. Gee, I was growed up. I can buy my own. I was still scared of my folks. (Laughs.) Now the kids is only 15 years old. They don't listen to us now.

Well, people drink, we see. They were bootleggin'. Well, I don't know. We didn't even know where they were gettin' it till '28. They were buyin' it right from the store. And that woman storekeeper was bootleggin'. They makin' the moonshine in Cache Creek. And she make the homebrew right in that store upstairs. And she bottled, you know.

Us kids look for bottles. She give us ten cents for little bottles. Any kind of little bottles. Well, we don't know what she was buyin' it for. We hunt for it. Just to drink a root beer. That's the only kind of drink I used to know.

They used to get — my stepfather and my Mom's uncle — get the moonshine. And they drink. Them two old men, havin' lots of fun, talkin'. That's the only time they talk to each other, I think, (laughs) is when they drinkin' moonshine.

My two brothers, they growed up. They didn't even drink like them kids do now. And they had money all the time. And the groceries was cheap. Everybody — we used to have money year-round. We never go broke ... Only thing that we spend money on is root beer. In the store, 25 cents a bottle.

Only way I could remember is they catch lots of fur. A couple hundred dollars — with that you'll be a rich man. Sometime we used to make 75 dollars. Me and my sister, we never used to go broke. Sometime we spend 15 dollars in the summer. Just two — two dollars and ten cents in the train from Willow to Talkeetna. And that's the only money we spent. The old folks buy groceries. But we don't know how to buy grocery.

I wish those days come back ... I want to get back out of town. Now we lost the place where we been raised. It not filed.

Gee, in Anchorage there was nothing. You know, Ninth Street up there on C Street? Ninth Street was way out of town to us. You know where the graveyard is on First Street? That was long walk to us. 1936 was when I first come to Anchorage.

I worked ... down here in the cannery ... I think I make 75 dollars, and five dollars for house rent. And now I still had 50 dollars before I went back home to see Mom and the folks. Just for the trip, you know. I still had 50 dollars.

The grocery was cheap. House — it's five dollars a month. Light and water (laughs), gee. We used to even snare rabbit on Ninth Street. People used to have a bunch of rabbit snare around there every morning ... And horse delivering the milk and delivering the wood.

That was 1936 ... There was one taxi ... Gee, I used to don't like to ride in there. I had to haul my stuff, and I don't like that guy sittin' in there. I didn't know he was an Indian. (Laughs.) I thought he was a Eskimo or something.

When I first got married — well, I been raised in the woods, anyway — he took me across the inlet to Point Possession. Year round. I still didn't mind. I still hunt, go trappin' with him. And my brother and them was still alive. The oldest one was married. And they ask him, "How come you keep her out of town all the time?"

And I asked them, "Why? Don't you like?" Because he was working railroad in Whitney here. So they thought I was glad to get out of Deshka River. And I wanted a city. But I wasn't. And I didn't even try to go to a movie or anything. I used to go to a dance, though.

They said, "Don't you like to see people? You get lonesome out in woods?"

"No. More I like it hunting, that's all."

So that's the way, since me and him we separated. Well, Mom got killed and from there I been raisin' my kids. And I'm grandma now. And I'm too old to go move back out of town now. So I don't know what I'm going to do. I have to stay right here now, I think, forever.

In summertime — I got my pickup out there. I got no license for it. And I didn't get it. It's going to be tied out there, I think. I didn't get insurance for it. Summertime I hire somebody else drive for me. Go to Willow and fish and hunt.

I like my hunting. Trout fish and everything. I still like the way I been raised. (Laughs.)

I used to get my own moose. Shoot him and butcher him myself. I even tanned the hide. I make slippers, gloves, do some beadwork. I still do beadwork, though. I used to make my own living with that. Then I lived at Matanuska. I think I started sewing when I was 14 years old.

Seems like old-fashioned material was better than them new ones come out now. We never used to get raggedy or anything.

I don't drink, you know. He (a former boyfriend) sure like his drinkin'. He can't stop. Whiskey! Whiskey! He finally drank himself to death. His liver busted. He lie in the hospital with it once.

I told him, "... Next time you get sick,

you not pull through." Ah, he don't believe it. He didn't have to drink too long. He used to work in Icy Bay. We go out to States every fall. And we just come back from States in March — March 29, I think. I got it written down.

He finally got sick again. I told him, "You're not pullin' through." He last only four days. And he died.

I'm glad I didn't marry him ... He was beggin' me to get married. I told him, "You drink all time. You gunna die most any time."

"Oh, no. Oh, no. I'll go back to work." But he didn't.

Gee, that whiskey — night and day. Too much. Sometime I used to steal his bottle and I take that much out and I fill it up with tea. Tryin' to save his life.

I used to drink. 1945 — my kids was about this big. My sister-in-law — I started smokin' in 1945, too — "Gee, taste that beer."

"No."

"Wine? Loganberry?" Loganberry wine. Gee, tastes good. I told them, "Gee, that tastes good. I want some more," I said. My brother laugh. He said, "Katherine, that thing got lots of alcohol in there."

"This thing tastes too sweet to have any alcohol in it."

He laugh. Pretty soon I feel dizzy. I don't want it. I quit. Boy, next morning I was sick. Sick, sick. No more drink for me. 1945, tried again.

Then from there I take bottle beer,

I get sick. And about 15 years ago, this friend of mine, you know, say, "If I drink like you — you had only two bottle beer — are you still sick? If I drink like you, I woulda quit."

I told her, "I'm gunna quit."

"Gee whiz, I'll bet you next week I see you in the bar," she said.

I didn't really need it, you know. I thought to myself, "I'm not gunna take it no more." I did. No more. It's no use try, you know, when just a few drink make you sick. Ever since I start, I get sick. I keep tryin', I get sick. Try it again. Sick. No use try. I quit it.

I like it (church). I think I'm baptized when I was really small ... Since 1935, I went to church — Orthodox church in Eklutna. From there I learn how to go to church and pray.

And I'm still goin' to church and prayin' all of the time. Sometimes I don't go to church here in Anchorage, I go to Tyonek — just for the church. Go on the plane. And the preacher proud of me. He like it.

And over here on Turpin? From here to there it's five dollars in taxi. I still go. My cousin live up here, and sometime he pay one way and I pay one way. And my kids are baptized — Orthodox ... So ever since 1935 ... I like it from there and I'm still going to church.

I don't think I'm going to quit. I never go to no church except Orthodox.

I think I better stop now. About my bedtime.

Southeast Alaska

Francis B. (Frank) Haldane is a Tsimshian who was born at Metlakatla on Annette Island in Southeast Alaska.

He was born on June 21, 1926. Today he lives in Anchorage and is a retired air traffic controller. He spoke in his home.

Mr. Haldane is a striking man who looks younger than his age. He has battled many problems in his life, including severe illness as a child.

One of the biggest battles of his life has been trying to find a way to reconcile his Native background with the white world.

Francis B. (Frank) Haldane

". . . Accept yourself for what you are. Realize you are as good as anybody that ever walked the face of the earth. You have as much potential as anybody."

My name is Frank Haldane. Real name is Francis Boyd Haldane. I was born June 21st, 1926. Place? Metlakatla, Alaska, which is on Annette Island, just a little south of Ketchikan. Born and reared there. My group is Tsimshian.

I'm recently retired, since March 19, '84, after 38 years with the government, 35 years with the FAA (Federal Aviation Administration), three years military. Out of which is 24 years with air traffic control and one year of which was computers. I've been here in Anchorage for 24 years, came up here from Annette Island in 1960.

I'm married to the former Mary Katherine Fisher of Independence, Missouri. And I have five offsprings. The oldest is Mark Francis, age 28, and Sandra Lynn, age 27, and Steven

Anthony, age 24, and the next is Corbin Cole, age 22, and our youngest Mona Kristine, age 20.

My parents — Mom is Lucy Verney Rainman, former, of course, Haldane, married a second time. My father, Boyd Anthony Haldane died in June 1953. He was very hard working and fun loving. Mom is a very staunch Christian person, and is a strong believer.

Well, as I said, I was born and reared in Metlakatla. Grew up there, went to school partly through elementary. I missed a couple years of elementary school due to illness. And I never did complete the full elementary grades. And I went to Sitka — Sheldon Jackson (a private boarding school) — in 1942, until part of '44. I got expelled for being rebellious. (Laughs.) So I didn't finish high school, either. So my academic education is basically incomplete.

I'm basically a rebellious person — it seemed like most of my life until fairly recently. For whatever reason, I don't know. Rebelled mentally, mostly, against regimentation or the requirements, restrictions of law and order. It's not that I was an extensive lawbreaker or criminal, it's just that part of my problem was not being able to conform to man-made laws.

I dearly enjoyed my time digging ditches, working in the lumber mill, fish cannery, and fishing boats. I dearly love the waterfront, the water and boats. And, in fact, my chosen hobby — my surviving hobby — is old-time ship models. And while I was in the hospital, Mom brought around a little model airplane, which sparked my interest in model airplanes that lasted for quite a number of years.

I'm at the present time with Toast-masters International Group. I am a former council governor for all of the state — Alaska-Yukon Toastmasters Group, which involved about 350 members in over 20 clubs. That was quite an experience in itself.

As I mentioned, although being rebellious in nature mentally, I nevertheless consider myself being very fortunate in reaching the areas that I have. And accomplishing what little I think I have. Primarily not so much on my particular burning desires or fantastic skills, but primarily because of Mom and Dad and some significant people that I can recall at the moment.

One is a high school teacher who was at Sheldon Jackson, Gladys Whitmore.

(Laughs.) I seemed to gravitate toward a group that appeared to be basically free and fun loving. So we went off campus once too many times to go see a movie. Because we were only allowed off campus certain days and certain hours. But we elected to sneak on downtown to see a movie, during the evening. And, of course, we were caught.

And I done that once too many times. I think you're allowed being caught once. And then the second time you're expelled. So that ended my high school career. I was a junior, or the first couple months into the junior year.

Any more, I've just accepted that particular trait, as such, and not fight it so much. I used to spend a lot of time fighting it, in mental anguish.

I think all youngsters are rebellious to certain degrees, mainly of the natural instinct of the desire to be free. Nevertheless, the end result has been good.

I first began to realize I was a "Native," or realize I was born an Alaskan Indian — Native — early in high school. If I was aware of it before high school, which was 1942, I didn't pay attention to it.

I saw Dick and Jane books. I saw books of the white man and in the movies. And I just associated that with something remote.

But I started to become a little more aware of being somebody different — Alaska Native, somebody with a different color skin — oh, during high school when I began to notice attitudes — different attitudes and possibly different treatments from other groups. Namely the white man.

It's not so much there was outright discrimination that was obvious. But I just began to notice attitudes. It didn't bother me, because for most of my life I've grown up and worked with and alongside the white man. Which in spite of this and in spite of that, were it not for the white man, I would not have gotten as far as I have. Namely in air traffic control and eventual retirement from air traffic control.

I was taught and I was shown an awful lot by the white man. I'm not saying that the Alaska Native is insignificant. I've accepted the fact that all people are, of course, equal. Discounting the color and the race and the creed, we have all the same potentials.

When I first noticed the difference it wasn't bad. Here again, we were young. We lived our own life. We didn't really care. And the impacts of noticing that I was different didn't have an immediate effect until a little later — until I begin to become a little more sensitive and a little more aware of the treatment of the Alaska Native, of the American Indian, of the black or the minorities.

And then, I began to build resentment in those areas because of the lack of equal treatment. Equal opportunity. As a result, I did become basically resentful with life. I was caught in between I guess, I suppose you might say. I'm married to a white gal, and growing up in a white man's world and culture so to speak, which was technological. And yet, I seemed to be stuck, in a way.

I thought many times of returning back to my hometown, my home country, and picking up where I left off, enjoying nature. I felt that it was easier to do, but to me that would be running away.

I chose to stay, primarily because I needed to face the issue within myself and around me. And possibly to help any person, preferably Alaska Native, or a minority, if and when, where possible to share what little I've learned about survivalship, so to speak.

I have learned to survive. I know what's required to survive. And, it's not always easy because I'm always torn between a lifestyle that I remember as a youngster. And then, of course, looking around to see what's happening in the modern world. And what is happening among the minorities.

I do feel that some of the values, as from being reared as a Native, or from growing up in a good environment which involved nature is the value of live and let live. Of respect towards property, respect towards the family, respect towards brothers and sisters. And, if possible, respect towards fellow humans. Not so much the competitive political structure as we know it. Which is more often than not dog-eat-dog or stab-in-the-back, unfortunately.

This is one reason I have elected not

to become involved in things political. And, as a result, I had a difficult time with promotions, and eventual promotion to supervisory capacity. I had to force myself. And, I had to fight for that.

But the basic values are, again, basic things that I remember from my mom and dad, the family.

My hometown of Metlakatla is a little town that I remember 24 years ago of living and let live. Helping one another to help themselves. Helping others in need, sharing foods, sharing clothing, or just giving to the poor.

I can remember a friend of mine, a good friend in earlier years. We helped one another whenever we found jobs or whenever we knew of a job, would tell one another, and, of course, spread the word among our friends. That seemed to me pretty significant because that illustrated to me closeness of friendship and interest in one another. We were always supporting one another through buddies and friendship.

Direct assistance. It was just a part of life with us. Families sharing foods, seafoods mostly, you know, just because for the sharing. But mostly because not wanting the food to go to waste.

If the person brought home too many clams, more clams than they can use, they'll give them to the next-door neighbor. Or crabs. Or whatever. It was just that way. That's the way it always had been, helping one another.

I wasn't rebelling against that. I accepted that. The things I rebelled against were the musts and the must-nots. And the regimentation. (Laughs.) The restriction. I guess maybe I just carried that too far. Maybe I just never outgrew it. Maybe it's because of my early childhood illnesses. Maybe I had a resentment against that.

The illnesses started with flu, measles, chicken pox, and complicated into internal organ disorders requiring hospitalization and surgery. Of course, that was way back in 1937 (in Ketchikan General Hospital).

I was so darn sick by then, I just kind of drifted like a dead leaf on the water.

Some of the people I do remember and I really feel good towards was a person that did save my life from drowning. I fell overboard, playing around on the boats at the waterfront. And my friend became panic-stricken, frightened, ran away for whatever reason. Maybe to get help. Or just panicked, thinking I was already drowned.

But I did fall overboard. I do remember the scenery. I came up and started to climb back on board. I don't know how old I was. We were very young.

But I started to panic when I couldn't climb back up on the boat. And I started hollering for help. The only person within hearing range was a fella down the beach, cutting wood a couple miles away. He heard me. And, of course, he ran down to the dock and pulled me out.

I must have been in the water for quite some time. Because of what we know today of hypothermia, I had started reaching because it took me a long, long, long time to warm up and quit shivering.

I feel good toward that person. Of course, he's long dead now. But nevertheless, I really feel real good about him and towards him. Were it not for him, naturally, I wouldn't be here.

The illness and the hospital were traumatic, of course. That's just only a memory of being sick, and having to spend time in the hospital. And the surgery. I don't know what kind of an impact that does make, except possibly a keen appreciation for health. (Laughs.)

Mom. I remember her visiting me as much as possible. Coming over by boat, whether it's sunshining, stormy, rainy or blowing. Always coming to visit me, bringing fruits and whatever she can.

I guess I was supposed to have been near death a couple times. And she stayed by the bed, you know, just about 24 hours a day. So there was that undying support that only a mother can give, I suppose.

I didn't really remember my dad too well, again because of my rebellious nature and partly because he was out and about, making a living, hard-working outdoors. But I do remember him as a kind, gentle person. I remember only two times — specific instances — where he got angry to us kids for bickering, as we normally do. And he got tired of that and he gave us a spanking.

But it hurt him so bad that he cried with us. (Laughs.) He actually cried because he felt so bad about spanking us. But he was a beautiful person.

The people that made a direct impact on me — there was another one, the son of a minister, who I befriended. I think it's because of the bullying that he had been receiving from the bigger boys at school. He was a youngster my age. And these people were picking on him, pretty much, because he was new to the community, and to the school.

And he was small and kind of scrawny, so to speak. In other words, an outsider and a Cheechako. And I felt sorry for him. And I don't know whether that's the reason I befriended him, but we did become friends, and good friends.

And we did a lot of things together, went a lot of places. And eventually joined the Boy Scouts together. And built a lot of model airplanes. He was always envious of myself because I did a much better job that he could ever do (laughs).

So those were good years. The friends, the groups running together. Just living in peace and harmony, mostly.

(Mr. Haldane talks about discrimination.)

It's hard to put my finger on that, except that I just became more and more aware of it through the years. And where I became more graphically aware of discrimination taking place in our world, namely in the government — FAA — was when I chose to become an EEO (Equal Employment Opportunity) counselor. And, of course, this required numerous courses, people-to-people relationships. Ah, but, primarily reading of books.

In fact, that was so devasting to me, and compounded by rebellious nature, I found myself disliking intensely what had been done to the American Indians, to the Alaska Natives.

(Mr. Haldane talks about World War II.)

Basically, World War II for me didn't have too much of an impact. Because we were basically remote from the actual exposure. And, except for the blackouts, the Territorial Guard, the building of the airfield, the RCAF (Royal Canadian Air Force) fighter planes being stationed on Annette.

For myself, I was too young. I was still in high school. Just as World War II was declared I was an eighth grader, in fact. Of course, the following year I went to Sheldon Jackson in '42. But I was still too young.

So there was a delay — for whatever reasons. I have my own theories on that.

People would refer to them as fate. But I have learned since that a lot of things that happen to us is not fate. It's workings of what we call spirit. And, oh, I can show you an example if you want, but it's a long and involved story.

Had all those things happened or not happened I wouldn't be here. I would not have joined the Air Force to learn communications. And as a result of communications experience — if I had not obtained that in the military — I would not have gotten a job with the FAA. And through the FAA commun-

ications experience I eventually moved into air traffic control, and then coming to Anchorage, learned a little more about what life is all about.

Had I not come to Anchorage, I wouldn't have learned all that. So it is significant. I don't think these are accidents.

Let's put it this way: I got drafted in 1945, October, and then, eventually got into the military in 1946. And took part of my basic training up here in the Army. And part way through the basic, somebody asked where we would be shipped to. And they told us the Aleutian Chain.

Well, we didn't care for that. (Laughs.) I mean that wasn't very attractive. That wasn't romantic enough. We wanted to go overseas in Europe or the Oriental Theater. But they weren't taking any more because this was in early '46 — the war has been over.

Then we asked, "How do we get out of this?" And they said, "Well, the only way you can get out of it is join-ing — picking a branch of service of your choice, sign up for three or four years." I did, wanting to be an aircraft mechanic. But I didn't get that. Instead, they gave me communications.

Making a long story short. Were it not for that — my choice to join the Air Force and become involved in the military and had I remained in the draft system and gone out to the Aleutian Chain — I would have gone home, picked up where I left off on a fish-ing boat, become heavily involved in alcohol.

I did in later years, but fortunately I was able to break that. But I have no doubt that because of the simple hard-working lifestyle — involvement in alcohol — I have no doubt I would not be here. I would have been crab food a long, long time ago, as did happen to so many of my friends.

But I've learned enough of why we're here, a little bit about the journey of the soul, the requirements of life, so to speak.

(He discusses his problems with alcohol.)

A few years after I came up here, after my training as an air traffic controller and I got settled in the profession of air traffic control, I found myself more and more and more gravitating towards alcohol. A lot of it is through frustration. Some of it is my inability to accept or handle pressure. Again, possibly back because of my unwillingness to abide by regimentation.

But, anyway, I did become involved more and more and more in alcoholism, and spent some time in and out of the bars along Fourth Avenue. Some friends down there. And it just started to become a way of life.

Part of it was a desire, too, to escape. I was caught between two worlds, one technological and one as I remembered — a simple, enjoyable lifestyle. And I really couldn't accept mentally the harsh requirements, the impersonal nature of our society as we know it today.

So I chose to escape by way of alcohol. But only recently was I able to break away completely from alcohol. I did it for a period of years, off and on. Mostly off. But it became a problem.

I got away from that basic bar-hopping because it was expensive. So I became involved in alcohol more at home. So that was, again, because of not being able to accept totally the harsh requirements of our technological system. I was fighting it, up until the time I did accept it as fact. So long as I'm going to live here in a technological society, metropolitan area, then I'm going to have to abide by the requirements.

I know about the laws of success — discipline and requirements — punching the clock. But, mentally I kept fighting that. It was a conflict.

What it was like to be down there? Before that I had tried to live the good life in the churches. You know, being a "good" Christian. I wasn't able to. I just couldn't seem to be able to conform to the requirements. But that convinced me of the fact that perhaps maybe I was not destined to be one of the lucky people, the good people.

So I resigned myself to the fact. I said, "Well, fooey, I guess I'm not the lucky few." So I became a little more involved in alcoholism. And mostly down in and out of the bars on Fourth Avenue.

But, the thing I did notice about Fourth Avenue or any other place like that is that so long as you have the money you're more than welcome. Plus, and, more important to me, though, was the element of fellowship. Regardless of why, you know, we are along Fourth Avenue the bottom line is fellowship, acceptance and a feeling of belonging.

To me, that was the important factor. The friends and the fellowship. Any and all people. We were equal, no matter what color. Oh, there were fights, you know. There were resentments and harsh words. But, what the heck? Who cares when you're snockered? (Laughs.)

And, money is money. The other thing I noticed is nobody really cared what you looked like. I was from one extreme to the other. I could dress first-class and go in and out of the bars. Which was seldom. Or, I could be looking like a bum, raunchy and dirty. And nobody cared. Nobody noticed. Nobody asked questions.

You know, so long as you were able to pay for your beer. And, to me, that was sort of a freedom. No requirements. Except for cash. So that was the acceptance area. To me, that was pretty good.

I had then given up on changes of life. Although I guess I was living two lifestyles — one technological in air traffic control and the other extreme is, of course, bar-hopping. I guess that amounted to moving towards alcoholism.

Later on I did acknowledge as being an alcoholic and eventually doing something about it. I had finally broken away — with a lot of help — from alcohol.

Those are my recollections, my experiences with Fourth Avenue.

(Mr. Haldane talks about the reaction outsiders have to Fourth Avenue regulars.)

Yeah, there's a lot of that thought: Disgust. Disappointment. Whatever you have towards the residents of Fourth Avenue. It's kind of sad. And it's sad, too, what those people do to themselves. And there's a lot of reasons, some good and some invalid.

But nevertheless, they're still human beings, and I'm positive to this day that you'd find the spectrum of all humans down there — from the fisherman, the ditch digger to the simple Native, to lawyers and doctors.

As in any skid row, as in any bowery, in a large city you'll find these elements. Again, this is a problem with alcohol. This is what alcohol does.

One real drastic illustration is that in bar-hopping you meet prostitutes out looking for business. I couldn't help but recall chatting with a few of them. And we'd kinda get off on a topic, one being parapsychology or religion.

And every one of those gals, I remember, when we'd get to talking about life and whatever, would seem to drift towards the desire to return to society. The desire to return to church. The desire to become re-established in their relationship with their God. And that was really interesting. They yearned this. And a lot of those people yearned this.

But, here again, I'm talking about the

prostitutes, they were convinced so strongly that they could never return to society or the church. Because society and church, they were convinced beyond a shadow of a doubt, would never accept it.

And I tried to tell them, "Well, you know, nobody would ever know. You know, you dress like everyone else. Who would know?"

But they kept saying, "Well, yeah. Somebody will know. Somebody will know, and they'll spread the word."

Here again, two conflicts, I'm sure. Two choices of lifestyle. But nevertheless, the illustration is that a lot of those people yearn, you know, for the good things of life. Yearn for the church, yearn for society, yearn for a relationship with God, possibly feel lost down there.

But they all have their dignity, their human values, their human dignity. But they have resigned themselves that that was their lot in life. I don't think so. They do need a break. More than a break — encouragement, convincing them they got as much potential as anybody else — if they could be convinced of that.

As I've said, Mom and Dad were strong Christians, deeply involved in the church. But I rebelled against that to a certain degree. I went to church because I had to. Because Mom made me (laughs). But nevertheless, I grew up with the awareness of the requirements of religion. And I did not understand religion fully until, of course, long after

I got up here in Anchorage.

I — eventually up here in Anchorage in one of the Presbyterian churches — I did become an elder for a few years. And through certain people in that congregation, I became introduced to parapsychology, which answered for me a lot of my questions, experiences with what we call ghosts. There's no such thing as ghosts. There are spirits only, individual spirits.

And then, prayer, of course, understanding a little bit about prayer and a little bit about healing. With that again, had I not come up to Anchorage, I would not have learned all those good things.

So religion, yes, is a significant, very critical element in our growth. Because it is food for the soul. As we would take food for our bodies, so is religion and church involvement nourishment for the soul, for the spirit. Which is a natural thing. That's the way it's supposed to be.

The journey of the soul, of course, is the lessons we learn here on earth. Earth is the school. Life is a series of experiences. If we can get through them without self-destructing, then we have learned. We become stronger. The soul, perhaps, has learned its lesson, whatever it might be. It might be a requirement. To become stronger. To overcome the adversities, I guess, is what I'm trying to say. To learn to accept and live with adversities in whatever form.

And not go off on the deep end of drugs and alcoholism or crime or violence or self-destruction or whatever. To come through all this adversity in the best possible shape.

Part of that relates to the early lifestyles of my group, as I know it. The totem poles are again, another long, long story. But religion and the association with God, called — way, way back then long before the missionary came along with the introduction of Christianity — the Heavenly Chief. And there was an awareness of spirit being in everything: the blade of grass, and the trees, and the animals, the birds and the fish.

The early people referred to these elements as Brother Spirits. And they were keenly aware the spirit was in everything. And there was the Heavenly Chief. Also acknowledged was the son of the Heavenly Chief. And, also, the early people — long before the missionary came — were known to pray. To pray to the Heavenly Chief and spirits. They also — when they shot an animal for food, caught the fish and the bird — they prayed for forgiveness of that Brother Spirit. Plus, before they ate or they took their first bite when they were cooking, they would throw a chunk of their game into the fire, offering burnt offering to the spirit.

As I mentioned, religion did and always has played a very, very critical part and a natural part of the Alaska Native and the American Indian life.

And we believe in reincarnation to a certain degree. And we were aware that people really didn't die. Their spirits just went elsewhere, so to speak, and came back to visit on occasion. Because we've had experiences of water faucets, lights turning off and on, and doors closing and footsteps. Not all the time. But on rare occasions.

In fact, my dad used to be fireman at the old church where he used to go, taking care of the boiler in the wintertime. He said he would hear the choir singing in the middle of the night in church. And then he would hear the organ playing. And so, here again, spirits returning.

You asked about some of the mythology. I've learned a little bit about totem poles. That's a real long, involved presentation in itself.

The totem pole did not and does not represent religion in any shape, way or form. It only stood for the basic history of the individual, or the family or stories on mythology or mixed. They're long and involved.

Initially, the totem pole came as a mortuary column to mark the place where the person was buried and what tribe or what clan that person was associated with. Later on it became complex, with the introduction of the carving implement — steel. One quick illustration of mythology has to do with the Raven and the Sun.

I might just tell one mythology story and one story based on religion. The mythology story involves the Raven and the Sun.

The Raven, one of the sons of the Heavenly Chief, got expelled from heaven because he was so mischievous and was such a troublemaker that something had to be done. So they expelled him from heaven.

But in their haste to expel him from heaven, they overlooked withdrawing his magical powers. So when he came to Earth, he retained his magical powers. He was able to turn himself into anything — and, of course, cause all kind of mischief.

Well, there was stored in a big powerful chief's lodge in a large storage box a bright ball. And above all else, the Raven dearly desired and wanted this ball. But he had no way of getting it because the box was guarded 24 hours a day by the chief's guards. So he was watching the lodge for weeks and months on end, and wondering how he can get in.

Finally, he noticed that the chief's daughter came down to the spring to pick up her bucket of water and take a drink of water. Every day. Every morning. So he thought, "Well, hmmm, I'll turn myself into a pine needle, drop myself into the cup. She'll swallow it, become pregnant and give birth to a baby boy." Which she did.

She swallowed the pine needle, or spruce needle, which was the Raven, and gave birth to a little baby boy, which, again, was the Raven. And the chief was happy because he had no direct male heirs to his throne.

So the baby grew, rapidly, and later on he kept crying after the ball. And the people living in the lodge, the chief

and his family, just wasn't able to get much rest or peace. And, finally, they did decide, "Well, okay, we'll give him the ball. But we'll watch him very closely." Which they did. And he was happy. He just cooed and cooed and gurgled all over the place.

But this went on for quite a few months. And every time they took the ball away from the little baby, he cried. And they knew no peace. So finally, they was able to give him the ball, and didn't watch him as closely.

Finally, one day there was a requirement of a potlatch that it was mandatory for everybody to attend, including the guards. Except for the baby boy, who was naturally directly associated with the ball at that time. They couldn't take him because there was no way they could get him away from the ball. So, anyway, they left him. They figured it was safe. And so they all went to this potlatch, and nobody was around finally.

Everybody was gone, so he saw his chance finally. So he turned himself back into the Raven, grabbed the ball, flew up into the smoke hole. And then when the air hit the ball, it burst into flames. And, of course, scorched the Raven. Naturally, it was so hot that the Raven let go of the ball. And the ball just drifted higher and higher up into the sky, grew bigger and bigger and bigger. Of course, that is where our Sun came from. And that's why the Raven is black. (Laughs.)

That's just an illustration of some of the myths. There's a lot of myths, and they involve various and sundry things.

The other I wanted to illustrate was more along religious lines, an illustration of beliefs. And the story goes — of course it's paraphrased:

Once upon a time there were two villages that were in constant conflict with one another. Finally one village overpowered the other, killed all the inhabitants.

But it just so happened the old woman and her daughter were out gathering berries a few miles away. And the old woman became aware of what had happened. So she didn't go back to her village because she didn't want to be killed.

And so she thought that there was a survivor in the woods somewhere else, so she went out through the woods hollering, "Who will marry my daughter? Who will marry my daughter?" And no response until eventually a squirrel answered, and said, "I'll marry your daughter."

Well, the old woman was going to ignore the squirrel because it was ridiculous. But just for kicks, she wanted to hear what qualifications the squirrel had. Because the old woman had high standards.

"Oh," the squirrel says, "I'm industrious. I'm busy all the time gathering food. And I store it in this hole in the tree. We're safe from the enemy, and we have food all winter. So we have no worries."

Well, that wasn't good enough, the old woman told him. So she went on, continued hollering out, "Who will marry my daughter?" and came across a bear. The bear says, "I'll marry your daughter." And she said, "Okay, Mr. Bear, what would you do?"

"Well," he said, "I'm powerful. I have no enemies. Everybody's afraid of me. My house is under the roots of a tree. We're warm in the winter. We sleep in the winter. Nobody bothers us."

Well, that wasn't good enough. So, anyway, the woman went through all the animal kingdom, and never did find one with the qualifications. Eventually, they came across a young male with a bright shiny face. And she knew automatically that he was the son of the Heavenly Chief.

And he agreed to marry her daughter. And, boy, she was happy. She knew who he was, and she was just really happy. But the son of the Heavenly Chief said, "I will have to take your daughter to heaven. And you can't come along because I have no way of carrying you."

She felt bad. She just begged and begged and begged. Finally, he said, "Okay. The only way you can come along with us is for you to hang around my neck very tightly. And under no circumstances should you look back on Earth. Because if you do, you will become weak, and you will never be able to hang on. You will lose your strength. You'll fall back to Earth, and you'll never be able to get to Heaven with us."

Oh, she promised. So, it came time

to leave, and she hung around his neck. And she couldn't resist the temptation of one long last look on Earth. And, as she did, she lost her strength. As hard as she tried, she couldn't hang on. She fell back on Earth, of course, there to remain.

The son of the Heavenly chief and the daughter got to Heaven, and bore three sons. And they each built for themselves. They grew up to be big, young good-looking boys and built big lodges for themselves, filled them with food and all kinds of gifts. And they were rich.

And these three lodges one day settled back down to the old location of the burnt-out village.

And the enemy chief, of course, saw smoke coming out of the lodges and wondered where they came from and who those people were. And, not wishing to risk any of the people of his group or tribe, he sent over his slaves.

And his slaves went on over — and came back pretty soon with an armload of gifts and food, and just really bubbling over with joy. They reported to the enemy chief they were treated so well. They were given all these gifts and all this food. These lodges just held all kinds of food and gifts and were really comfortable.

Well, the enemy chief wanted these things. So, being an expert in gambling, he went over to gamble for all their possessions. Of course, naturally he lost. Because these young boys were skilled in everything.

Well, the enemy chief naturally became angered and took together his army and went over there and was going to take all that by force. Well, a big battle followed. And the three boys, being also skilled warriors, defeated the enemy.

Well, anyway, the meaning of the story is that the enemy chief and his village that overpowered the good stand for the adverse elements of mankind. The daughter of the old woman represents the love in mankind. And the old woman represents mankind's dwelling in the past too much, thereby losing the strength that could be there.

Of course, the son of the Heavenly Chief represents the Christ that is in everybody. And the young boys represent the good that is in the good side of mankind and that will eventually someday overpower the bad.

The missionary came into the Tsimshians in the early 1800s. And he heard this story. And he naturally recorded it. There are different versions, slightly different versions here and there. But it has been known and told long before the missionary came among the Tsimshians.

(Mr. Haldane talks about the Alaska Native Claims Settlement Act.)

I think it's perhaps one of the good elements of perhaps justice finally taking place. The opportunity given to the Alaska Natives, naturally a tremendous opportunity.

And it's a way of the U.S. government, perhaps to varying degrees, making amends for the past treatment of the American Indians and the Alaska Natives. And to assure the Alaska Natives of some of their rights — rights to their land before they lost it all.

Yes, it is significant. It was necessary. And it is a must that eventually would have come along. Had it happened later it would have been much, much less, I'm sure.

(Mr. Haldane talks about what advice he would give to young Natives.)

Be proud of self. Accept self for what you are, in spite of the conditions, in spite of the feelings. To accept self for what you are. To realize you are as good as anybody else that ever walked the face of the earth. That you have as much potential as anybody else anywhere. Although perhaps there's a lot of obstacles — big and small — along the way.

To refrain from falling into the trap of alcoholism and drugs. You know, the running away and self-destruction.

To acknowledge and learn about the heritage. That's not to say that we should live like in the old days. Because that's virtually impossible, no matter how you cut it. Because technology is here, no matter how you cut the cake.

It's here to stay. Changes are inevitable. And the only permanent thing in the universe is change. And that we need to grow with change, to accept it.

To learn the dynamics of success, because after all, as was mentioned earlier, the name of the game in this final analysis, the bottom line, is survivalship. You know, we've got to face that. The name of the game is literally survivalship.

And how do we do that? Some, of course, are lucky enough, like myself, to survive in spite of this, in spite of that. Some do it naturally. Some do it because they want to do it.

It's not to say that we all need to become the white man. But the white man has taught us a lot of things. They have given us a lot of things, science, technology. So I suppose ideally to merge the two cultures, concepts or philosophies — one technological and one with Nature and God. It is possible. It is possible, contrary to popular belief, to mix the two, but, you know, in moderation.

These things are not easy. But they are possible. To establish yourself. To be a meaningful person to yourself.

Arthur P. Nielsen is a quiet man who lives in a simple and spartan fashion in an apartment complex for the elderly in Anchorage.

He is a Tlingit Indian who was born in Sitka on April 25, 1921.

He is proud of his heritage and feels a deep concern for his fellow Natives. He is also proud of his hard-earned education, which he completed as an adult.

After quitting drinking several years ago Mr. Nielsen said he has tried to counsel others with alcohol abuse problems.

He spoke in his sparsely furnished apartment.

Arthur P. Nielsen

". . . that was our Native heritage. Somebody's struggling, they help each other."

Hello, I'm Art Nielsen. And I'm Tlingit Indian from Sitka, Alaska. Was born and raised there. And my grandfather John Michael taught me how to carve Native totems, and as we grew up into school age, we was doing our carvings for the schools. And, also, while we was still in grade school, we was doing some carvings for my father.

And, as I went into the Army — after I got out of the Army, I started going to school. Went up to the eleventh grade after I got out of the Army.

And the reason I didn't go to school while I was at home was we was always out doing things during the school days — getting fish, drying fish and everything. That's the reason why we didn't go to school while we was kids.

And I waited until I got out of the Army before I start goin' to school. And after that I took adult education.

And after I went down to Sitka, I got two certifications for alcohol counselor.

As we started to grow up, started to break away from home, we went all different directions. Some went down to Seattle. Two of us went up to Anchorage here, and some stayed back in Sitka.

And then we kept contact with each other as we started to grow up. We was close family. We grew up in one house. We managed to keep contact with each other as we broke away from each other.

(There were) 11 of us. I was the oldest. But then we start — two, three, four of us died off. Two of them with cancer. The rest with tuberculosis, things like that. I had tuberculosis, too, but was cured by surgery at Edgecumbe Hospital in 1955.

(At home the language was) both Tlingit and English. We never broke away from our Native language.

Our grandfather used to teach us the Native history from the time he knew, the time that was passed down to him, and he passed it on down to us. And so he told us, "When you boys start growin' up you're gunna pass it down to your kids." And I think that's more than right. We just keep our culture alive.

My dad was a fisherman. My mother was a housewife. She was also a mid-mother. 'Cause nurses and doctors were hard to come by in our days. In fact, she brought a lot of kids into the world.

She knew what to do. In fact, twins were born still and she brought 'em back to life. She patted 'em on the back until they started cryin'. And them two twins, they treasured my mother for bringin' 'em into the world.

We had what you call old country doctor. And he took care of the whole village. Sometimes he can't be in all the place at once.

Course in them days, medication and doctor and schools were hard to come by. And we was glad to get any kind of education. But then, most of the time, we can't because we're puttin' up our food. And that was hard to come by, too, puttin' our food up.

In our house there was four rooms. And mostly we'd be in the living room. And we'd go up and play. There was just too damn many of us kids in the room.

That house used to be a mercantile store. And we converted it into a house. Make the kitchen and the living room and all our bedrooms upstairs.

And the foundation we put there was right down to the bedrock. And had concrete for pillars. Ah, we just had a lot of fun, kids just start growin' up. And we had the only RCA radio in the community — neighborhood. So we put it out the window, turned up high. And everybody in the neighborhood would listen to radio. (Laughs.)

Go to fish camp, put our food up. Let's see, go in August, come back in October. And most of the time, we lose our grades on account of that because we can't keep up with our grades, missin' all that school.

In them days, you know, we didn't have water in the house. We had to pack water. The water would be like community water. It would be out in the street. And everybody would pack water from that.

And as for wood, we'd have to pack our wood, have to get it from up in the woods and pack our wood. 'Cause we didn't have any coal. We didn't have any oil. All we had was wood for our fuel.

And sometimes we'd get a whole bunch of kids together and make play out of it. We'd get a log and put some ropes on it and start towing it like a sled. And make play out of it, instead of makin' it into work.

And when we get some logs — or somebody tow some logs in on a beach

— we all, say two, three houses, get together and start cuttin'. And when we get through, we divide the wood up. And that's like any ordinary community, you know. When they're doin' something they want to help each other. And that was our Native heritage. Somebody's struggling, they help each other. And I think that's the same with all the communities in Alaska.

We all grew up and went to our church. In fact, every Sunday we went to our church. Fact, if we didn't go to church we couldn't get our — we'd get punished if we didn't go to church.

Both our mother and father were both religious. Fact they used to belong to church choir, and we belonged to church choir as we started growin' up. Religion was our belief when we was kids.

There were (white people in Sitka), but they let us do with our own culture. 'Cause, see, the town was always divided up into our section and their. They never come into our section. We never go into theirs.

It's like boundary line. We can't go over that boundary, and they can't come over to our side. It's just the way we was growing up. And that's the way they left us. They didn't try to bother us. And we didn't try to bother them. I think that was good. Because they realized that was our heritage, and we weren't going to break away from it.

(At the movies) we'd sit on one side and the white kids would sit on the other side. See, we'd have to sit on our side and they'd have to sit on their side.

I thought they were somebody else when I first start growing up. Because they were white skinned, and we thought they were somebody else. But they never tried to bother us, and we didn't try to bother them.

But after I got out of the Army, then I had different feelings towards them. I knew they was Americans just like I was. And my parents tried to say, "What you doin' with the white people?" I says, "Mom, they're Americans just like we are. Can't be any different." So just left it at that.

(In World War II) I was in the Air Force. I was stationed in Anchorage. And Attu, Shemya. And I was crash boat service for the Air Force. It was good. In fact, I liked the boys I served with. There was two of us, Alaskans, in that boat.

All the rest were all whites. But then, they used to have fun with me all the time. They used to call me "Chief" and everything else. I knew they were just tryin' to be friends and everything else. And our skipper was a school teacher. And every time we were goin' on a crash run, he'd always tell me to take the wheel 'cause he knew I grew up on a boat. He knew I could handle the boat.

I started taking my training. After I got through with my training, I stayed at Elmendorf and cook in the Army there and for the Air Force for about eight months. And then I was shipped out to Shemya — Adak and Shemya.

We was on a crash boat. We was patrolling the islands.

While I was still in there — World War II was over when I was up at Shemya. And everybody was celebrating. Even our skipper. He broke out with eight fifths of whiskey. (Laughs.) I don't know where he had it. He was hidin' it somewhere.

It was in '46 before I got out of the service. I went home. They shipped me home. They asked me if I wanted to stay in the service. I told them no, I was needed at home. So I went home. They shipped me home. And when I got home, I went in started in fishing. And after I got out, I went back to fishing. And in between fishing, I started in carving.

In fact, there was no work. We relied on our carving for our living. In them days, work was hard to come by. But before I got drafted in the Army, I was workin' on the air base over in Sitka. I got drafted from there. I went into the service.

And after I got out, I wouldn't say I was lucky I got home. We didn't see any action up in Alaska. In fact, the action was already over with when we got there. See it was in '44 when the Japanese was in Dutch Harbor. We didn't get out there till '45. So, we was lucky. I guess it was just the grace of God that we didn't see any action.

I started in boxin' before I went in the service and continued boxin' while I was still in the Army. I was fortunate to win. I took heavyweight boxin'

champ of all Alaska while I was in the service. And I retired undefeated so I just stayed that way.

Where I got involved in boxing was my uncle got sick of seeing me get beat up, so he gave me his boxing gloves. He told me teach myself boxing. I liked it so much I just kept on goin' till I started winning.

When I took the heavyweight boxing champ of Alaska, and my general, General Johnson of the Air Force, he said, "Hey, that's my boy. Take care of him." And that was the proudest occasion of my life. In fact, that was. You ought to see the trophy I got, a four-foot trophy.

I don't know who has it now. You see, I couldn't keep it. I had to give it up for the next guy that wins. Unless I win it three years in a row, then I get to keep it.

It was a good feeling. In fact, they took my picture. And I gave that picture to my mother, and I don't know what happened to it ... My manager was from New York City — New York, Madison Square Garden, and he wanted me to go back there to startin boxin' over there.

But I never heard from him. So when I didn't hear from him, I just left it. 'Cause he didn't want me to go. If he wanted me to go, he probably would have notified me.

I had water in my brain. I had to quit. That's why I quit. My doctor told me to quit. That's why I retired undefeated ... It's almost the roughest sport there is, besides wrestling and football.

When I was working at the Pioneers Home (in Sitka) the Orthodox Church burned up (almost 20 years ago). What happened was the clothing store across from the church burned up — had faulty furnace. And it burned up all the clothing. And that burned our church up, too.

We had the Sampson Tugs, Coast Guard and all the other tugs was pumpin' water from the channel. There was no water in town. So they started pumpin' that salt water, so it would help put that fire out. And everybody in town was helpin' put the fire out.

It burned all night. And the fire was finally put out the next day. It burned right down to the ground. The only thing we saved was the icons ... And all the things that could be moved was moved.

(Mr. Nielsen explains why he became an alcoholism counselor)

That's what I wanted to do. I used to be a drunk myself. I was drunk for about 35, 40 years. Now I been dry for four and a half years. And it's taken me that long to dry out.

I used to see my folks drink.

(People drank) moonshine, them days. They used to buy it, ten dollars a pint. That's strong alcohol, too. That's 100 percent proof alcohol. And you don't know how that can burn.

When I was 15. My aunt is the one that started me on drinking. She used to drink. And she told me, "Here, c'mon, drink." Well, at that time I was

more or less curious to see what it would do. I found out. I found out the hard way.

That's a hard subject, that alcoholism. And it takes a lot of our lives.

(He explains when he stopped drinking.)

Four and a half years ago. When I was in Juneau I just had enough common sense. I just had enough money for bus to get to the hospital. And I passed out before I got there. And they carried me up to the surgery ward. And that's when I found out I had alcohol problem.

When I first started growin' up — when I first got introduced to alcohol — I used to laugh at it. Used to laugh at what it can do to a person. Now I'm serious. I know what it can do.

And I don't laugh at it any more. And I try to help other people that's got an alcohol problem. I can tell what's wrong with them 'cause I was there. I know what it can do. And they don't know what it will do. 'Cause that's a hard thing to fight by yourself. In fact, you need help. You have to ask for help — get cured from that.

(Fourth Avenue), that's where all the alcoholics hang out. Four o'clock on they start gathering on Fourth Avenue ... More or less they go down there to see if they can get some drinks.

I know one fella I took a likin' to him, I tried to keep him away from there. Soon's he dries out, he goes right back there. It's hard to break 'em away from that. 'Cause I knew what he was gettin' into.

The only thing I can say to them (young people) is keep up our Native culture. Teach 'em how to carve. Teach 'em the value of carving. Make 'em interested in carving. Keep up the Native tongue, and culture and keep it alive. And keep it goin'. And that's about the only thing I can think of.

Aleutian Crescent

Nick G. Elxnit is a retired fisherman who today lives in Seldovia. He is a quiet man, but enjoys telling a good story.

He was born on November 3, 1903, at Kodiak. He can recall clearly how the eruption of Mount Katmai in 1912 affected the island and the people who lived there. Mr. Elxnit is part Athabascan and part Russian and Finnish. He lives in a retirement apartment complex for the elderly in the community.

Although it is difficult for him to hear, he loves to carry on a conversation. He spoke in his tiny apartment, extolling the virtues of living in a small town and explaining that he once stayed in Anchorage for about a month. That was long enough to convince him he wanted no part of it.

Nick G. Elxnit

". . . We had to saw them by hand — six foot saw. Oh, work! But it was healthy job. Out in the fresh air, good stream of water."

My father was Harry Greenolf. He was a Finlander. My mother's dad was Russian. She was Alaskan. Her mother was Native-born, Native background. I still have pictures of my grandmother and my mother.

My mother was born in Kodiak. She used to tell us, she remembers when Russians sold Alaska to United States. She was around Kodiak when they hoisted the flag on the pole. She was there at the time.

My sister, she was born on the boat, they call Steamer Dora, used to carry mail and passengers to Unalaska along the Aleutian Chain. So the crew, the skipper named my sister. They acted as the nurse. They named her Dora after the boat. She goes by that name yet.

My mother used to speak Russian. Course we did. Pretty much at home used to speak Russian all the time. Course, Russian language, too — you meet some European Russians, they have different accent.

I met some Russians — I used to work down Port Graham cannery. They used to come down from Anchorage. They were from different part of Russia. I could tell that by his accent — when he talk English to me.

So I asked him, "Are you Russian?"

He says, "Yeah."

I said, "I speak Russian, too."

So we started talking Russian. Well, heck, some of my words, he couldn't understand. And I couldn't make out his words.

So finally we converted, talk English. Then we understood each other. (Laughs.) It's kind of a different accent or something. It's different country they come from.

They started Russian school, too (in Kodiak). They was going to give us teaching in Russian writing. That was kind of a church — priest was going to start that. But that didn't lasted long. They had to drop it. It didn't work. Got mixed up with the English language. So they just quit that Russian teaching altogether.

(Mr. Elxnit recalls the eruption of Mount Katmai in 1912.)

I remember it was month of June (in Kodiak). It was nice sunny morning like today. But towards noon hour, clouded up. It got darkness. And by two or three o'clock it got dark.

Of course, those days there was no such a thing as light plant. It was kerosene days. We had kerosene lamp. Ma had to light the kerosene lamp.

Everybody wondered what was happening, what caused it. And then sometime we heard maybe concussion of the Katmai blowing up. Just like lightning, maybe kind of shake like earthquake. Course it got dark. People got jittery.

Lot of church bells — Russian church bells would ring. A lot of people went to church. They thought the world was coming to an end. Course nobody know.

The only thing Army had was this wireless. That was on Woody Island, on that island where the Army had that communication. And nobody know till next day what happened, what caused it.

And then the ash start to fall. Ash was coming down like snow. And that was coming down for two, three days. And darkness.

Anyhow in a day or two the Army knew what happened. They got it through wireless. And then three Coast Guards come to Kodiak. They awake you, and loaded all the people in town onto boats. We were on the biggest one that was there. And the name of it was Manning. Kept us couple days on that boat. Course they were anchored out.

And then rumors were around, if that ash didn't brighten up, they was going to take us to Southeastern Alaska. But then one morning it kind of cleared up. Ash quit falling, and sun come up. So they took everybody ashore again.

But there was so much ash on the ground, all over. It was just like snow in wintertime. And rain afterwards — the weight of the ash — lot of flat roofs caved in.

But it was funny thing, you could walk outside, you could smell the fumes of the volcanical smell of the sulphur, whatever they call it. But nobody got sick from it. And didn't hurt the drinking water. But it was funny.

And then that ash that fell in the ocean. You could see, look down as far as tide went down, it was just flat white laid on the bottom of the ground in the water on the beach. You could look down. I guess ash went in the ground and things got normal again.

We lived in Kodiak permanently until 1912. And then we come to

Seldovia in 1913 because my mother's folks lived in Seldovia. And then Ma remarried. We adopted the step-father.

Of course he went by Elxnit. That's why our names changed. All my records went by Elxnit.

And then my stepdad — there was no canners, nothing in Seldovia — he used to row with another fellow up towards Anchorage for a job. A grub-stake, you call it, to get by your winter. They used to row up the Susitna River, and there was a place up there they called Cache Creek.

There was a gold mine up there, someplace up the Susitna River. They used to go up there, work a couple months or so, and then row back again. That was before our born days. And then he stopped — weather or tides — at Ninilchik Village at that time.

Of course, he talked Russian. And the villagers — there was some Russians there. And he learned quite a bit about the condition there.

In those days, salmon was plentiful there and coal on the beach, lot of game up in the woods. Moose, and winter months, ptarmigan. Of course, people in those days used to have gardens, and they had chickens and cow. They used to live pretty good.

Well, anyhow he bought a house there from school teacher that had a property there. She was my teacher also there.

We lived up there till 1919 in Ninilchik Village. Of course, nobody dreamt about highway or what it is today. It was just the village.

I went to our schools — you know, American. To start with it was Territorial days, used to be what they called Indian schools.

When we first come to Seldovia, I went to that school in Seldovia. Bureau of Indian Affairs, they call it. I still remember our teacher, his name was Nash. They was married couple, they had a little boy. And then on certain days, like Thursday, they used to have us make baskets.

I don't know, that was their idea of teaching kids. They used to get a lot of this straw, you know, making baskets.

But in Ninilchik when we went to school, it was public school then. Our tablets and pencils were furnished. We didn't have to buy our own. School was furnishing those.

Imagine in Ninilchik Village there was about 40 school children. We only had one teacher. Imagine what work she had to do. And then she had to burn coal in her living room — there was a partition. She had to check the coal stoves and fires in wintertime.

And then the well was back of the school house. Us older kids, we used to fill her coal buckets before we went home. She used to rotate that. There was no such thing as janitor in those days.

Those days we didn't have no gyms. But I would say those days we learned something. We learned the arithmetic and reading and geography, spelling. Myself, when it come to spelling — I never study — I was pretty good. I used to take interest in geography, arithmetic, drawing. I was pretty good in drawing maps. I was doing all right.

I didn't go very far. I didn't go to high school — about eighth grade is as far as I got.

It wasn't too important, anyhow. There wasn't no such a thing as high school in those days. Course we come out of poor family. Family couldn't afford to send kids out to school for good education.

Them days, used to have good times in Ninilchik. Wintertime, used to go to school. And then winter months, there's a steep hill there by that church. Our school house we used to go to was by that church up on the hill.

It isn't there now. That's where we used to go — climb that hill every morning to go to the school. And then moonlit nights — the village kids — we used to slide down the hill.

And then we used to make our own skis out of barrel staves. That was fun, too, you know. We didn't have the factory skis like today. We had to make them out of barrel staves. You know, like herring barrels used to have — they're kind of rounded a little bit. And then we'd put rubber straps over them and use them just for sliding. The road would get kind of smooth on the ridge.

And then we used to use moose hide, used that like a toboggan. Gee, that was fun, sliding down, pretty steep hill, bunch of us young boys and girls would get on that hide and slide down. Some-time the hide would get sideways, everybody rolls over on each other. (Laughs.) But you couldn't get hurt.

And then when we used to hunt moose we used the hide for toboggan to get our moose out of the woods to the camps. That were good, too. You could kind of lash the whole quarter onto it. And then you pull it like a sled.

It made it lot easier than packing on your packboard on you back. You walk in front with your snowshoes and drag that behind. And then, if you were going uphill amongst the woods, that worked pretty good. If you had a little incline, when you stopped the hair kept it from sliding back again. So it was real good. Good old way to do it.

Ninilchik when we lived there, a mailman used to pick up mail in Homer, and he had a contract to take mail as far as Kenai. That was before highway. He used to have a horse and buggy, go along the beach. Deliver mail to Kenai. Once a month, we used to get mail.

Those days there wasn't many people, and he handled it. But boy, didn't he have tough trips. He used to stop with us overnight, and then come back to Homer again with outgoing mail.

And then, when we was in Ninilchik we used to take fresh king salmon up there, you know about thirty or forty to sell, to make a little money.

My stepdad went to butcher shop there. He thought he would sell the whole load. But they wouldn't offer more than 10 cents, 12 cents a pound. So anyhow somebody advised him — we sold it to the Army, you know. So they bought the whole works for 15 cents a pound.

It was funny, too, my stepdad said when he collected to get the check, well, of course, he had a bunch of people at the desk.

"I'd go to one, they'd send me to one to sign this paper. Then they'd send me to next one. I went to about half a dozen people until I got my check." (Laughs.)

That's the way they work.

Anyhow, then Seldovia started to pick up — herring fishing. So we decided to move back to Seldovia. We bought property on the point next to the church down there in 1919. So we moved back to Seldovia in 1919. So I been around Seldovia — well, pretty much made my home since that time.

And then, of course, stepdad and I, we built a little 30 foot boat. Course we didn't have the power — one of those 5-, 6-horsepower engines, one of those one-cylinder deals, you know. Used to call them clunks.

You didn't go very fast like you see boats nowadays. You had to stop, wait for tides. And we made several trips with that boat to Anchorage.

Anyhow, we used to fish for canneries. And we fished for Port Graham. We had a fishtrap down there, above Anchor Point. We didn't make big money those days.

Salmon was very cheap in prices,

maybe eight cents for reds, two bits for kings.

And then I used to work for Alaska Packers cannery. They had Alaska Packers cannery at Kasilof River there. You could see the stubs there yet, last time I was there. Those days, canneries used to bring their crews and everything on a sailing ship. And then they would load their crews.

They used to bring up mostly Chinamen those days for cannery workers. And a few Mexicans. They didn't have any Filipinos those days.

My stepdad, he was working in a cannery with the machinists. I remember his wages were 65 dollars a month those days. Course they get meals in the cannery, three meals a day. Being our dad worked there, summertime we was in Kasilof, too. I was about 12 years old. We stayed in a tent out on the flats.

Anyway, they was short-handed — July when salmon was running strong. Those days, was mostly fishtraps. They used to bring in salmon on scows, you know. Tugs would bring them in and unload. They used to have what they call a beach guy, locals used to work. They called it beach guy.

And you know what? There was no such a thing as coffee time those days. Night-time, they would be called to pitch fish. 'Cause they had to bring those scows in on a tide to unload. And you know what you got? Their wages were? Forty-five dollars a month.

Anyhow, they asked my stepdad — they were short-handed, course help was hard to get those days — they asked if they could put me to work.

There was two-line cannery. Course my stepdad didn't like the idea of me eating (Chinese) food — rice. Still they used chopsticks those days. So he talked to superintendent, if I could eat in white man's quarters. So superintendent said it was okay. I could eat three meals a day where rest of them ate.

So those days they used to start seven o'clock in the morning. Cannery would start to can salmon. There was no such thing as coffee time nine o'clock or 10 o'clock. You would work till 12 o'clock noon. And then you went to lunch. And then one o'clock you went to work again and worked still six o'clock in the evening. That was a day's work.

My job was: cans used to go through the steam box. They didn't have vacuum-seal deals like they have now. Those days, salmon had to go through what they call steam boxes on a chain for 15 minutes.

Then they came — from steam boxes — they went into a lye wash. Wooden tank was made and cans went through this water on a chain. Then after they came out of the tank they went into coolers. Then they stacked them inside. Then it went to be cooked for 90 minutes.

My job was to watch for leaks or light-weights. And I had a pair of iron tongs. In case a can was light-weight — would kind of tilt or float up — I'd fish it and set it on a rim of this tank.

And then if there was any leak the bubbles would be coming out of the can. Then I had to fish them out, too.

And you know what my wages were? Dollar a day. I worked thirty days, I made thirty dollars. (Laughs.)

I often think about it, later years. Course those days there was no withholding. It was all take-home pay. And those days, you buy Hills Brothers coffee for thirty-five cents a pound. Fifty pounds of flour used to be $2.50.

Then in Seldovia used to be sawmill. I spend two summer working on what they call Powder Island. There was a sawmill there. Course it wasn't big outfit. I call it poor man's setup. Everything was beach-comb stuff. We had steam boiler. That was our power to run the mill.

When we didn't have breakdowns things used to go pretty good. We used to sell about 5,000 feet of lumber in a day. About four people working there.

Our wages used to be 90 dollars a month and board for eight hours work. That was pretty good, those days.

We used to go out to Tutka Bay. We had steam donkey used to take it up there on the scow, way up the head of Tutka Bay. Used to log, do our own logging in the summertime, month of June, July. We got the logs out of woods with the steam donkey.

You would pull this cable by hand to where logs were and then drag them out to the flats where the tides would float them. Then, to make steam for the steam donkey, we had to cut wood.

Those days there is no such a thing

as — nobody dreamt of chain saws. We had to saw them by hand — six-foot saw. Oh, work! But it was healthy job. Out in the fresh air, good stream of water.

I never forget, way up at the head there we had a cabin we stayed there when we was logging. There was a little short grass grows on the flat. I counted 40 porkies (porcupines) all in one bunch — young ones and old ones feeding on that little grass. There was a lot of game those days. Now you very seldom see one nowadays.

We had a telephone, too. Those days they had old-fashioned kind, just for town. Each house had long-short — certain rings. That's how you got in touch. But the funniest part was somebody else could be listening in to your conversation. Lot of people used to listen in, see what the conversation was about.

Those days, people kind of helped each other. Was friendly, too. Everybody helped each other. I would say they were most honest people, too. In early days, dollars was scarce. There was no job. But still, people had a little money.

There was two stores, for instance, in Seldovia. When people got a little short, used to go to the store get credit, see? But they paid their bill, too. Even amongst a few people we used to go borrow money. There was I.O.U. — piece of paper or something. Everybody trusted each other. But still, they paid what they owed. So there was no big loans or anything.

They kind of worked things that way in those days. Everybody kind of helped each other. Just like in Homer when a few people started to homestead, bought a few pieces of ground ... they used to get their logs out of the woods, built log houses.

Well, they all got together, helped to build this log house. When they finished, helped the other fellow. That's the way they worked things. And that was kind of the idea. I'd say they were more honest, too.

And then we had dances, around Russian Christmas. That used to be two weeks later than ours. We used to have what they call masquerade dances. Used to have dances for nine nights straight. And you had good music, too.

Like early days, there was some Scandinavians used to play accordians. And then lot of local boys used to play guitars, made good music for dancing. Well, we had good times, wintertime.

They had jail alright. They did have cops. They had marshal, those days. Like this town (Seldovia) had only one. But there wasn't much trouble of any kind. Once in awhile there was some case. Course Prohibition days, they used to have a jail. They'd get few for — moonshiners. Somebody complained, they would lock them up. There was no really bad violation, bad criminals those days.

They didn't have no hospitals. Like in Seldovia, before we had any hospitals, you always had some kind of a doctor in town. But they were pretty good, too, give you medicine. Course, later years when there was something serious — somebody had broken bone — they always took them to Anchorage. They had a hospital in Seward, too.

In my younger days I was working on Alaska Packers boat as a mess boy. I was young fellow. That was a tug. It was steam engine. They had a crew of fourteen on that tug.

Well, anyway, I got a job as cook helper, they called mess boy. And I was helping cook, wash dishes. And my job was peel potatoes, get things from — they had kind of a locker in the fish hold where the grub was stored, what cook needed for his cooking.

And then my job was to fix up rooms — skipper's room, engineer's room, fix their bed once a day. And mate's. Course they had what they call a wireless operator. They had that aboard.

Those days, the wages were small. Even skippers got one hundred and fifty dollars a month, those days. My wages was sixty dollars a month at the time. And the firemen that was shoveling coal, keep the steam up, and the deckhands, too, they took eight-hour turns at the wheel, four-hour shifts. And their wages were seventy-five or eighty a month. Course they got grub, too. But it was all take-home pay those days. There was no withholding.

As far as I ever got that time, we had to go down Southeastern to tow a ship, sailing ship. The name of it was Star of Greenland. So this tug pick up that ship outside, and they put the towline on it.

Well, they took that boat into little cannery. Alaska Packers Cannery — they had a cannery in Loring, a little community they called Loring, fishing town. That's where they had one cannery. So they took the ship there, tied it alongside dock, unloaded supplies.

And then when they unloaded we towed it to Wrangell. Alaska Packers had a big cannery there. And there, the ship was left there for the whole summer till season was over in the fall.

After we took the ship in, tied it there, they had to go into Ketchikan to fuel up, get coal and water. You know, supplies so that we could come back to Cook Inlet again.

And then when we went to Ketchikan I went to a picture show. That was during Charlie Chaplin days. I still remember that show that I saw. (Laughs.)

You remember what you see. I think that's the first talkies that come out. I think it was talkie show. So anyhow, some of the crew, we went and took in a show. I did anyway. I kind of enjoyed it.

That's the farthest south I ever got, was Ketchikan. Never got to (Lower) 48.

During World War I, I was too young. They didn't take me. Then, World War II, then I was a little old. Course I registered. And I put a little time in town here. They organized kind of a home-guard deal. And they dished out some rifles ... used to do a little target shooting. And they gave us some Army coats, shells to practice.

And then during black-out days, they used to have a little cabin out on the bluff on the end of the town. We used to take turns to watch outside the bay. You're supposed to watch for Jap boats or something.

The town was supposed to be blacked out. But it was kind of funny, too. The harbor light — the blinkers out there — was burning. But still in town we had blackout. (Laughs.)

I used to be up in Anchorage. I figured life would be the same. I was in Anchorage — when was Eisenhower president? I was in Anchorage, drawn on a petit jury. I stayed there a month.

Of course, Anchorage grow up then. And I didn't want no part of it. You couldn't cross the street. You had to watch them stoplights before you could cross. And traffic. Noise. They could have this. (Laughs.)

I still think the old lifestyle was better than what it is today for people. We went a little too far with everything. Lot of guys I meet, like some politicians, they say "progress." But progress went a little too far for good things in my opinion.

We got to go back to make things normal. This can't go on because this ain't going to work out.

What do you think?

Of course, you've got your own opinion.

Helen E. Malcolm is part Aleut and part Swedish. Her mother died when she was less than two years old, so she had almost no contact with her mother's Native culture in the faraway Pribilof Islands.

Even if she had been able to afford a trip to either St. George or St. Paul it is possible Mrs. Malcolm may have had difficulty visting her mother's home. Until rather recently the islands were completely controlled by the federal government, which ran the seal hunting.

Mrs. Malcolm was born March 3, 1901, at Unalaska. She grew up at the Jesse Lee Home on the island, which seemed far removed from the Aleutian Islands' culture.

She discusses some disturbing concerns about the way she was raised at the home and the lack of preparation she had to live her adult life.

She spoke in her Anchorage apartment.

Helen E. Malcolm

". . . we made our own clothes, underwear, stockings, aprons . . . we worked all the time."

My name is Helen Malcolm. I was born at Unalaska, and at a year and a half, my sister and I were put into the Jesse Lee Home where we grew up.

My father was a Swede from Stockholm. He was Charlie Swanson from Stockholm.

And then we'd get apples or oranges or candy (from him). He'd leave enough there till he came back the next year. And that's the only way we knew him. He was a nice fella as far as we knew. (Laughs.)

We didn't know him very well because we were young then. By the time I was 12, I guess, he got drowned. We didn't know him when we grew up. So we were without parents nearly all the time.

Oh, we loved it when he came. And he wouldn't stay too long — maybe a week or two. He came for groceries and things like that. Because he lived out in the islands, I guess. So he'd come to get his supplies. And come to Unalaska where we were.

He looked like Papa. Just a Swede. Blond and blue-eyed — a real Swede.

Then he'd leave money at the store so we could get candy and whatever we wanted. So much, I guess, till he came back the next year. He didn't leave it at the home because he was pretty sure we wouldn't get much of it, you know. They'd keep it. But at the store, you know, it was on his account.

Oh, he came probably in May. Because he had to sail. See, they didn't have motors then. In their little boats, he'd sail up there and get what he needed. And he'd come up and visit with us.

And we all just looked forward every day to see him coming. (Laughs.)

He'd take us on his little boat. Give us things, you know, eats, different things. Because at the home we just had regular menu, not much of anything. But he would have different things — fried potatoes, which we never had (laughs).

He probably had about a 30 foot boat or something like that. Just a little one. Enough for him. He was alone. He sailed. I don't know how long it took for him to sail up from King Cove to Unalaska. Must have been quite a bit. Must have taken quite awhile to just sail.

He was the only relative we knew, you know. We didn't know our mother, either.

But then he lost his life to the sea. A ship wreck. And we never did know anything about his people. We did have an aunt in Stockholm that wrote me once a year or something like that. But we never did see any of them or hear much. We were, oh, not too much interested because we knew we couldn't go see them.

My mother was from Pribilofs, I guess. I never did — at that time you had to have permission from Washington to go to the Pribilofs. And we didn't have any money because there was not much work there. So we never did find out anything about our mother's people.

No, never did learn it (Aleut). When children came there that spoke it, they were forced to forget it and learn English.

So we never did learn only maybe a few words.

There was a little girl that when she came, I guess she was about five years old. And she only could talk Aleut. And she just sat on the bench and listened. She didn't talk.

But when she did decide to talk — I don't how long it was — she talked English! 'Cause she listened. She never spoke, but when she did finally after a few months, why, she just talked. English. We just marveled at that, how she could talk. She came from the Bristol Bay area.

It was usually orphans (at the home). Or with one parent. Seemed like most of them were the fathers. It was for the orphans, really, the Jesse Lee Home at that time. And for the Native people.

And most of our workers — the teachers that were there — came from Massachusetts. Nearly all of them. Finally when I was probably about 10, we did have someone from Colorado.

But the rest of them were all from Massachusetts. I guess that's how it started. That Jesse Lee was from the East, you know. And that's how it started. They got their workers from the East, mostly from Massachusetts.

Well, that's the only life we knew. And we went to the public school there, which was up to the what? Not even to the eighth grade at that time when I was going. About sixth grade was about as high as it went.

And after we grew up, then they finally got a high school there. But it was way after we were out on our own.

They had boys and girls, between 75 and 100. We didn't mix too much. There was my sister and I. And then there was the Peterson family. The two families together mostly. There were a few Eskimos, but not too many. Most of them were Aleuts at the time I was there.

They wanted us to forget our ways and our people. So we just didn't pursue it. Because they didn't want us to go amongst them — even in the village where the Aleut people lived, you know. We weren't allowed to go into their homes or anything. They just kept us there. That was home and that was our place to stay. We didn't get out.

We just, our group there, that was our life.

We didn't do anything. They didn't do much about entertaining or ... Work! We made our own clothes — underwear, stockings, aprons, things like that. We worked all the time. Every day we had to knit. We had to knit for an hour every day.

Then we had to mend the clothes. Iron and wash. Everything was put up. Every day was like that. Monday you washed. And then Tuesday you ironed the underwear and everything.

Then Wednesday we had to do mending because there was a lot of it. Then Thursday we had an embroidery class, or like that, which they sold. We worked them and they sold them, and we got a tenth of what they sold them for. (Laughs.)

And Friday, we didn't do anything particularly on Friday. And Saturday, we had the afternoon when we could play or read or whatever we wanted to do. And Sunday we went to Sunday school, then to church in the afternoon, church in the evening.

We got punished. We couldn't do too much mischief or you got put in the closet and have to lay down and go to sleep. For nothing. I mean really nothing but they'd make something out of it. I don't really know what I got put in for.

That's the way our life was.

I'd hate to have to see children grow up like that. Like we did. With nothing. I mean we weren't encouraged to do anything. We had to learn after we got out how to manage, to make friends.

We just grew up there. And we had to make our own ways afterward. I mean we had to learn to make our way.

And then when you were 18, they looked for someone for you to marry. And you were married off at 18.

Only one girl that picked her own. And he was in the home, too. Most of us — my sister — well, her husband was in the home for awhile. But then he went out to Oregon, where his brothers were. And when he came back, why, he courted my sister. And they got married. And they were married for 57 years.

The men would come to church and pick out the girls they wanted. (Laughs.) And then they'd encourage us and tell him to come.

(Her future husband) — he came to

Unalaska, bought a home. Then when he came, in the early evening, they'd say, "Helen, someone downstairs to see you."

Well, we weren't allowed to mix with the boys, so it was all strange to meet a man. But then he kept coming, and they'd send me down. And, finally, he asked me to marry him. Well, they wanted me to get out of the home, so I got married.

(Laughs.) And so, I still lived in Unalaska, then, with the man I married.

I didn't know anything from home life. We didn't know anything of home life because I was so young when I was there, and stayed there until they married us off.

He was a good husband. But he contracted TB when I had my two-year-old son. So then I had to go on my own. And I worked at the home for awhile — for fifty cents an hour, and tried to keep going. Didn't have much of anything. You just couldn't. And it was an island where you couldn't buy anything. You had to depend on the catalogs for your clothing and things.

I didn't know anything from home life. We didn't know anything of home life because I was so young when I was there, and stayed there until they married us off.

(She explains that life was particularly difficult for her right after her husband died.)

I didn't even sell my house. I was so ignorant about anything like that because we didn't know. I just left it.

(Laughs.) No one told me anything, you know.

I went back to the Jesse Lee Home with my son, and they didn't tell me anything. So I just stayed there until when? When I was at the home there was a woman at Harrisburg, Pennsylvania, that used to write and send me things.

So then I went to Pennsylvania with my son. I didn't have the girl then, just the boy. I stayed there for a couple of years, I guess, before I came back to Alaska. I used to call her Milady. I never did hear from them again, even after I left. Because I didn't write. I didn't correspond. I was so ignorant.

(Pennsylvania) was okay. I was far from home. Didn't do much of anything 'cause I didn't know how and I didn't have much money. So you couldn't do much of anything. Go to church and stay home. Cook for them.

And then I worked in a place where they took in boarders (in Seattle). Helped around in there. But I didn't get paid. You know, I told you I was so ignorant of the ways, I didn't even expect pay.

From there I came back to Seldovia. My sister was living there. And I worked in the canneries, and I did housework in Seldovia. Got along, fairly well. I mean I didn't complain. I got enough to live on till I got married again.

My husband operated a cannery in Seldovia. And that's where I met him. And that's where I married him. And we lived in Seldovia then for about 18 years. After he passed away I moved to Seward.

I was cooking at the hospital there. And I had my little home. Walked to work, and walked back every day. I cooked at the hospital. Cooking was what I did, you know, wherever I was.

My children, they both had cancer and died.

I read a lot. People used to say, "Where did you get your education?" Well, through books ... I about read the library in Seward. (Laughs.)

(Mrs. Malcolm says she has noticed some discrimination against Natives through the years.)

Well, you weren't accepted in many places. So we got so we didn't care ... Like clubs and things. If you were a Native they didn't want you ... I don't know.

But I know we weren't accepted in many places. Natives. They don't want Natives. I said, "Well, I'm part Native, I'm part white." They take the Native part mostly. They don't think of the white part ... But now, they're more lenient. You can get into some of the places we couldn't before.

(She talks about when she was happiest earlier in her life.)

I think it was when I came back (to Alaska from the Lower 48), and I went to Seldovia. And I was free then. I mean, I could do as I pleased. I could work at the cannery and make enough to live through the winter. And be free.

Alice Larsen Nutbeem is part Aleut and part Danish, English and Russian. She lives in Seldovia in a small apartment.

Mrs. Nutbeem was born on September 15, 1899, at Unga in the Shumigan Islands. She was shy in talking about her life as she spoke into a tape recorder in her home. But she frequently asked that the machine be turned off so she could describe her feelings about past events.

She is a friendly and gentle — but very private — person and found the idea of sharing her recollections with others a difficult one.

Although Mrs. Nutbeem had no children of her own, she was the fourth oldest of 12 children and helped raise her siblings.

Alice Larsen Nutbeem

"And my husband said to me, 'You want to go back?'
And I said, 'No. I made my life. Now it's
with you.'"

I'm Alice Nutbeem. I was born in the Aleutians. The Shumagin Islands.

There were 12 of us. Most of them are not here any more. Clara and I are the only two girls left. And two brothers in Washington. There were 12 of us, seven girls and five boys. I was the fourth one. Clara is a twin. And she's the tenth one.

My parents were wonderful. My dad was a trapper, and he was a guide for the different ones that came to hunt bear all the years back. He trapped. And then later on he fished. And my mother was a housewife.

My father was 17 years old when he came to Alaska (from Denmark). And he never went back. An awful lot of them came like that. Found their way.

Our hills were full of berries. We would go berry picking and hiking on the hills. It was fun. Our mother used to take us over the hills in the summertime. She'd cook up some fish or make something to take with us. And we'd go over the hill.

And we'd go on the beach and would pick up little pieces of driftwood. And we'd have little packsacks and we'd carry that on our back. We'd go to a stream where we could wade. And we'd have our lunch. Then we'd play and could do what we wanted.

Then she'd bring us home, and then she'd fix a light supper. We'd be so tired, would go to bed gladly. We'd have little packsacks and bring our wood home. Because we didn't have any wood there. No trees. We picked all these little sticks to build a fire in a hurry. We smoked our own fish in the summer.

Dad would be on a trip, taking some people out bear hunting. He was a guide in the summertime. I have to tell you this story. It was cute.

Dad came home one time, and he says, "You know, we went to the Valley of Ten Thousand Smokes." You know where that is? Katmai? And he says, "We were walking, walking."

A couple packers that was supposed to pack their supplies in were not there to put up the camp when they were ready. And so they were pretty hungry!

And Dad was walking, and he said out of his pack pocket he pulled out a prune. And he handed them a prune apiece.

And they walked some more. And he said they looked like they needed something. So he gave them another prune apiece, you know. And they sucked the pit.

And they said, "This is one time our millions don't do us any good."

And Dad thought that was the biggest joke. He come home and told it. He said that was good.

Language at home was all English. My grandmother never spoke a word of English. But she understood it in later years. But we learned the language of Russian. Her language.

My mother spoke English always. But she wanted us to learn grandmother's language, Russian. So she'd speak to us in it. But the boys would say, "Why don't you speak English?" You know boys.

Her father was English. And our mother was part Russian.

Our house had lots of room! Dad kept building. We had a lot of room. We all had rooms. Dad hunted. And he fished. And he trapped. Our fish house was always full.

And we had plenty to eat. We had our fish. We had our meat. We had everything. Of course, caribou was very plentiful up there, too. And we had that hanging up. Fresh meat in the winter, if you kept it cold.

Sourdough yeast and good bread, too. You can't fail there. You made your own yeast. And after once you had a starter, you keep building that up. And you had your yeast for the winter, as long as you wanted. Just like you do sourdough hotcakes.

We used to set the bread in the evening and pan it in the morning. And it was beautiful bread. It was good. Mother made all that. She was really good. She saw that we had plenty to eat.

We had a druggist up at the mine that done what he could for the people. But otherwise we had no doctor. My mother was a midwife. And she brought a lot of babies in the world. My mother never lost any, either, of all the babies she brought into the world.

There was a lot of families there in Unga. Then the fishing — there wasn't so much fishing going on anymore. So all the families moved out to Sand Point, where there was more work there. In the meantime, no one went back because there was no way of making a living there.

In the early days it was codfish that they fished and made a living on, our little stations around the bay. The fish seemed to disappear. They started to disappear in the '20s. And then everybody started moving out to go where they could find work. And they never went back again. They went to Squaw Harbor near Sand Point.

That (a painting) is a sailboat that Dad had. He took us wherever we wanted to go around the islands. It's called "Alice." I had a friend here in Seldovia paint it for me, going out of Unga Bay. That's a beautiful boat. He was just learning how to paint when he painted that about five years ago.

It was just a little village. It would be like here, I suppose, with houses here and there. We had a Russian Orthodox church and another one. Most of the people in Unga were Russian Orthodox.

We had one little school. It was a little red building up on the hill. I only went as far as the fourth grade. And we had a room adjoining. It was a library. And we had a pool table and a punching bag and all that.

So when we had our class we'd go in there and get out of the way for the other classes. And go in there and play pool. I learned how to play pool, too! Then we had a nice big yard. And our teacher lived in one corner. It was real nice.

I didn't go very far in school because I went to school only two days a week. I had to help Mama with the washing, you know. Take care of the babies. I was so far behind in my school that I only went for the fourth grade.

There was a mine about three miles up. It was supposed to be gold, I guess. Well, anyway, this picture of Unga was taken from the mine. It was three miles, we used to walk up there.

So then when it closed — everything was from San Francisco, you see — and when it was closed there was a great big tank they called a cyanide plant. So the town bought that and put it in the middle of our town. And we had that for a dancehall! So we'd have square dances in a round hall! We had more fun. We danced a lot.

We had this steamer that came twice a year from San Francisco. And then we had a mail boat that came once a month with our mail.

And I was married in February of 1920. There was lots of snow in February. We were married on Lincoln's birthday. We thought he was very special. And so we were married on the 12th of February on Lincoln's birthday in the afternoon, and the creek was frozen. And then we went across and danced all night in the round dancehall.

We read a lot about Lincoln. I did anyway. I liked history very much. I really did. Of course, I absorbed everything that I read.

When we were leaving on the little mailboat, leaving Unga, I was looking home. And my husband said to me, "You want to go back?"

And I said, "No. I made my life. Now it's with you."

And I turned away from home, turned my back on home. And I said, "Well, I'm with you now."

And I got over it then. It was hard leaving the family. And all the relatives.

So I started my own life. After we were married we went out to the States.

We got a little place to live back of the Orpheum Theater in Seattle when I first went out there. And I didn't care for any of it. I wanted to be back in Alaska, anyway, that's all. Too many people. Then we got on a boat called the Dora. Got out of Seattle.

We went out that fall after we were married, for the winter. And we were coming home, you see.

And they loaded fuel under one place. And then I noticed at Port Blakely, the other one, they loaded liquor. And, of course, that night they were all tipsy on the boat. We were going through Seymour Narrows.

And I said to my husband, "We'll never reach Alaska." Sure enough, four o'clock in the morning we hit the reef. Piled up on the reef. They got off and went about six miles and beached her. And there was a logging camp. And we went ashore there. There was a couple watchmen there.

And we started cooking breakfast, and flagged the Canadian boat. And we went back into Seattle. And the Dora sunk. They stayed there till they drank all the liquor. And then they came back into Seattle themselves.

Then we went to Seldovia and a friend came down from Halibut Cove.

And he told us there was a place where we could get a homestead up there. So we went up there. Looked around and we did file on a homestead. We had 13 acres up there. Cleaned it, cleared it and built our cabin. We lived up there about eight years.

Then the fishing all disappeared up there, too. You know, herring. And then we came down here to Seldovia. I've been here since. I'll never leave.

I had been to Kodiak a couple times when I was little. The funny part was when I was going to school, my girl-friend and I, I told her, "You know, I'm going to live where there's lots of trees. That's my wish." Here I am. And it was all barren country up there at Unga. Just barren.

And Mama was so good about keeping in touch.

My mother came to be with me when my husband was very ill in '44. She still lived in the Aleutians. She passed away later on in '45.

After my husband died I worked in the cannery. And then I got a job up at Libby's in Kenai, Libby McNeil Cannery. I was a waitress in the cook-house. I paid all my bills like that. Of course, in them days it wasn't too expensive.

The wages were not very big. You worked. But you worked hard for what little you got.

I never had any children. But when I was a girl at home, they used to say, "There comes Alice and her chickens." I'd have about seven or eight of them little ones behind me. And I'd go all over the hills with those little tots. And I always had children with me. I babysat when I was just little. Rocking the cradle when I was just little.

I was around a lot of children all my life. I love to be with children. I love all the children around here. I never fail but that I don't put my arm around one of them and give them a hug.

My motto is: Live each day as if it's your last. Tomorrow has no promise.

Albert Wilson is a retired fisherman who today lives in Seldovia.

He was born on April 15, 1929, in Seward. He says his mother had a serious drinking problem and so he spent much of his childhood in the homes of friends who looked after him. Despite his mother's problems, however, Mr. Wilson has fond memories of the times he was able to live with her.

Mr. Wilson is an unassuming, quiet man, who is part Athabascan and part white.

He lived Outside for about ten years, beginning in 1972, but he says he is glad to be back in Alaska. Mr. Wilson disliked the hustle and bustle of the Reno, Nevada area, especially heavy traffic.

He spoke in the office of the Native village corporation for Seldovia, a hub of activity in the village.

Albert Wilson

". . . While you were skating around, you just put your line down there and leave it there and go around skate awhile and come back and see if there was a fish there."

My name is Albert Wilson of Seldovia. I was raised in Seldovia and brought up here. My mother's name was Mary Hunter, and she was raised in Kenai, moved to Seldovia in the early days. She settled here in Seldovia and stayed with George Ritchie behind one of his houses. And then we moved to her mother's place.

There was three of us, my brother and sister and me. But my brother and sister was raised in Jesse Lee Home in Seward. So I was the only one that stayed with my mother. My mother went to the Orthodox Church here in Seldovia. And I went to school here.

They were older than I was. I didn't get to really see my brother and sister until they were old enough to leave Jesse Lee Home. My mother was married four different times.

She was married to Jimmy Wilson in Kenai. She left Jimmy Wilson and moved to Seward, and she was staying with Albert Sundberg.

Albert Sundberg was supposedly my dad, but they were never married. So when I got my birth certificate I found out I was Wilson, and I thought I was Sundberg all the time.

She worked in the cannery. She was a cannery worker, sliming fish most of the time. That's what most of the women did here in town — work in the cannery in the summer months.

She was a nice person alright. But like most Natives there, she got into drinking a lot. She'd get into heavy drinking a lot of times, and that was why I was always on my own, why I had to be taken care of by other people.

That's the biggest thing I have to put

up with today is that so many people get into drinking. Wherever you associate with people, it seems like it's in that kind of conditions. I drink, but I try to keep it under control. I try to never let it get out of control.

Drinking ruined more Natives than anything else. They got to drinking and they couldn't control themselves. The Natives then were awful weak. They never did have a very strong will-power, you'd call it. Somebody'd offer them a drink and they'd get started, and they never could quit.

They never knew when to quit. I was brought up that way, under those conditions. And I've learned a lot about it. That's what made me stay in so many different places in this town here. I stayed with so many different people in town because my mother — a lot of time — wasn't with me. She was always somewhere else.

You couldn't ask for a better person when she was sober. But it's something I had to put up with. And my brother, he drank himself to death. My brother and my uncles and most of my family, that's the way they went, drinking so much.

When we run out of money it'd be credit, we'd live on credit. Then do a lot of hunting all the time, go out hunting for rabbits and porkies (porcupines) and occasionally go moose hunting.

She did hunting with her second husband. They went out hunting a lot, go out duck hunting, rabbit hunting.

I went to Seldovia school here, and I went to the seventh grade was all in the old school house. I liked school all right, but what was hard on me was I had to walk all the time in the wintertime, especially walking to school there — deep snow.

I had some nice teachers, and they always treated me nice. And it was hard for me to communicate, I'd guess you say. I never speak my language there. My mother did, and a lot of her relatives did, but I've never learned too much of it.

I used to go to church with her all the time, the Russian Church, but I never really understood it. I stayed with the church all the time my mother was raising me. Then after that I didn't go to church any more.

My mother passed away in '45, and then I was on my own. I had to take care of myself, and then I had to go out fishing. I become a fisherman then. I started out with a little skiff and outboard and a small seine, and I'd go out fishing and catch a few fish and take them to the cannery. And I made it that first summer there.

I can't exactly know how many fish I caught that summer, but I made a few dollars anyway. But then the second summer there I went with Tony Martin and we went up the Inlet drifting, and I drifted with him and fished with him that year. And I made enough there to get through the winter pretty easy that time. I was able to buy whatever I needed then.

I was young. I quit school, too. I

couldn't go to school any more. I had to make my own living, so I never did go to school.

A lot of my education was from elderly people. They tell you more about things that's real, their experience in life, going hunting and mining and fishing and all these things. And they tell you a lot more than you could ever learn in school, I think.

(Mr. Wilson talks about the food he ate when he was young and the house he shared with his mother.)

Clams and fish. I stayed right up in the slough there, in the lagoon, and we'd fish in the lagoon all winter and catch herring, whiting and go out clam digging on all the minus tides. And do a little hunting — go out and snare rabbits and shoot ducks. And that helped us a lot, getting by.

It wasn't too good of a house. I think it was a two-room house that we stayed in. It had a wood stove in it. I'd say it was livable, but a lot of times it was cold when there was nobody to go out and chop the wood. The way I been brought up is to put up with all these hardships.

The happy times? Well, going to school was about the happiest time of my life because I got to know the teacher so well, and she thought the world of me. She had me come over after school and make ice cream for her (laughs).

And she seen me since I was a kid; she watched me grow up. Mrs. Grudoff. I'd say there was about 200 kids at the most. There was different grades. Twelve grades. And I just went up to the seventh. She was the first and second grade teacher. She was the one that seen me grow up.

There was never any discrimination that I know of. I've never seen any of it. It never bothered me, being a Native. In fact, I wish I'd learned to speak the language better myself.

All the big events around Seldovia was always at Joe Hill's place. Yeah, he was a colored guy. And I stayed with him when I was a kid there for awhile. And he'd cook breakfast for me and send me off to school.

But he was making so much money that he would never pick up anything off the floor. He was making money hand over fist because he was doing all the work himself and taking care of the whole place himself. And us kids used to sell wine bottles to him — gallons and half-gallon jugs. He'd buy them back for 25 cents apiece and we'd sell four jugs to him and go the show with it. And the first show was in Joe Hill's place.

They showed the first movies I ever saw in my life. I can still remember the movies. I seen one movie — the first movie I seen was a volcano. I think it was in the Hawaiian Islands. It was a scary movie.

This woman, she was on a boat, a luxury liner. But anyway she got in the lifeboat and she lowered herself down off the ship. Her and her kid, by herself, and she got the motor started and she went ashore into the volcano. And she started climbing up that hill until she couldn't go any farther. Just walked up into the volcano, you'd say, and that was it.

And they tried to rescue her and they couldn't get to her. I never forgot that the rest of my life. It was scary.

And then the next movie I saw was a ranch movie where there was a lot of horses — beautiful horses. And the barn caught fire, and all these darn horses was in the barn. And they tried to get the horses out of the barn.

That was another story I could never forget the rest of my life. You see all the timbers down and the poor horses jumping around and all this noise.

This here Joe Hill, we used to sell the jugs back to him to go to the show. And he'd sweep all his sweepings off the floor. He'd just sweep all the dust together and throw it overboard. And we'd go down there and look through there and we'd find quarters and nickels and dimes, fifty-cent pieces, all kinds of money in there.

He'd throw it right down the beach. And all this money, we'd always be finding money down there. In fact, I found my first 10 dollar bill down on the beach there. I took it to my mother, and it had a cigarette hole burned right through the middle of it.

I remember that 10 dollar bill just as clear as could be. And that's where I got my first pair of boots from. She bought me a pair of hip boots with that 10 dollars.

And then there was the old schooner that was across San Juan Beach over

there. I got a lot of souvenirs off of that. San Salvador was the name of the schooner. I guess that boat there was — it was a herring boat, is what they tell me.

They used to process herring. They'd salt them down. And it hauled timber. But, anyway, they anchored it up by San Juan cannery over there. That was during the Gold Rush, and most of the crew left to go up for gold.

And they just left a few people on there, taking care of it. And a storm came up and the anchor drug ashore. And the people just got off and left it there.

And there was nothing wrong with the boat. It just drug ashore and they got tired and walked off and left the darn thing. And that thing rotted to pieces. It was a big sailing ship. It was a two-masted sailing ship. And it laid there and just went to pieces.

We used to go ice-skating in the moonlight all the time, after dark. It'd get dark early in the wintertime anyway. But this here one time, we went ice-skating up at the lagoon. It was salt-water ice. It was beautiful there.

You could build a fire on the beach, a little smudge fire on the beach. There's a lot of trees around. And skate out in the moonlight. And fish, too. You cut a hole in the ice and catch whiting. While you're skating around, you just put your line down there and leave it there and go around skate awhile and come back and see if there a fish there. (Laughs.)

Everybody in Seldovia used to go up there and catch whiting. Chop a hole through the ice and catch whiting. In later-on years I started selling whiting to the Filipinos. The Filipinos around town, working at the cannery, they'd buy a dozen. A dollar a dozen I'd sell it for. And then herring, I caught herring up the lagoon that same way.

I used to jig for herring up there, too, with a single hook, a lead sinker on the line, and I'd shine the lead up and move it fast in the water. And they'd go after it in the water.

I've caught as many as a five-gallon can full of herring that way of jigging for herring — when they were thick out there when the tide was coming in. The tide'd have to be moving. That's when they were feeding in the mouth of the lagoon.

When I was a kid I was always crazy for fishing. Then we used to go out on the bridge out here — in the slough — and jig for dog salmon off the bridge. A whole bunch of kids, we'd get out on the bridge and we'd catch dog salmon. They still do it; the kids still do it in the summertime here. They jig for fish off the bridge.

And then another thing we did — me and my cousin — we used to go up Fish Creek. There was a lot of dog salmon go up Fish Creek. We used to go up there.

We'd club every fish, and kill every fish and drift it down to the mouth of the lagoon and pick out the two brightest ones and go home. And next day the creek was all full again, full of dog salmon. (Laughs.)

And then there was a dog — Prince. It didn't belong to us. It was a neighbor's dog. Prince, he was a water dog, anyway. He used to go and grab the fish and pull them out of the water. He'd grab them by the fins and pull them out up on the bank all the time. He'd chase fish; he'd be soaking wet, just chasing fish all day long, just having a ball.

I went one year over and stayed with my brother. He moved over to Iliamna when he got married and he had five kids in all. But I stayed with him and took care of his wife's mother.

That was Frances. Frances was his wife's name, and her mother, she was a Native and she talked nothing but Native language over there. They went out caribou hunting, and I had to cook for her. She was an elderly woman, and I had to cook hot cakes. I start making sourdough hotcakes — she liked the small ones, three in a pan. And I tried to make big ones, and she didn't like that.

But anyway every Sunday they'd go to church all the time and they wouldn't eat until they come back from church. So I always cooked breakfast, and when they came back then they'd eat. That was when I was about 16-17 years old.

(Mr. Wilson discusses poverty in Seldovia.)

Yeah, I guess there was quite a few people. But they could always go out and get clams. There was nobody that couldn't get out and get fish and clams for themselves anytime they wanted to go.

I mean it was just because of their laziness or drinking habits that would cause them to not get out there. But there was always enough food to go around because everybody would go out fishing and they could always share it with somebody else.

World War II? Yeah, I was still here in Seldovia. I was still staying with Ed Danielson in World War II. He usually listened to the radio all the time. It really didn't have too much of an effect on me. I didn't get into the service until '52 was when I got drafted into the Army.

And I spent most of my time up at Fort Richardson. We went up to Lake Louise and did some road building. I was in the engineers, and we built roads into Lake Louise. It was a recreation site in there. I spent my two years in the service there.

When I was in the service we went from Girdwood over the mountains and came out at Eagle River. We was on a march through there.

And that was a two-day trip. It took us two days going over the mountain. They took us up on the mountain, and we stayed up on the mountain there above Girdwood. And we had to sleep under our ponchos.

We didn't have no tent. And it was pouring down rain. You couldn't sleep at night because that water would sag the poncho down. And you'd have to keep pushing the poncho up to get the water to come off there. But we dug holes in the ground on the mountainside and the poncho over us, and that's the way we stayed on the mountain overnight.

And then we started marching the next day and we had to cross a glacier. On the side of the glacier there was solid rock — it was all solid rock there — and the water had worn on down through rock. I think it was channel almost two feet deep, just like a chute.

And anyway, we marched for two days and was given rations when we started. And that was supposed to have been enough to last us all through the hike. People got so tired and miserable, they started throwing their rifles away. They started throwing their rations away. And a lot of people were just mad. I couldn't believe the march they put us through.

And we just about got over to Eagle River, coming out of the woods we was on private property. And the guy came out there with a gun and stopped us.

"You're not coming through my property."

And they had to get a colonel from Fort Richardson to come over there to get the guy to let us through the property, to back up the trucks and take us back out of there. (Laughs.)

I was so happy I got out of there I had tears in my eyes. I was just that happy. And hungry and tired. We had to go through a swamp just before we got to this property. It really was a rough go, I'll tell you.

The funny thing that happened to

me on that hike, we was going through a grass field — there was a whole regiment of people ahead of me and behind me — and a bumblebee came and stung me.

I was the only one had a hole through in my khakis, and the bumblebee got in there and stung me. I took my helmet and smashed him. (Laughs.) All these people marching and I was the only one that got stung by the bumble-bee.

That was in the fall of the year. I think it was in August.

And then when we went up to Lake Louise, we went up there and started building cabins for a recreation site at Lake Louise. I was still a bull cook, helping out in the kitchen all the time, helping the cook out. We'd have to set up camp in different places.

But the ground was all frozen solid. It was just a muskeg. We was staying in these like quonset huts. We went up there in the wintertime, and then when the ground thawed out all these floors started to buckle. And then there was a lot of mosquitoes coming out of the muskeg.

And the only way they could get a bathroom — an outhouse, a hole through the ground — was blow one. They took this big charge of — it's made for blowing holes in the ground, I guess. They set it over there and they blew it. And you look down there and there was a small hole on top, and underneath it was just like a big cavern in there (laughs). That's what we used for a latrine.

They gave me nicknames. What was that? Caldonia from Seldovia. That was great.

We went on another maneuver down in that same area down by Portage. It was beyond Portage there, Turnagain Arm area. The Army came in there and what it was, it was supposed to be a park in there.

We got in there with the vehicles and we cut the branches off the trees, and the vehicles skinned the bark off the trees. And then the parks people came in there and seen what we done.

We had to repair everything that we done! (Laughs.) We had to put the branches back where they were, to make it look like natural again. And the trees — where the bark was off — we took moss and we covered it up to make it look like it was nothing wrong with it.

They kicked us out of there. We had to get out of that area there. We spent a whole day patching up what we'd done. Anything we cut down we had to get rid of it so they couldn't find it.

That was at the head of Turnagain Arm there, a park area. But, boy, the parks people were really mad about that. We had to repair everything that we done and make it look like nobody was in there!

And after I got out of the service I went to work on the railroad. I worked down at Portage. They call it Moraine. That section isn't there any more. It's between the two tunnels there, right out of Whittier.

And I stayed on the railroad there for about nine months. It was opening and closing doors in the wintertime. When the train come through you had to open and close them doors, you know, to keep the ice from freezing inside the tunnel.

There was a lot of water in there. They got doors, big doors that open and close for the train. And a lot of time the freight train would be coming through at night-time, so you'd have to stay up and go up there and open up the doors when they'd telephone through the train was coming.

That was an interesting job. We stayed in a quonset hut. The quonset hut was below the railroad tracks. The wind would blow and rocks would fly off above, and you could hear it hitting the roof! (Laughs.)

In fact, there was boxcars that blew right off the track at one time. And then wintertime there was a lot of moose there. You'd have to go out and chase the moose off the track. If the train hit any, then you had to go out and get the moose and bring it in. Shoot it or whatever and bring it in.

When I first went on the railroad there, we shared the grub bill. They'd go to town every once in awhile and order all the grub and bring it out to the section. But the first grub I had was GI grub.

The GIs came through the tunnel and they threw all their rations away. They were stationed there at Portage

Glacier for months and months. But when they got taken out of there, they took all their rations and they threw them all along the inside of the tunnels. We picked them all up and we had enough food there to last us months and months! (Laughs.)

I liked the work on that (the railroad), but one guy was sort of prejudiced against me. That's the only time I run into anybody prejudiced. He wanted to get my job. I was a bull cook is what I was — opening and closing doors and then maintaining the stove.

I didn't have to go out with them and work in the tunnels. They got out there and chipped ice, and they'd come back black because they were trying to melt the ice by burning it.

They'd take a drum of diesel fuel and a drum of gas and pour it on there and set it afire after they'd chip most of it out. And they'd try to melt it away that way. And they'd come back all full of soot and all black. And I was staying at the mess hall there and helping the cook out.

Being a bull cook, I didn't have to do that. And he was jealous of my job. Besides I was getting two hours of overtime — every night, opening and closing the tunnel doors. I was getting overtime and they wasn't getting any. They just worked their regular hours, and they were all getting dirty.

That's why he was mad. Because I was putting in my eight hours and getting two hours of overtime. It was just the job, the overtime I was getting in. That's what he didn't like about it.

We had a coal stove, and it was my job to bring in the kindling and carry water and haul in the coal. The cook there was an elderly woman. She was from Wasilla. She lived in Wasilla quite a few years. But she got to work on the railroad, and her and the boss fell in love and got married. And they left me to do the cooking while they went to town to get married.

The first morning I made French toast. That's the first compliment I got! The crew liked it. (Laughs.) I was cooking for about eight people, I guess. There was eight of us. They liked my French toast.

But then when it came to dinnertime, I took out some steaks, some — I think they were Swiss steaks. Anyway, they were all frozen together. I took them out and they were frozen together. And I tried to pry them loose. The butcher knife — I slipped — I just tried to pry them loose and I slipped, cut my finger right down to the bone right down here with that butcher knife.

I just wrapped it up. There was no doctor. I never did go into a doctor or anything. I just wrapped it up and kept it wrapped up until she came back from when they got married.

She was sort of a nurse, too. I'd say she was in her fifties. And he was only in his 20s. He was younger than I was. And they went and got married. They just fell in love. It was great. But he was a nice guy, Gordon was his name.

And that was the extent of my cooking. Anyway, when the boys went to town, they went and got one of these stamped tokens — they had a token machine — they put "Moraine, Alaska, Albert Wilson, bull cook" on there. It had a penny in the middle of it. It was a lucky charm. They used to have them up in Anchorage during the war.

Then after I quit on the Alaska Railroad, I went down to Seward and got a job there in Seward at the Seward Sanatorium. I was janitor down there. I stayed there that whole winter in Seward and worked at the Seward Sanatorium. And then they put me to work — for awhile I worked in a service station.

I got married and I went Outside. I went Outside in '72. I stayed Outside in Reno for about 10 years out there. I got married to a woman that was from out there. We went out there and settled down.

I was going to go on a vacation is all I was doing. When they built this new schoolhouse, I and Edna worked and made a few dollars there. And she was working for Paulson in the restaurant. We got money together, and she asked me, she said, "What do you want to do? Take a trip or fix the house up?"

And the house was pretty well rundown, too. It was outside the city limits. I said, "I want to take a trip. Because I never been outside of Seldovia. I never did much traveling."

So we went Outside and we met her relatives. We stayed out there and, of course, she was taking care of all the money. I never knew how much was in the bank. She was making the checks out.

Finally, we went broke. Of course, her dad then got us a job there. He was living in Lemon Valley. So he helped us buy a trailer. He went and put some money down on a trailer and we started staying out there in Reno. We moved and stayed in a single trailer and we worked there for about two years.

We worked for an old guy that was connected with the Mafia I guess it was or something like that. And I went in there to get a job from him, and he just looked at you and asked you a few questions.

And if he checked you out and you were okay he put you to work. And he paid you off in cash. (Laughs.) He never had you fill out no forms or nothing. I worked down there as a cook's helper a long time. We had different hours. Edna, she worked there as a waitress, and I worked there as a cook's helper.

But we worked there for about two years, I believe it was.

I liked the working, the jobs I had. But I couldn't stand traffic, driving back and forth to work. There was too much backed-up traffic. Sometimes you had the sun in your eyes when you were driving. I seen too many accidents, and that's what made me nervous. And that's what made me want to come back to Alaska indefinitely because I can't handle traffic.

When I was out in Reno before I came back here I stopped and stood by a dead body on the highway. I worked for a K-Mart, and I was going to work about six o'clock in the morning. And here this body was, laying on the freeway. And I had to stop my vehicle and get out and direct traffic around it. And I felt his pulse, and he was already dead. But he was a guy that worked right there where I worked. He was a part-time worker. It shook me up so bad that I'd never want to stay out there. As the population increases you get more traffic on the freeways.

But my wife, she done all the driving Outside while me and her was together. She done all the driving. It never bothered her because she was school-bus driver to begin with.

She didn't want to come back. She become a purchasing agent. She was putting in long hours — 10, 12 hours, she was always gone all day long. I sort of got tired of that because she had her mother stay with us, and her mother was a school teacher. And she had arthritic spurs and a bad heart and diabetes, and we had to take care of her.

In fact, my wife bought a van — a one-ton van — just to haul her around with. There I'd come home and I'd have to do all the house cleaning and take care of her and do the cooking. And she would never get home until eight, nine, sometimes 10 o'clock at night. So that sort of broke our marriage up.

I never paid too much attention (to the Alaska Native Claims Settlement Act of 1971) before I went Outside. I heard about it, and everybody was ranting and raving about it. And every time I come downtown people were talking about it.

But I never really got into it. And then I went Outside, and all I got was newsletters out there ... It wasn't until I came back that I really got into it and learned all I could about it. While I was Outside I didn't pay much attention to it. I didn't really get the meaning of it until I came back.

I think it's been a great benefit to the Natives in Alaska. If they take an interest in it, I think it'll be something that they can really look forward to.

The young generation can get a good education. And they can make life better for them.

They don't have to go through the misery that they did in the early days. They used to catch all these different sicknesses, and they didn't know how to take care of themself when they got sick. Now these things are something they know more about.

It's like when I moved over the Iliamna with my brother, and over there the people were dying an average of one a month. And it was all from TB.

And I told the people, "You know where that's coming from?" They didn't understand where it was coming from. They had flies and mosquitoes all around the village. And the flies and mosquitoes were getting in the house, and the mosquitoes were biting these people. And the dogs, tied right outside the house, the flies would land on the dogs. And these people were getting this sickness. I said that was the cause of it.

(Mr. Wilson discusses advice he would give to young people.)

Today in this changing environment, kids has got a chance to learn more. And they should take advantage of everything, all the benefits they got.

I think if they don't get into alcohol, they would be able to learn more. They got a great future ahead of them. Always ask questions. Ask elderly people about their life. When you talk to elderly people they can give you a pretty good idea what life is all about.

Western Alaska

Otto Thiele Sr. is the son of a Prussian father and a Yupik Eskimo mother. He was born in Bethel on September 8, 1921.

Mr. Thiele is a retired tugboat captain, but throughout his working life he has worn a number of hats. Today he lives in the Anchorage area.

Although Mr. Thiele himself never contracted tuberculosis, the disease took a terrible toll on him because many of his young friends were struck down by it.

He has many concerns about the Alaska Native Claims Settlement Act and fears that it was a mistake on the Natives' part to participate in it.

He spoke in the home of the interviewer.

Otto Thiele Sr.

"I got a church. It's the whole outdoors. And the goodness in people. You'd be surprised how many nice people there are. . ."

My name is Otto Thiele Sr. I was born in Bethel, Alaska, September the eighth, 1921. My mother was half Eskimo and half Scotch and Russian. And my father was a Prussian.

And I led a very interesting life. The only language I spoke until I was seven or eight years old was Yupik Eskimo and German. I understood English, but I heard my father say one day, "Mother, we've got to get out of this town because look at this kid. He's eight years old. He doesn't even speak English."

But I didn't need to. My mother spoke Eskimo, and father spoke German to his friends. And I understood both.

German is the most exacting language ... You can't misconstrue anything said in German. In English, you can talk all day, and nobody knows what you've said. Very tricky language.

And Yupik, it's a shame to say, I've forgotten most of it. Because I haven't used it since I was 12, I guess, 13. If somebody from Bethel or the right surrounding area talks real slow I can understand what they're talking about. But I wouldn't try to compose a sentence. 'Cause it'd come out wrong.

Yeah, Yupik is a very difficult and a complex language. And it changes all the time. Even in my lifetime, it's changed. Words have changed. They've shortened words or changed 'em completely. In just the little time I've been here.

And it's a very difficult language, even according to the linguists at the University of Alaska. It took 'em years and years to construct an alphabet in Yupik. And even some of that's a mistake because of pronunciation. If you learn to pronounce a letter or a sound in one language, it should apply to another, shouldn't it? So I can sit down. Like "Qiana" means "Thank you." And you look at it in English.

And in some printings it starts with a "Q" — which it should start with. Others, it starts with a "K," and it's completely mixed up. How can you teach a language or even write it down, if you can't be consistent?

No, it's a difficult language. So, I've never had the need. My brothers speak it. And they didn't speak it when they were kids but they do now through association. They fish down in the bay. Reinholt and George has flown all their lives up here. They're airline pilots.

So from flying all these people in and out of Bethel and all the villages, they speak Eskimo real well. And they didn't as children because Carl and I were the only ones who spoke it when we were children.

And I grew up on the Kuskokwim between Bethel and McGrath, with a couple years in Seward and Kodiak Island and Afognak. We moved a lot. We moved so much I had a brother, Reinholt, who was born aboard the USS Tupper in the middle of the Bering Sea.

My mother used to tell us stories in Eskimo. They're hard to translate, you know. All the time we were children she'd tell us stories. But they're like little fairy tales. I can remember the gist of them. It was always like a little Grimm's fairy tale or something. Only people would become other things. They'd become needle fish, swimming up the stream, you know. And they always sang little songs with all the stories.

And they always turned into beautiful princesses and handsome princes, and all this stuff and they always lived happily ever after. And they created everything. And it was gorgeous. But it's just like fairy tales in English or German or anything else.

They're all the same, Eskimo, Yupik legends are. Because people are first something else — they're fish — and they're always singing a little song as they're swimming up the stream.

And they always meet a princess or something. And either they get that princess to become a little fish or they become a prince. Or handsome man. It's either one or the other.

And they were always happy little stories. All the little kids, I remember, would sit around and listen to beat heck, you know. Yeah, they're like bedtime stories. Little fairy tales in Yupik.

I was the oldest, the first surviving son. We lost two before me in infancy. And mother had eight altogether, six surviving. We lived a real nice life. We grew up in the woods, and hunted and fished. It was nice fun to run down to the fish trap in the wintertime, and bust the ice out and dip some fish out. Take out the ones you wanted to eat that day, and throw the rest back in.

And then I got big enough — when I was six, I got my first gun. And mother used to take me out and show me how to hunt ptarmigan and arctic hare. So from then on, I had a shotgun and a rifle. And I got to hunt. The rest of my life at home I got to hunt all the meat.

It was a great way to get food. You know, you couldn't run to the supermarket. There weren't any. The NC (Northern Commercial) Company — primarily what you got there was spoiled, really, unless it was canned or smoked. And you know how long you can eat canned meat. Or smoked meat. It's good for breakfast. But there's nothing like a fresh ptarmigan or spruce hen or nice good moose or something.

We had fresh fish, salt salmon. We didn't have freezers back in those days. You know, in the summer you couldn't possibly freeze salmon, so you had to smoke the fish or salt it down or can it, you know in Mason jars and stuff like that.

So we had a certain amount of salt fish and potatoes and moose steaks and liver and potatoes, more potatoes. We had big root cellars in them days with carrots and rutabagas. We had all the good stuff — cabbages. And we always had a big barrel of sauerkraut. Father being Prussian, that came pretty easy, you know.

And it was nice, and my father gave us a basic education, with the exception of a couple of years in the Anchorage school here, and part of a year in

McGrath. But we were educated at home by my father, who spoke seven languages. He was like a computer.

He was a tool and die maker, primarily. He left home when he was 20 after he got out of the Prussian Army. And just wandered around until he met my mother. And he was 38 and she was 16 when they got married. And he outlived her, spoiled her rotten, and refused to leave her side after she died.

So I come from very loyal type stock. And I've got three brothers and two sisters. They all stay married forever.

The house was nice and warm. We always had a great big pile of cut wood. In those days, nobody had running water. You know it was just strictly great big barrels, and you filled them every so often. And it was rather primitive.

But it was a nice way to grow up. Oh, heck, a couple of us guys to a room, and the girls had their room, and the parents had theirs. And then there was a living room and a great big kitchen and a huge Lang woodstove — always smelled fantastic. There was bread on the table everyday, and pies and doughnuts and cookies and cake.

Father was gone most of the time. Up to the mines. He used to run two or three mines. He'd be the master machinist for two or three mines, placer mines or a dredge or whatever he was working on. So he'd be gone half of the year. The rest of the time he'd be home.

And then if we had nothing else to do, ever since I was 13, we'd run out into the woods and cut 300 cords of wood for the mine, you know. And they used to have steam donkeys in strip mining instead of the modern drag lines. In them days they had a big "dead man" on the other side of the valley and then the donkey engine on this side, and they'd have a drag line.

And they'd strip dirt with the drag line. And it burned wood. So we used to cut hundreds of cords of wood in the wintertime. Nothing else to do, between classes and sleeping. And, all in all, everything was fine.

It was a beautiful way to grow up. And then we trapped. I used to trap marten and mink and otter and beaver.

We had a lot of close calls. And no doctors. There were cases where you had to put on your snowshoes and run 90 miles, you know, to get a doctor for your brother, or something. So that's the way we grew up.

I've chased dogs across from Susitna Station, across the Susitna, going into the Yentna. And the dogs would fall through in the spring, with the brown water bubbling up. And one dog would fall through, and the rest would drag him out, and the sled would break through and pop up again.

We used to come very close to being dead every once in awhile. And it was all just a matter of chance you had to take, every now and then, by circumstance.

I can tell you about losing all your friends. You know back when I was a kid — in the '30s — tuberculosis was killing all my friends. And I'd watch 'em die. And I'd have a friend for a few months and — it got so bad that I was depressed.

And I can remember names of a dozen of 'em. Just got to know 'em, and they'd be sick, and they'd die. Everybody died from tuberculosis in the '30s on the Kuskokwim River. And I never could imagine why not me, you know. Or my brothers or sisters. And that made a terrible impression on me. And looking at kids that obviously were as healthy as I, they'd be here today, and gone before I knew it. We were always burying these kids. And I used to think about that a lot.

And I never ever got any religious flashes or nothing. My father didn't believe in organized religion. Mother was a devout Catholic until she married him. She was a dear and gentle woman. My father was a gentle man, too, but he wouldn't allow organized religion in the house.

Absolutely not. Even when the traveling preacher — Father Gallant, who was head of the Catholic Church from Holy Cross, had recourse to stop at our place a time or two. Weather or dog teams.

Father would tell him, "Fine, Mr. Gallant, you can stay. But the baloney got to stay outside, you know. And there will be no praying at table. There will be no mention of anything religious. My kids ... when they grow up and they need a crutch, they can find one of their own. But I'm not going to have one imposed on their young mind until they grow up."

And every one of my brothers and sisters are fine as wine. Honest as the day is long. And moral. Good. You see? And all the religious people I know can do anything they want because Sunday they can go get their sins forgiven. But we can't. Anything we do, we account for.

And anything that young people should know, first of all, is that they are totally responsible for everything they do. And they are going to have to pay for every mistake that they make in growing up.

And they've got to know that they got to organize themself to be responsible for themself alone. Nobody else is responsible for them but themselves. And whatever they become is gunna be through their own choice.

I'm as religious as anybody. But I don't believe in organized religion as it's practiced, told to me. I know there's something far greater than us. But I'd be stupid to imagine I was smart enough to know what it is.

I got a church. It's the whole out-doors. And the goodness in people. You'd be surprised how many nice people there are running around.

Well, Bethel was a lot of Natives, but the commerce was all white people in them days. Except for my grandfather. He had trading posts. Old Max Clark, everybody called him Kyakshook, that's his Eskimo name.

He was revered by all the people down on the Kuskokwim-Yukon Delta.

And to this very day, old, old people recognize me and they defer to me. Because I was the Old Man's grandson. And I don't know why because I never liked him.

No, he wouldn't even talk to my brothers and sisters. I was the one. He'd throw me on his shoulders and pack me up to the store and I could have a handful of bingles. He printed his own money.

It was, you know, out of aluminum. I wish I'da kept some. It's collectors' items now. But he wouldn't even give my brothers and sisters any. So I didn't want the money, either.

And he was afraid of thin ice and rough water. And he refused to speak English.

(He talks about discrimination against Natives.)

No, none at all. I mean, not me. We were never discriminated against. Of course, I was blond and blue-eyed, you know. That was a strange-lookin' Eskimo kid. Nobody's ever discriminated against me that I can remember. I never even knew Natives were discriminated against.

Oh yeah, the real obvious Eskimos, you know, that would come up the river in their rain clothes. They were all made out of animal skins, and intestines, you know. And stuff like this. And they smelled fishy. You know how they are. Well, naturally they'd have a different part of the store they had to go to and stuff like this.

But we were never discriminated

against. And all the children in Bethel were all mixed. We were all mixed.

I guess I was a little spoiled. It was being the first child to survive in the family. I was kind of doted on and as I grew up I didn't like it. But you just take what comes along.

And it was nice, a nice way to grow up. I had a beautiful childhood. I never ever worried about anything. I didn't go through any crises when I became a teenager. And I've always felt this very same way.

Yeah, I've never ever had any anxieties. Oh, when I chased my wife for three and a half years, yeah, I had a lot of anxieties then. But that's the only time.

(The family left Bethel) in 1931. Father didn't get along with Grandfather, and he just up and moved us out of there one day and up the river to McGrath. And we've lived in Sleetmute, and different places up and down the river.

But we moved into McGrath for three or four years. And from there we lived in Innoko. A winter at a time, we'd go some place in the winter and he'd educate us.

We had a schedule that was rigidly adhered to. And we had to go cut wood every day, or do something. We could play after the sun came out. I mean the moon at night in the winter. Then we could go out a play awhile, you know. If we could clear off a piece of ice, we could skate or something.

In those days there was no welfare. Everybody had to go out and work. And they were all happy. And they worked like crazy. And they had fish traps. And they run snares. And in the fall they'd go to fall camp and get all the ground squirrels — sik-sik-puks — and ground squirrels for making parkas. And in the spring they'd go to spring camp for muskrats.

And they just lived beautifully. And they didn't have welfare checks. And they all had beautiful warm clothes they made themselves. And they dried a lot of fish. And, boy, they could string up those smelt. You could see them hangin' in the trees like jewels. They'd string them up through the gills on long willow ropes that they'd make. It was just beautiful.

And they'd dry muskrats in the sun for three or four days, and eat them. And they were delicious. In New York you have to pay a lot of money for a meal of marsh hares, you know. But, no, they were fine then.

And alcohol was no problem, with very minor exception. As a matter of fact, there were more drunken white men around than there were Eskimos and Indians. With the exception of the guys that were taught to work for wages, way back when at an early age.

But I never noticed. Because everybody was busy, hunting, trapping and fishing, and feeding the family. And they were healthy — at least the ones that survived the flu epidemic in 1918, you know. I remember seeing whole empty villages along the Kuskokwim that were wiped out by the flu. There used to be just an empty space on the bank with high grass.

And I found out real early that all those people died of the flu during the First World War. But with the exception of that, the survivors were fine.

Hell, they were all men that worked hard and supported a bunch of kids. This alcoholic problem was never a problem until they started giving them welfare checks.

(World War II), aw, it was just another war. What the heck? I had a little problem a couple of times with some super-patriots because my name was German. But other than that there was no problem.

Well, they drafted me. Yeah, I had a little time with the Army for awhile. And we had a disagreement. They drafted me when I was married six days. And I absolutely refused to go.

So, yeah, I had a little round, a little hard time with the U.S. Government. They decided after throwing me in the stockade — my attorney and my wife would come out and get me right out again because I refused to swear in.

I done that, and just stood toe-to-toe for a few months. And they threatened me with a corporal and a shotgun and a shovel. They put me in a coal car, and the corporal said, "Shovel." And he had a shotgun. And I just refused to shovel. He refused to shoot me.

And the lawyer and my wife come out and got me out of there again. He said, "You can't incarcerate this man unless he's sworn in. No, he hasn't

sworn in." So out they'd get me again.

So they finally threw me out and said I had a constant psychopathic state of mind — totally unfit for military duty. And just right after that I went to work out at the base, driving truck.

A few months later I was a truck foreman. A few months after that I was general superintendent of transportation on Fort Richardson. I stayed there until the war was over.

So I think it's kind of strange that they should tell me I'm nuts on the one hand, and then make me superintendent of transportation, you know, next month.

And, yeah, they sent me some correspondence, saying that in the event of martial law that I should buy some uniforms. They gave me specifications, and told me that my job required me to be a colonel. And I was 24 years old.

That's the way it was.

And in between that, getting married, ever since I was a kid, all I did was enjoy life. I still do. I have very few difficulties, other than losing my wife. I lost her the eleventh of May — it'd be three years next eleventh of May (1985).

But other than that, everything's been fine. I disassociated myself from my own kids. They have to go shovel for themselves. So I've got to the point now where I got to learn to live free. I never have, since I was a kid. Because I always had responsibilities to someone — to my father, mother, wife, children.

I've lived all over Alaska. I'm a tug-boat captain. And I've run freezer ships, fishing boats, crab boats. I'm a seaman, licensed tugboat captain. I was a big-game guide for a few years in the spring and in the fall. Used to go out, my brothers and I, and kill wolves from an airplane.

We used to solve our own wolf problem in them days, kill a couple hundred of them in February and March. And the more we killed, the more wolves there were. They get so smart, you can't shoot 'em anymore.

I don't know why everybody complains so much. People from the States come up here and tell us we can't shoot wolves. And they don't know nothing.

Anyway, I've done most everything. I've been a truck foreman for construction companies on the Slope.

(He talks about close calls he had as a tugboat captain.)

In the middle of the winter on the Gulf of Alaska? Yes, we have. Did you ever fight with a barge behind, and a small vessel? We're talking about a boat that's 90 feet long. And it's blowing 85 knots southeast, and it's making ice all over. And it's 70 foot sea, and you stand in one spot and go backwards for two or three days.

And you ice up and you think you're going to turn over. And stuff like that. There's no reason why I should be here. All the people that I used to fish crab with, back in the '50s and early '60s, they're all gone. They've all drowned. Or, fell overboard, drunk off the boat float. They were all divorced, heart-broken.

You know, women only put up with that for so long, and then they'll run off. They don't care about money. You know I used to make so much money down there, and my wife said, "That's it. If you want to go back to Kodiak now, you can stay there." So I quit.

See, I was lucky. I was henpecked. (Laughs.) But all the rest of the guys. I mean damn near all of them, they're all gone. They've all drowned. Some dear good friends, old acquaintances, they've drank themselves to death, fallen off the boat float. Nobody left.

But that's in the days when we had wooden boats. You know we used any kind of a boat we could get ahold of — old sardine seiners, and power barges, anything. And get out there in the wintertime and ice up and roll over and sink. That was tough. But we thought it was lots of fun because we didn't know any better, you know, before radar.

(He talks about whether he sees himself as a Native or white.)

No. Just a human being. And once I said to my father, I said, "Father, sir, you've got to realize that I'm not all Prussian." He said, "Yeah, I realize that. I'm aware of that son. And it's possibly your only saving grace."

But he said, the only thing was, he said, "It's a wise child that knows its own father. But nobody denies their mother. And if I ever discover that you've been ashamed of being part Eskimo, you're in fact ashamed of your mother. And I'll kill ya."

So, I've always been a nice good

Eskimo. Or German. Or American. I'm just a human being. It's never bothered me. No aspect of it has ever bothered me like it's bothered a lot of people I've known. I know people that pass and lie, and are ashamed of what they are. And that makes me feel sad.

I'm not greedy. And what I abhor most of all is greedy, self-seeking people. I could name a whole bunch, but I won't — both Native and non-Native and mixed.

But basically Eskimos are not greedy. They're the biggest hearted people in the world. They'd give you half of everything they got. Yup. Makes 'em feel good to give. Makes me feel good to give.

And I think that's the nicest part of being part Eskimo is that I've never ever lusted for money or power. I've just been content all my life. I'm just a — I guess (laughs) you could call me a ne'er-do-well or something. But I've been terribly happy. And I've done everything I wanted to do in my whole life, with a minor exception or two.

(He discusses the Alaska Native Claims Settlement Act of 1971.)

Oh boy. Well, I was one of the few that started it way back in the late '50s. When we started the ANB (Alaska Native Brotherhood) camps north of Yakutat.

But it's a mistake. In one way it's fine because it's given young people an opportunity for an education. And that, in itself, should be enough to satisfy me.

But it's not. It's the Lawyers' Retirement Act, is what it is. And that's what the attorneys all over the West Coast, Washington, D.C., and Alaska call it, laughingly — the Lawyers' Retirement Act. Because there's lawyers, whole firms, that don't do nothing but represent Native corporations and villages. And they wind up with all the money.

And I told 'em not to sign that thing in 1971. I said, "You guys, in 1991 it's designed to self-destruct. You guys won't have nothing. The corporations will be bought out by non-Natives or crooked Natives that will be running them." I said, "They will take control. And you guys will have nothing. Your land will go right down the damn tubes."

Nobody listened to me. Oh man, all they could see was a few bucks on the horizon and signed the act. So I go out to the (Alaska Pacific) University. I watched them sign it.

Sure enough, everything I told 'em was going to happen, happened now.

But nobody remembers me telling them. I screamed and yelled, "Don't sign it." I said, "Sue 'em forever. Tie and lock the land up forever and ever. Tie it up. Don't sign it. Because, you guys, look at the thing. It says 1991. In 20 years, it's done for. Because they can sell it, trade it, give it away, steal it from us — everything. (Snaps fingers.) Just like that.

"And for the resource alone, big corporations, self-serving companies are going to buy it. Stock! They're going to run up and give you five times what your stock is worth. And you gunna be thirsty for a drink. And you gunna sell your stock. And there goes the whole thing. The land base is gone. Your subsistence lifestyle is done for, everything."

But they wouldn't listen. And see what happened. It's happening now. And everybody can see it in the last couple years. Hell, I knew it then. As soon as they put conditions on it, it was a mistake.

Northern Alaska

William D. (Bill) English is well known in Alaska for his years as a Wien pilot, flying throughout the state's North.

He has become a spell-binding storyteller, recounting many of his experiences as one of the state's early pilots. He is extremely articulate.

One of his most fascinating stories concerns a forced landing near the present-day village of Anaktuvuk Pass. It was 1948 and the people were still living in huts in much the same way their ancestors had thousands of years earlier.

Mr. English's mother was Inupiat and his father was white. He was born in Wiseman, Alaska, a small mining community in North Central Alaska, on January 31, 1923.

He spoke in the home of the interviewer.

William D. (Bill) English

". . . No matter who we are, where we live in the world today, we can sustain a way of life for awhile. But if we are static, the world will pass us by."

My father's family was from California, and fortunately for me he saw the value of an education. And so he insisted that I continue in school. And I'm thankful that he did.

I was born in Wiseman. My mother was from the Kobuk, and she came over to the Interior of Alaska in the days when the Eskimos wandered around the country, searching for food. And so they had, the people she was traveling with, gone up the Kobuk River and eventually over into the Koyukuk, where Wiseman is.

I can remember my first trip to Fairbanks from Wiseman, looking down, flying over Fairbanks, and looking down and seeing people from the air, and such a thing as a car, which I had never seen before. And a bridge, a lot of new things. But I think I was more filled with wonder.

I was quite young at that time. I'm not sure whether I was with my mother or my father when I went to Fairbanks, but undoubtedly I felt safe with whomever I was with and comfortable in that respect. No, I can remember looking down on Fairbanks in wonder.

I was a boy from the village of Wiseman at that time, and I flew in an airplane before I ever saw a car or a railroad, or any of the other modern forms of transportation that existed. So all these things were new to me. But seeing them at a young age, I suppose I didn't regard them as threatening, just with wonder.

Most people are subjected to big changes in their lives, their lifestyles. And their culture's going to be subjected to those changes. It's not just the Native people who are subjected to those changes. As a member of the human race, we're all faced with making decisions on which way the world is going to go.

While the pace of change was slow, say five, six hundred years ago, there was still change.

The one thing that's been different in our lifetimes, and particularly here in Alaska with the economic development that's taken place, that pace of change has stepped up. It's accelerated. Perhaps it's come much too fast for a lot of people to assimilate. It's something that becomes confusing.

My education started in a one-room log-cabin school. I think there were about 10 or 12 students in that school. And grades were from one to eight, so I imagine that in some of the grades there was only one student.

The teacher that I remember was Miss Carpenter, Miss Clara Carpenter. And I remember her with a lot of fondness. I think I was probably one of the students that gave her a bad time. But nevertheless I do recall Miss Carpenter with cherished memories.

I don't know how the Wiseman school of that time would compare to the schooling of today. When I went Outside and started school I don't remember any particular difficulty making the transition. So I suppose, based on that one factor, I could say that my schooling in the early days was adequate enough, at least to go out to an Outside school in Oregon and continue without any problems.

Mostly I remember school as being a fun place to go. I don't remember having to drag myself off to school, so to speak, unwillingly, dreading the day.

Wiseman is a gold-mining town, and when gold was discovered there just before the turn of the century, why, the miners started coming up the Koyukuk River. And Wiseman was established because it was about as far as the river scows could get up in the summertime. And the river was the only reliable means of transportation.

There were too many mountains and hills between Wiseman and Fairbanks, which was about 200 miles away. And, of course, the airplane wasn't flying into Wiseman in the early days. And so the river in the summertime was the only reliable means of communication with the outside world.

The larger steamboats could make it up the Koyukuk River at its mouth to Bettles. But from there freight or passengers had to be transferred to a shallow-draft scow. And the scow was motor-driven, except in the shallow places and in the riffles. And for getting over the riffles the scow had, oh, three or four horses on board.

The horses would be taken off, hitched up, and the scow would then be pulled on over the rough places when the motor could take over again. So although it was only about 80 miles by river, it was quite a journey in itself, just getting that far. But Wiseman was just about as far as the scows could go, and it was just about centrally located in the areas where gold was being found.

So it developed as more or less of a hub for the gold-mining activities that took place around there. The Natives arrived on the scene. My mother came over from the Kobuk, up the Kobuk River, and then into the Alatna, which flows into the Koyukuk.

And that was all country that was used by the Natives at that time for hunting and fishing. And, of course, the Natives were great wanderers in those times. They might stay at a location for a year, perhaps two years. If it was a good fishing location and the fish began to dwindle or be fished out, the Natives would move on to another location. And I think that moving was an integral part of their lives.

And eventually some of those Natives that came over from the Kobuk moved on up the Koyukuk River to Wiseman. Some came from the Yukon. And some came down from Barrow.

The ones that came from Barrow, to me, really were explorers. Anyone who has been up to or seen the North Slope knows it's a long expanse of seeming nothingness. Although there are things there, to the casual eye it might seem as though, especially in the wintertime, like looking at a white sheet that stretches on forever and ever and ever, with no visible means of making a living.

And the Natives that came down from Barrow or the North Coast traveled to Wiseman by dogsled. And so they started out over this vast expanse of nothingness. And, of course, they didn't have compasses. They didn't have modern means of navigation or guidance. Starting out over that on what would be a long, unknown journey must have taken a lot of courage and a willingness to face whatever occurred out there, in the hopes of discovering something. Or just plain curiosity, I suppose, of what was there.

Of course, they would eventually see the Brooks Range. And that, itself, would arouse a great deal of interest. But those Natives travelled probably down the Colville River and possibly up the the Anaktuvuk River, through Anaktuvuk Pass, and then on through to Ernie Creek, which flows into the North Fork of the Koyukuk, and then over some lower passes into the Middle Fork of the Koyukuk, where Wiseman is located.

But it must have been a journey filled with uncertainties. Once they started out and got to the halfway point they probably still didn't know where they were or how far they had to go, or where their next meal was coming from I imagine in a lot of instances.

In flying over that country I feel a sense of pride in seeing and imagining what those people had to go through in order to make such a trip.

As I said, I saw an airplane and flew in an airplane before I ever saw a car, or a train, or a boat — a big boat. And I think that probably from the very first there was something there. I, undoubtedly, was very interested in flying, wanted to fly, made little toy airplanes out of sticks when I was a youngster. So, undoubtedly, the desire was there at a very early age.

My mother, among her friends, spoke the Eskimo language a great deal. And, when I was younger, I could follow the conversation. I didn't speak it as the language I used to communicate. But probably that is the reason, and now I regret not knowing more or forgetting what I did know.

Of course, I took French in high school, too, but I (laughs) know very few words now. And I think it's because of non-use.

But, in connection with my own language, had I stayed in Wiseman or stayed in the village and stayed with my parents, I probably would have retained much more than I have. As I said, my father recognized the value in education. And so, when he left the store business in Wiseman, we went Outside to Oregon, and I started grammar school there.

That was during the Depression. And we ended up on a ranch. One of the reasons for that, I think, is that, and I heard this many times over, the old-timers that were in Wiseman, the miners, universally, when they struck it were going to go Outside — back home, wherever it was. And buy one or two acres and have a cow, a few fruit trees, a few chickens, and settle down and just enjoy life.

And I think my father had the same

dream. He came from California. I never heard him say he wanted to go back to California. But I think he was caught up in this having a little farm and a cow and chickens and few fruit trees. And that was a repeated desire that I heard many times from the miners, what their goal was.

And I think my father was right along with them. So when he felt that he could, that's what he did. He retired. And we went Outside, and it was during the Depression. Instead of a two-acre ranch, we ended up on a 160-acre ranch. And my father didn't know anything about ranching. (Laughs.) And so he found himself involved in all the mechanics of running a ranch. So he had to hire people to do this.

Well, he lost of lot of money. And so it was necessary for my parents to come back to Alaska. And he sent me down to his sister's home in California where I continued my education.

But at that point, well even before that, the intimate contact with the Eskimo language was broken.

After I finished high school I started college, a junior college at the time. I had graduated from high school when I was 16 years old because I was advanced in the early grades. My aunt felt that I was very young and she was correct in her assessment. In high school there were people in their 20s. They were grown men and women, and I was still a boy in many ways.

But, anyway, I started junior college. They felt that it was better for me over in Marin Junior College in Kentfield, California. I graduated from Marin, and then World War II came along.

Another friend and I were taking engineering courses at Marin Junior College, and signed on as engineering aides to come to Alaska. Of course, when this job became available in Alaska, why, I gravitated toward that. And my friend followed me, so to speak.

It was a job with the Public Roads Administration, and we were to work on the Alaska Highway. The War Department apparently wanted another route to Alaska other than the sea lanes, which they thought might be broken or interrupted. So the Alaska Highway was funded.

We left Seattle on a yacht to Valdez. On that boat north in coming across the Gulf we ran into a terrible storm. And almost everyone on the boat was sick. They went below, and I can remember walking by the galley (laughs), and seeing that everything in the galley that the cook was cooking on the stove had come off the stove and was upside down on the floor.

And the poor cook was lying on his back, sliding back and forth in this Mulligan stew of food and slippery stuff that covered his floor. That scene remains with me to this day.

Anyway, the captain of the boat had to put in behind Cape Saint Elias for some shelter. And we stayed there for a couple of days until the storm subsided, and then went on to Valdez.

So, anyway, by the time we had gotten to Valdez, one of the supervisors or managers of the highway project learned that I was from Alaska. Our original job was to go out with survey crews and work on surveying the route. But as soon as they learned I was from Alaska, they ordered me to go up to Fairbanks to report to a certain individual. So I was separated from my friend, Burr, who went out with a survey crew, and I went on to Fairbanks.

And the job they wanted me to do: they were in the process of buying all the equipment that they could lay their hands on in Interior Alaska. They needed drag-lines and bulldozers. And since I was from Alaska, they assumed that I knew a little bit about getting around.

That was the job they put me on. It was a nice job because I had to go out to many places, locate a bulldozer or a cat, and find out from the miner if he was interested in selling the equipment. If he was interested, the Public Roads Administration would send a mechanic out to look at it to see if it was suitable. And if it passed the mechanic's inspection, then Mr. Clarkson, who was the boss up there, would go out and make the deal.

But my job was to locate the equipment, which was fun. It really was. I was able to either drive or fly out to these places in the Interior. The equipment had to be in a position where it could be transported to Fairbanks. And then on down to the highway.

In those days there wasn't much

heavy equipment out far from Fairbanks. Like in Wiseman, for instance, just before World War II, some heavy equipment had just started to come in. The ground — the shallow ground — that the miners in the late 1800s and early 1900s worked was fairly shallow because they were doing it by hand methods.

They were either shoveling the gold-bearing gravel into a sluicebox or sinking a shaft down to bedrock and hauling it out in the wintertime and stockpiling it, and then putting it in a sluicebox in the summertime.

But by the time World War II came along, or before that, the production of gold in the Koyukuk started to dwindle. And there was one outfit that brought in a cat — walked it in in the wintertime from Fairbanks.

It was quite an event in the history of Wiseman and the Koyukuk. I mean it's been done many times since. But that was looked forward to with a great deal of anticipation.

But, anyway, they walked the cat in and they used it in uncovering some marginal ground down on Myrtle Creek. And they were very successful. With that bulldozer they could remove 20 or 30 feet of overburden, get to the gold-bearing gravel, put that through the sluiceboxes and do it on a scale that they were never able to do before.

And so that aroused a lot of interest in getting more heavy equipment into the Koyukuk. And it started to come in. And then World War II started. Well, when World War II started, the younger men left Wiseman, either to go into the service or work someplace else. And, when World War II ended, why, the price of machinery, the price of fuel was so high and the price of gold still low that many of those miners never went back. The younger people either stayed with the jobs that they had or whatever.

Getting back to Fairbanks, my job was within, say 125 miles of Fairbanks, just searching for equipment in those areas where it was accessible. It was an interesting time for me.

Discrimination existed. There's no question about that. I think that one of the things that helped me was I had begun to acquire an education. And I say begun, even though I had had two years of college. In looking back over quite a few years I think my real education began after that. But nevertheless I had some of the tools to work with.

The impact of discrimination, while it probably was there in some instances, was minimal with me. But I knew it existed.

For instance, in the court system in Fairbanks I think it was well known that any Native who was arrested or hauled up for trial in the court system that existed in Fairbanks at that time got much harsher sentences than white people did for the same thing. I think it existed in other ways, too, in hiring.

I spent a couple of years with the Public Roads Administration. World War II was on, and they had virtually finished the highway, and our job was winding down.

Burr and I ended up in the same camp down in Gakona. We spent several months down there, not doing much, doing office work. And at that time we both decided to go into the service. I went to Fairbanks, and enlisted in the Army Air — they called it the Army Air Corps. It was a branch of the Army at the time. And Burr went Outside and enlisted in the Navy.

It was in the middle of the war, I guess. I went in April of 1943, and the war had started in December of '41. I spent the whole war at Ladd Field in Fairbanks.

I was one of a few selected to go before a board to select a candidate to go to West Point from Ladd Field. So I made that choice, and the board selected me to go to West Point. But I didn't know what all the rules were. And after I was selected they said I had to make a seven-year commitment.

Well, I never was enamored with the Army in the first place. (Laughs.) In fact, I can remember going through boot camp, and charging up the hill with a gun with a fixed bayonet on the end of it. And I said, "I will never use this thing." (Laughs.) Those were my own private thoughts at the time, but I certainly wasn't taken with military life.

But, anyway, the seven-year commitment was a formidable thing with me, so I let that go.

In the meantime, I probably would have tried to enlist in the Aviation Cadet Program. And shortly thereafter, before the West Point thing came along, why the aviation cadet program was closed. So I spent my entire military career at Ladd Field.

I started out by running the swimming pool in Fairbanks. That was for two summers, and the rest of the time in the post office. It was a good job, as far as having to be in the military was concerned. But I was happy to get out in '45 after the war ended.

And before I got out — several months — I had started to work part-time for Alaska Airlines. I think it was called Alaska Star Airlines at the time. And I had started taking flying lessons on my own. I had to pay for those. So I was already involving myself in an aviation career.

I used to work for Hutch (pilot James Hutchinson) in the hangar there at Alaska Star Airlines, kind of as a mechanic's helper and general cleaning boy, and taking flying lessons. Of course, there weren't any established flying schools at the time, or anyone involved in instruction. So I walked into the Lee Brothers' office in the Nordale Hotel, and asked them — they had one airplane, a Rear-Wind Sportster — and asked them if I could take lessons.

They were just getting started in business, kind of doing charter work and whatnot. Neil Warren was their pilot. And I guess they were looking for business no matter of what nature, so they agreed to give me flying lessons.

I started in their Rear-Wind Sportster. I kind of think — they've never said this — but I kind of think that they never expected me to stick with it for very long.

But I did, and I soon found myself ready to solo. And this is all something that I've thought about later — that this really presented them with a problem. Here was their only airplane, (laughs) and they had obligated themselves to giving this boy flying lessons, and now he is ready to solo and are we gunna let him take our one airplane out and fly it? (Laughs.)

And so, I think as I see it looking back on it, they started dragging their feet. And that went on for awhile. But they finally relented. They saw the rightfulness of my position. They relented, and I soloed. But that was the end of my career as far as flying with them.

I've been good friends, I'd say, with Richard and Allan Lee. I haven't run into them for a number of years, but I've been good friends with them ever since. And they must have really been agonizing over whether to let me solo.

But then another young fellow and I bought an airplane called an Aeronca-K. It was a two-cylinder, single-ignition plane with a 10-gallon gas tank. It didn't fly very fast, didn't have any brakes, didn't have any tail wheel. It had a tail skid, which acted as brakes.

But, it was very economical to fly. And it didn't cost very much. And Dave and I were both trying to build up hours, and we did.

It was a good airplane just to build up hours in. And we used it just for that purpose. Dave, my partner, was subsequently killed in an airplane crash. Had he lived, I think he would have been.... He was one-quarter Native, Eskimo. Had he lived, I think he would have had a fine career in aviation.

He and his brothers had gone moose hunting. He had two brothers. The three brothers were all moose hunting south of Fairbanks one morning, and they had gotten a moose, and two brothers — Dave was flying — were coming back into Fairbanks the next morning after getting the moose. And Fairbanks was foggy.

There were some communications towers out where Fairbanks International is now located. And they had guy wires. It was a pretty high tower. I forget how high. But they had these wires going out from the top of the tower to the ground. Dave ran into one of those wires. And, of course, the airplane just plunged right into the ground.

And, I was staying with Don Gretzer at the time, who was the one CAA — the forerunner of the FAA. And, of course, he got a call not too long after that. So we went out there, and sure enough, there were Dave and George. Nothing could be done for them.

And it was our sad duty then to tell his mother. I was a good friend of Dave's, and I'd been over there a lot. And when I walked into their home, the phone was ringing. And she had just, she had just started to get up. I walked back to her. And I didn't have to say a word. She knew.

Well, anyway.

But I built up my hours, got my commercial (license), and as soon as I got my commercial, Wien put me to work. Pilots were scarce. That was one thing about my career.

Pilots were scarce in those times, in Alaska. And I had the advantage of being born here and knowing the people. And, also, I did my training in Alaska, and I'd been flying out to these villages already to get experience. And, so that was an advantage.

My low hours — just having gotten the commercial — they probably were concerned about that. So they put me to work. They rented an airplane. And I was out — mail and freight and whatnot — for two or three months.

And not too long after I started that, why, Northern Airways, which was one of the forerunners of Northern Consolidated needed someone to fly co-pilot on a DC-2. Pilots were scarce.

It wasn't like it is today where if you want a pilot you can get one with thousands of hours and lots of experience. Here I was with no experience, but a commercial ticket. So Northern Consolidated needed a pilot on the DC-2, so they hired me. Here I was on an hourly basis for Wien, and I was on an hourly basis for Northern Airways.

The DC-2 is a forerunner of the DC-3, which you've probably heard about. The one notable thing I can

remember about it is the gear had to be pumped up. Modern airplanes today, you have a hydraulic system that raises and lowers the gear. But in a DC-2 you had to hand-pump it up. It was a lot of pumps with the left arm. That's one thing: if you ever flew in a DC-2 and had to do that, you'd always remember having to do it.

It was with Terry McDonald. His run was down to McGrath, Aniak and Bethel — quite a few landings along the way. And I think Minchumina might have been in there, although I'm not sure of that. It was a lot of work — took all day — but I enjoyed it.

But not too long after that, I don't really know what entered Wien's mind, except that maybe we better put this guy on full-time or else Northern Airways might. And pilots were scarce. So that's what they did. A couple of months later, they put me on full-time with a salary.

So I flew around with Wien the rest of the summer there in Fairbanks, and the next spring they sent me up to Umiat to fly a gravity meter in a Cessna-140. A gravity meter is a device that can measure masses under the surface of the earth. And in that way they can tell what the contours of some of these domes are and whatnot.

So I spent all spring and all summer, just doing that — landing every two or three miles on the North Slope. And I got to know it. In fact, talking about intimacy with the terrain, you got to know the significance of twigs and the way that a creek would cut into a riverbank, or the shape of lake. All these things were landmarks, and they eventually loomed as large as a large mountain in your navigation up there. Because there wasn't really too much to go by. So these little features on the earth became significant.

I remember when I went up to Umiat. Sig Wien was there to check me out. So he took me out and told me to fly this way and that way and this way and that way. And then he said, "Okay, take me back to Umiat."

And, of course, I didn't know where I was, really. I was just out there someplace over the tundra. And it was all white — in the wintertime. But there was one significant landmark that you couldn't miss. And that was the Colville River. So if you could remember where that was, and if you could hit the Colville, then you could find Umiat. And that's what he wanted to see: No matter where you were flying around out there — and you might not know where you were, exactly — that you could find your way back to Umiat.

And that was my test with Sig. I guess I passed it, because he turned me loose. And I spent an enjoyable time flying the gravity meter.

For one thing I can remember, there was a wolf. We had landed at one of those sites where we were going to take a reading. And a wolf came up and sat not too far away from us, just watching us. And, of course, I suppose this is something I wouldn't do today, but my culture up to that time had taught me that here was something to be taken. And I didn't have a gun. But I had an ax. And so I was going to go and knock the wolf in the head. (Laughs.)

Well, that didn't work because the wolf was too smart, you know, to let me get that close. It was amazing. And the wolf had a kind of a limp in one of his front legs, anyway. So that may be one reason why he stuck around and watched us. I don't know. But maybe we were so foreign to him out there that he wasn't afraid of human beings at that time. Because certainly anyone with a gun could have hit him pretty easily. He just was sitting there looking at us.

So I started up the airplane, and the fellow that was running the gravity meter and I were going to try to run over him on skis — chasing him around there. And so we went right at him, trying to hit him.

And the wolf, on the first pass he jumped aside. And from then on he realized he could outmaneuver that airplane. So he showed the same non-concern that he was sitting up there watching us. He'd let us come at him, but he'd just simply step aside.

I realized that was fruitless. So I said, "Pete, I'm gunna get that ax ready and I'm gunna get him." The wolf got so he would kind of trot along right beside the airplane underneath the wing, just right there. Yeah, I mean he, you know when we missed him, why, he'd just trot along there. We could probably just go on over the tundra there for miles, and he'd just trot, right there.

And so, I said, "I'm going to get the ax ready." Of course, I had to have a little power on in order to make the airplane move. "With the wolf trotting out there. What I'll do is I'll chop the power, and I'll jump out, and I'll whack (laughing) him."

But he was even too smart for that. So the wolf got away. That's the end of the story. The wolf got away (laughing) without my harming a hair of his head.

But I tried. I really tried. I tried throwing that ax at him, and everything, but I just didn't. So the wolf got away, and I'm not unhappy today that he did. But I suppose if that had occurred around Wiseman or one of the villages that wolf wouldn't have gotten away.

Another instance with an animal happened with a wolverine up on the Slope. I had never seen a wolverine live around Wiseman — or any place in Interior. They're very good at keeping concealed. But they're also a very destructive animal. They can break into a cabin, for instance, and bite holes in all your canned goods. And, if you have meat around, they'll, of course, gorge themselves on that.

But worse than that, they destroy whatever you have. Let's say that you have a quarter of meat or something of that nature. They will come along and eat what they can, and then they'll urinate on the rest of it. And, of course, that destroys it for any other animal or for human consumption.

And so they were really a hated animal in the village, I'd say. Wolverine. Yeah, they were really hated.

When we saw this wolverine we were flying, making our gravity meter stops every two to three miles. We saw this wolverine, right out there on the tundra, in the open. I couldn't believe it because I'd never seen one in the open. In fact, I didn't even know that they were up there. So we landed and we were going to run over him.

And, of course, he was running. Just full out. And we came up behind him. The airplane passed over him. And, as we passed over him I heard this terrified scream from the wolverine. And, if you know anything about wolverines, they never show any fear. They never show any fear of a bear or anything. They're just fearless animals. But this wolverine showed fear.

It was a terrified scream. As though someone were just doing him in. In actuality we never touched him. The plane passed over him. The skis missed him. The propellers missed him. Everything missed him — never touched him.

But just that experience, I guess, terrified that wolverine. He just screamed.

And we could hear that scream inside that airplane. And for some reason, even though it was taught to me that here was an animal that everybody hated, nobody liked, not even any animals in the animal kingdom liked them. And here was a chance to do one of them in. In that instant of revealing his own terror, it did something to me, and, we decided not to go ahead with our plan to try to run over him.

But we followed him for miles on the tundra. Just followed him, watching him run, thinking that well, maybe he'll slow down and just turn and look at us, maybe. But he never slowed down once. He just kept going. This amazing strength and vitality of a wolverine, it was displayed in that, well, it wasn't a race anymore because we were just following him.

But he displayed what a wolverine has — physical characteristics and attributes. It was amazing. He never slackened. Just ran. When we finally took off, why, he was still running.

And I can imagine in my mind, to this day, that that wolverine is still running.

Uh, I guess I have a little different attitude toward wolverines now than I did when I came out of the village. And probably a slightly different attitude toward most wildlife. I think that the Natives view game — all game — as either something to wear or something to eat. And that's part of the culture. Getting back to the North Slope, another experience I had. We caught a loon in a little pond. The ice melts differently. Where there's reeds sticking up through the shallow lakes in the spring-time the sun will melt the ice around that reed. And it might be three or four feet across. And the rest of the ice is still solid, maybe seven, eight feet thick.

And we landed to take a gravity meter reading, and here was this loon, sitting in a little pond over there — three or four feet across. And so, while Pete was taking the gravity meter reading, why, I ran over to that loon.

I really expected him to fly. But he didn't. He dived. And I said, "Well, gee, what's he going to do?" And I stood on the hole, and I could hear him underneath the ice, going off in another direction. I looked over, and here was another hole. And it was quite a ways over. I don't know, 50 or 60 feet or more.

So I went over, and I stood on the edge of that hole. And sure enough, soon the loon came up in that hole. I mean he had maybe done this before, or knew that other hole was there, and had enough sense of direction in order to find it underneath that ice. Because if he couldn't find it, you know, he'd be done for.

So I went and stood on the edge of that hole. And he came up. As soon as he saw me, which was in just an instant, he went back down. And he started over to the other hole. 'Cause I could hear him going underneath the ice. (Laughs.)

So I walked over to the hole, and I stood on the edge of the ice. When he came up, there I was again. So, back down he goes. And not time enough to take a breath. I mean they can stay down for a long time. So we did this. We repeated this thing several times, just going back and forth.

And, finally, the loon ran out of breath. He could not — the last trip — he just barely made it, apparently. So when he came up, and I was standing there, he must have said to himself, "To hell with it." (Laughs.) 'Cause he just sat there with his bill open like this, going ... (Breathes hard.) So we sat there — eyeball to eyeball — looking at each other while he was catching his breath.

But that was another little experience that I remember up there. Because I've never been so close to a loon in my life, either. I've seen them out on lakes, maybe 100, 200 yards away, you know, calling, and whatnot. But, not eyeball to eyeball with a loon.

One other interesting experience I can remember is, it was the end of the summer season, and I was told to bring an airplane on floats back to Fairbanks. And so I started out from Barrow to Fairbanks. And when I got into the Brooks Range, why, there were snow squalls and snowstorms there. And it got pretty bad.

And I'd already passed Chandler Lake, just west (26 miles) of Anuktuvuk Pass, on the way. I was trying to get into the John River. And I couldn't do it. So I had to turn around and go back. I didn't want to go all the way back to the Colville. So I decided I'd go to Chandler Lake and land and wait for the snowstorm to subside. It was already starting to get dark. I would have had to stay there all night.

But, anyway, I did turn around. And went back to Chandler Lake. And I was looking for a place to land because the wind was blowing. It's a big lake — and the waves were pretty high. And I was kind of apprehensive about landing in those big waves, unless I found a sheltered spot. Well, in looking around, I flew over this small Native village there, right on the shore of Chandler Lake. And so, I decided that that was where I was going to land.

And there was kind of a smooth spot there in the water, relatively smooth. I landed there, and I was still maybe 150, 200 feet from shore, taxiing around because the shoreline was very rocky — fairly large rocks and boulders. And I was trying to — in the growing darkness and the snow and the wind and the waves — trying to find a place to park the airplane on floats so it wouldn't get battered by the wind and the rocks.

And I could see the people on shore, watching. They knew I had landed because they heard me when I flew over. They were watching. And I was taxiing around out there, and all of a sudden I ran on to a sandbar that was underneath the surface of the water. And I was stuck out there, you know 150, 200 feet from shore, I guess it was. And I put the power on. It wouldn't move. And I put the power off, and hoped the wind would get me off. And I tried to rock it back and forth. Nothing.

I was stuck. And it was cold. The water was cold. I could see that. And the waves. And, I thought, "What am

I going to do now? Just what am I going to do?"

And I sat there thinking. And, I'll be darned. Pretty soon I looked out at the shore. And here were two men. They were walking out toward the airplane. And it was windy with waves. What they were walking on was a narrow sandspit that I had run into. But there was a narrow sandspit they were walking on — out to help me.

And if they had fallen off — I mean they didn't have a boat or anything else. And I would guess that they didn't know how to swim. They were really risking their lives to go out there.

Anyway, they got to the airplane. And they pushed me off the sandbar. And told me where to go. So we went in and parked, and secured the airplane. And then one of them introduced himself to me. It was Frank Rullund. He said he was a cousin of mine. And so Frank invited me to stay in his hut. I gladly accepted, because it was, boy, it was cold out there. And it was fine with me. I was happy.

And the huts that the Eskimos of Chandler Lake lived in — now these were still nomadic peoples. They were really the last of the people that lived a nomadic life. This was in 1948. They had very little contact with the outside world. They had truly a subsistence lifestyle. There was very little money exchanged. They had no money at the village. But Sig would stop by there once in a while on his flights to Barrow. And maybe pick up some furs, take

them into Fairbanks, sell them. And then they'd buy ammunition, tobacco. And that was about it.

But they really lived off the land. They were camped along the shores of Chandler Lake because Chandler Lake provided the fish that they wanted. There were sheep in the mountains. And there were caribou that came by there. So they had a good site for the time being. These same people, subsequently, started the village at Anaktuvuk Pass. And they're living over there now. But they have permanent dwellings now. So it's a permanent village. They have an airstrip and a school, post office.

But, at that time, there were just these skin huts. And they made the huts by tying willows together, and then looping the willows in a half-circle, putting the ends into the ground, or sticking them down into the ground. And doing this all the way around, maybe with 20 of those loops, tied together. So you had a dome, sitting on the tundra. And then over that dome they would lay the caribou skins — a layer or two of the caribou skins.

And then, of course, inside they had a little stove. Their stove was about the size of a five-gallon gas can. If you know what that is — not very big, maybe 15 to 18 inches long, something like that, maybe 10 inches by 10 inches. Little door on the front, small stove pipe.

And the reason for that was that there was no wood, no wood in the vicinity. It's all barren, very barren.

Now one of the impressive things here that we think nothing of — when we want heat in the house or to cook a meal — is to go turn a switch. And we have heat. But these people, in order to sustain their lifestyle, had to go 60 miles, with a dogsled — in the wintertime — in order to get fuel for the fire.

And that 60 miles was down to the Colville River, where they would cut willows. There were not trees. They'd cut willows and bring them back. So they used this very sparingly. It was as though it were a, well, it was a commodity, but a very precious one.

I don't know what you would compare it to, but you might imagine yourself in some remote location for 10 years, with a limited supply of a medicine that you needed. And you would ration it. And so they were very careful about the use of the wood that they had to go down to the Colville to gather.

Anyway, we went to Frank's dwelling. And it was actually quite cozy inside. It was Frank and his wife and two children, and two dogs and myself. And the hut was probably 12 feet across, something like that. It wasn't very big. But it was cozy. I was surprised at how well I slept, with the storm raging outside, how warm I was. I had my own sleeping bag.

And his wife fixed a dinner of the meat along the, the tenderloin, I guess it is. Yeah, she fried up some tenderloin, and mixed up a mixture of flour — kind of like a biscuit mixture, which I don't imagine that they did all the time. That was just because I was there, probably. Yeah, I was company.

And it was all very tasty. And I enjoyed my stay there with my cousin. And, actually, looking back on it from this point in time, it was a privilege. You couldn't find a like situation again. Because their life has changed. Their life is — for whatever reason, in some cases they have opted to change it because of some of the modern conveniences they've seen, they wanted.

But I remember that experience at Chandler Lake with people who lived in the skin huts. And they still carried on the old, nomadic way of life. And it's about as close a picture to, perhaps life that existed maybe two or three or four or five hundred years ago. Yes. Because there was very little change, I believe, in the way of the life of the Natives before the white man came. Because they had established a method of existing in very harsh environment.

(Mr. English discusses his feelings about the Alaska Native Claims Settlement Act of 1971.)

I think in selecting the corporate form, it was one of many that were considered. How can anyone at this point say that it's really good or bad? In the case of CIRI, CIRI has been very successful. And, in the case of Bering Straits, they've been very unsuccessful. And I suppose you could derive two different and very strong opinions from people who belong to both corporations.

And I think there are people within

CIRI who would prefer that it be administered differently. There are people who would like to see the land divided up. There are people who would like to see all the money used for cultural purposes, for health and welfare. So there are divergent opinions as to how these resources are to be used.

I think that as long as we're a part of America — a part of Alaska — we are really not a society unto ourselves. We are part of a larger picture.

I don't think we can take a purely provincial view with anything that's been granted to us or anything that we have now — and say, "This is mine alone. We're going to use it for our benefit alone." I don't think we can do that and be successful.

No matter who we are, where we live in the world today, we can sustain a way of life for awhile. But if we stay static, the world will pass us by.

So the preservation comes in say, art, the art form, or museums and things. But if there's a better way, and I think that this is evident, well, ever since I've been flying. You can go back to the dog team. Where are the dog teams today? Because the Native people themselves see that there's a better way. Or, they feel that it's a better way.

Now there are people out there running dogs. But they're running dogs more for the fun, for the sport. But they're not running them because it's an economically feasible thing to do. It was in the old days.

And, to me, it's good if you can take the good from another culture and use it. If there's something good in our culture that another culture wants to use, fine. But to freeze a way of life at a certain period of time, I don't think is possible.

Who knows? At one time you might have a whale. And the village is wealthy at that point. And another time you might have a lot of fish or a lot of caribou. But you would adapt to that change as it comes along.

I'd never quite thought of it in that way. But, yes. The Natives were living on the edge of nonexistence most of the time. It was feast or famine, I think, many times with all the other hazards, weather and terrain that they were presented with.

I think the Native who looks down the road very far can see that the Natives are very few in number. Their society is small compared to the society which surrounds the Native society. And it's inevitable that the larger society is going to have a great impact on how the Native population lives. In my own mind, there's no question about that.

Laura Beltz Hagberg Wright is an energetic woman who looks much younger than her years. And she always has a ready — and beautiful — laugh.

Mrs. Wright, who was born on October 8, 1908, is part Pennsylvania Dutch and part Eskimo. She was born in Candle, a former gold-mining community in Northwestern Alaska.

Mrs. Wright has owned and operated her own business making parkas for many years. She is well known throughout Alaska for her talents. Today, she lives in Anchorage, after having sold her business to a relative.

She spoke in her home, recounting many of the happy and sad times she has experienced.

Laura Beltz Hagberg Wright

". . . I sold my business to my granddaughter and her husband . . . I'm trying to retire. But I can't, I don't know what I'd retire to."

My name is Laura Wright. My maiden name was Laura Beltz. And I married a Swede. His name was Albert Hagberg. And he passed on, and so I married five years later to Dallas Wright from Coeur D'Alene, Idaho.

So I guess I'm supposed to tell you more about my life when I was a kid. I was born in Candle, Alaska, in 1908 — October 8.

My mother was full-blood Eskimo. And my dad was Dutch. Pennsylvania Dutch. He came up during the Gold Rush in 1897. He came up with the horses. He was always with the horses.

A lot of them died on the way. He climbed the Chilkoot Pass at the same time when they carried the piano over that Chilkoot. He used to tell me all these stories. I paid no attention to them. Wished I had now! And then he went clear up to Nome. Walked. He walked.

My dad — he was a prospector. And he cooked on the dredges. They had gold dredges. And he was a teamster. And he hauled freight and took care of the horses. During the winter he would be a jailer.

My mother — in the summertime she had a fishnet she made by herself and would set the net up the river a little ways, about a half a mile from Candle. You can see the net across there and when the fish are jumping we'd go up there in our boat and take the fish out of the net. I was about seven or eight years, and I'd go around town peddling fish (laughs).

My mother was a very hard worker and took care of us kids. Boy, she would never let us come to the table without making us say a prayer. And never allowed us to talk at the table. Just kept quiet and ate our meals.

When I was a child, being raised in a white community in Candle, there were about a dozen families where the Eskimo women were married to white men. And their families were accepted. All the families were accepted into the white community and joined in with everyone there. And there was no conflict between the Native women and the people there. Everybody got along.

When the Eskimos came in from Buckland, Deering — Deering was a mining community also — and Kotzebue and all the northern towns and villages — they all worked. All those Eskimos. They were pretty well educated.

The Eskimos were very industrious. All of them owned their own reindeer — two or three thousand head of reindeer. And they took care of them with the Lapland dogs. They'd have their reindeer roundup and corral them and butcher them and took very good care of the reindeer.

Even my grandfather — his name was Egokpuk. He was a well-known trader amongst all the Eskimos. And he'd go to Nulato and the Yukon and trade with the Indians.

Then he'd go back and he'd go up to Point Barrow and trade. At that time my grandfather had a lot of wives — all along wherever he traveled. His real wife — my grandmother — was Niggloo-ruk. And she was from Selawik.

My mother was born in Selawik. And my grandfather was always traveling. He was a huge fellow — handsome and well dressed. He had fur clothes on.

I have never seen anyone dress so pretty with furs as he was. And all the old Eskimos remember him. They said he had lots of wives. This old Eskimo would remark, "And they'd take him back, even when he had other wives!" I'll never forget that expression.

And then his wife divorced him — in their way. I don't know how she divorced him. And then she married again to a Foxglove. And they had two sons. We went up to visit them in 1917-18, during the First World War.

I remember he had holes on each side of his lower lip — my step-grandfather. And I was scared to death of him when we visited Mom's mom. And he had these Worcestershire caps — those glass caps from the Worcestershire bottles. And he'd stick them in there. That was stylish. He'd put them on each side where he had the holes on each side of his lower lip. And I was scared of him! I couldn't get over that.

In 1916 and '17, my mom used to take us up to visit her old friend. She must have been pretty close to 90 years old at that time. And she lived in a little igloo. Not snowhouse. No! They never lived in those snowhouses.

It was an igloo where they built it with sod. And way up the river from Candle. She had a little cabin on the river bank and she burned willows for her wood. And her little house was so warm. Mom always went up there to visit her. Her name was Foster. The last name was Foster, but I don't remember her Eskimo name.

She used to tell stories. Every time we'd go there us kids would follow Mom with the dog team, about five or six miles from Candle. We'd go there and she'd cook a pot of rice with raisins in it. And that's what us kids thought were so great! We're going up to see Dick Foster's mother.

She was white-haired. A little white-haired old woman. Very old. And she used to tell us that when she was a young girl, over in Buckland, the Indians and Eskimos fought. They had war. The Indians came there. She got so scared because they take the women, steal the women. She said she'd run out into the Buckland River, down into the bay between Candle and Kotzebue.

And she went out into the deep water and took a blade of grass. She'd go under the water and breathe with that stem. She'd stay out there until their fighting was done. She said that's true. Eskimos are still scared of the Indians. These are the old, old Eskimos ... Fear. But the younger generation — we're all mixed in together. We have no problems.

But they have a place near Kaltag, this side of Unalakleet. They call it the battlegrounds, where they fought. If all this is true, I don't know. And in those days they couldn't dig down to bury their dead people in their graves. So they built a box out of lumber and put four legs on it. And had it in the air.

And that's where they stayed — in those boxes.

We used to peek in those boxes and just see nothing but hair (laughs) and cloth and bones. Us kids were curious. And then the boards would warp, and you could peek in and see in the cracks.

Candle was a thriving gold-mining town, smaller scale than Nome at that time. I remember all about a lot of people and what was going on there in Candle. We had five stores. And there were five saloons.

And they had a big hospital. They had a blacksmith shop. Of course, they had a lot of horses in town. They did all the hauling and freight. And there was a tinsmith's shop where they made smokestacks and all kinds of things that were needed for homes.

They had four or five restaurants. They had a Japanese restaurant there and a Chinese laundry. And they had a barber shop and a candy store. They had a judge's mansion. And a marshal. And a jail. And they had a bowling alley. It was made of wood. And you could hear the bowling balls rolling down the wooden — whatever — troughs.

And they had wooden sidewalks. And they had two large horse barns, which kept the horses.

One thing I will say about Candle — they had everything there but a church. I was never raised where there was a church.

They had Mrs. Perkepile who had a Sunday school in Candle. And that's the first time that I went to a little place where they had Sunday school. A lady had it in her home. They were from the States. She had a big family.

We used to fly kites, back in 1913-14. Big kites. And they'd celebrate the midnight sun up there every summer. All the people from Candle would go down to the sandspit on the boats — on that big stern-wheeler. They'd have a big celebration.

All the freight was sent up in big steamers. They came by Dutch Harbor from Seattle and Tacoma, and on to the coast of Alaska and went into Kotzebue. And before they got to Kotzebue they'd stop off there near the sandspit about 10 miles from Candle — from the ocean. And then they'd have a river boat haul all the freight and mining equipment.

Mining had been going full blast since 1900. And that's the time they had the Tent City in Nome. That's where my mother met my dad. She was housekeeper for Judge Noyes at the time he met her. And then they went to Candle and got married by Judge Campbell.

They had all kinds of entertainment that kept people from getting cabin fever. And they had beautiful homes up there. Mahogany. And they had maple furniture. And rugs, tapestries. So pretty. And they had just as nice a place as anywhere.

They had a nice school. They had a public school, and teachers came in from the States and taught school.

They had about 35, 40 children going, maybe more.

And the people — they had vaudeville shows. They had masquerades. They had all kinds of goings on. And then at Christmas time they had all kinds of entertainment. They paid attention to children. They gave them all kinds of gifts.

There was a lot of money flowing from gold mining there in Candle. And most of the stores were run by Jewish people. And it was really nice. They had the Laplanders there. Their home was right in the middle of town. They had a great big huge building where they hung all their reindeer harnesses all around the inside of the interior of the building. And a big pot-bellied stove right in the middle of the building.

All the Laplanders had their reindeer nearby, and they kept the whole town — it was quite an industry — selling carcasses of reindeer meat to the whole town.

And that's what we lived on besides all the canned foods from the States that the boats brought up. Then they had the root cellars, which kept the potatoes, oranges and apples and onions and all that perishable stuff across the river.

And the oranges were real tasty and sweet by March and April. By that time they were getting a little bit soft. Us kids would always watch when they started throwing those oranges out on the river on the Kiwalik River on the ice. And we'd all run out there and take all those oranges home. And they were just sweet, really good by that time. And the eggs were good until then. Then they would start getting ripe (laughs).

But we lived good up there. And people were just great. And most of the older people were out there skating on the Kiwalik River right in front of town. And then they'd slide down the hillside on big toboggans. The old people, oh, everybody, joined in and did all this.

In Candle, with their Eskimo wives, these white guys, they'd go up the Kiwalik River in the springtime by dog team. And then when the breakup comes and after the ice goes out, all these men had their rafts built. Three tiers of wood — timber ... And they had three rafts, each family. One for the dogs, one for the kitchen, one for the bedroom. Tents, where they slept.

Then, they'd tie down their rafts at a nice camping spot, after they'd build the rafts. And then they were going down on the high water — takes them into Candle. And that's how we had our wood for the whole winter. They'd sell some of it. People wanted it ... And there was reindeer on the hillside. They had all the meat they wanted. We had roasts and steaks, everything, good.

Like that movie — "The African Queen" ... Our rafts were big and we came down on the high water. And that's how we had our wood for the winter, besides coal.

I worked in this restaurant when I was 10 years old for Mrs. Smith, an Irish lady. That's where the rich gold miners ate. They had mirrors all around the dining room in this ritzy restaurant where I worked.

On their table they had linen table-cloths, linen napkins, cut glass bowl in the middle of the big long table full of fruit — oranges and apples. And silverware. Everything was just rich people. That's what these gold miners ate on ... I'll never forget that.

First World War in Candle — propaganda on every building about Berlin and Germany and children piled up like cord wood. Starving to death!

That's all I could see all over Candle. All that stuff was hanging on the buildings. And I was so scared the Germans were coming into Candle to shoot us. A little kid. I was small. It was scary. We had all that up there. And I thought that we were going to be like that, too.

They didn't allow them to talk German. And if they heard anybody talking German in Candle they were arrested. They wouldn't allow that. I'll never forget that. Candle was big town.

During the War, the First World War put a damper on gold mining in Candle and all parts of Alaska. Everything ran down and it was never the same. People left for the States. They made their stake. And lots of them moved out of Candle.

And then in 1918 they had a big flu epidemic in Nome, which killed most of the Natives there. But Candle did not get it because it takes about two weeks for a dog team to get to Candle. And by that time, it was gone. And at that time they had a cabin about two or three miles away from Candle up on the hillside where the mail carriers were. They'd have 15, 16 dogs, 500 pounds of mail every two weeks that would come from the States and Nome.

The mail carriers had to leave that mail — all that mail — in that cabin. And they had food and dog food — everything for him — while he was there. And he unloaded his mail there. They had a bed for him and everything.

And then he'd take our mail and take it on. And while that mail that he delivered was in that cabin, they fumigated it before it was delivered into the Post Office in Candle. They were very careful about anybody coming in. And so that way even every letter was fumigated before they opened it. And we did not get the flu in Candle.

And they had their own dog teams in Candle in those days before the airplanes. There was one car — one Ford that came into Candle in the 1920s. That was the first car we ever saw. A Ford. I got a picture of it, too. (Laughs.)

They had telephone service at that time from Candle to Nome. And all the telephone poles were wired, clear to Nome. And that's where you see a lot of ptarmigan flying. They'd hit the wire. And all these foxes and animals would go along the telephone line and eat ptarmigan. (Laughs.)

Candle was quite a prosperous town. People would flock in from all over the world — from Europe — everywhere. They were there in Candle. And they had a stern-wheeler boat with a paddle wheel that came up the river, the 10 miles from where the big boats landed from Seattle ... We'd all run down to the water front and watch this big boat coming in with the paddle wheel.

And here there were women dressed in bustle skirts, bonnets tied with ribbons. High-heeled shoes. Button shoes. And tight corsets. They had narrow waists. And they looked so beautiful. Everybody was welcoming them in. Men, waiting for their wives and sweethearts. Everybody was just all excited.

And then they'd give a big dance. They'd have dances about three times a week. They had a big hall. And they had music — by the piano, banjo, mandolin, violin and guitars. And everybody joined in. Everybody had fun. There was always something going on.

They always served their liquors. But they had the saloons. The townswomen were not allowed in the saloons. Only the dance-hall girls. And they had spittoons everywhere in there. Kept up really nice. I used to peek in the door. Every time someone goes in there, there I am, looking to see what it looked like.

They had two-story homes. And they were built really pretty — painted up real nice. I remember when my brother and I used to go into the garbage dumps and look for men's pants. Because they had gold money.

The twenty-dollar gold pieces were the size of a dollar. And a ten-dollar gold piece was the size of a fifty-cent piece. And the five-dollar gold pieces were the size of a quarter.

And we'd always look when they'd throw those pants away. We'd run over there in the garbage ... We'd look in the pockets. And we'd find gold money (laughs). We got smart and that's how we always had show money!

We had silent movies at that time where they'd show Charlie Chaplin, Fatty Arbuckle and all these old movies. My dad used to tell us kids, "If you want to go to the movies, you go out and pick a pot of berries." Blueberries. And we did. We'd go and sell them — fifty cents a bucket. And that's how we learned ... whenever we wanted something we had to work for it.

Any time that any crime was committed, they'd give them a blue ticket and 24 hours to get out of town. That's how they did it. If they don't there was a marshall and dog team and everything to ship them to Nome. They'd ride on the dogsled — tie them down.

And whenever there's an insane person or a prisoner, they'd put them in a strait jacket — put them in the sled in a reindeer sleeping bag. They'd take them all the way into Nome. They'd have a matron or a caretaker — a man or a woman — and they'd have a marshall and a dog team. There's at least three on that dog team. Take them

into Nome — to jail. Or hospital.

It was tough in those days. And they had to stop in all the different towns. It takes about two weeks to get into Nome, traveling by dog team.

And there was one woman from up north that got loose out of the strait jacket. And she got out of there and ran — bare feet — towards the ocean. Bare feet in the snow! All kinds of funny things happened.

(Years later) there was one man and a woman got into a fight in an airplane. And she was always drinking ... I forget the name of the pilot ... And she opened the door of the plane, and she was going to jump out. And he was hanging on to her, same time driving and trying to hang on to her.

And then the other passenger was trying to hang on to her, too. She was hanging out. And they were holding her arm, and she wanted to jump out of the plane. They said they flew around and flew around. And they found a soft spot in a snow bank. Soft snow, that's what they found. And they let her go. And she lived! (Laughs.)

We had seven (children) in our family. I'm the second oldest of the seven. I had five brothers and one sister. And all my brothers passed on. John, my brother, had a broken back. And he was chewed up by dogs when he was young, and had a plate put into his head.

When he grew up he was a pilot. John who was crippled owned his own airplane (John Beltz Airline) and so did Bert. John passed on with emphysema when he was about 71 years old. Another brother, William Beltz, he was our first state president of the Senate in Juneau. And he had a nice family.

His wife raised the children by herself when he passed on. My sister Hazel is living in Fairbanks right now. Hazel Moneymaker and her nice family. And they're all doing good. She has a lot of grandchildren, too. Like I have. I had six children, and their dad died when they were young.

Oh, I better go back to my family again. Bert was a pilot. Bert Beltz. And his wife Fredrica in Kotzebue. And they had five children. And Laura (their daughter) was married to Neil Bergt. And she passed on in Hawaii.

And Tom, he was married to Ruth Kern. And he passed on. They have five children. He died in Hawaii. He served in the Second War in Attu.

My youngest brother, Harry Beltz, was married. And they had 12 children. And a drunk driver was going along the road while Harry, my brother, was on the stop sign, ready to cross. And this drunk driver hit him and killed him. So we had a lot of hard times.

And then my little brother ... We moved to Haycock from Candle. My dad got a job over there in 1921. And we went there near the breakup time. Two weeks later, the ice went out on this stream. And he and my brother John fell in with the ice. And he drowned.

And the whole town stopped working at noon to look for his body. They couldn't find it. They had hooks and everything to see if they could get him. And then finally this one old fellow, George Leonard, noticed all of us running along the creek bank and yelling.

We didn't know exactly too much about the town that we moved to. And so this George Leonard told us that there's a dam down there, a little ways. So we ran down there, followed him. And he grabbed my brother John by the hair and got him out before he went down into the dam.

It was too late to grab my brother Albert down in the middle of the stream. They hunted all over the creek bank, clear down from Number Six Bench. All the claims were numbered. And so, this fellow saw his hand moving. It was above the water line.

He was caught in that dam on a nail. His clothes, I guess, hung on there. My dad took him home, and we all followed. And then my mother, she had a nervous breakdown from all this. And slept on his grave every night during the summer. And she would not come home until about four or five o'clock. And that's all I could hear — her crying. Cry, cry.

She was never the same after that. That's when we moved from Candle to Haycock. So then I had to take over the whole household when I was 13 years old. Cooked for my dad. Took care of the kids from then on. Until I got married. I married Albert Hagberg on my 18th birthday.

I only finished the seventh grade

because I had to take care of the others.

Then I thought — I took care of kids all my life. I thought, "Now, I don't want any more kids." But I had six! (Laughs.) And I'd never part with them, neither!

Now with all my six children, Bob Hagberg; Bud Hagberg; Babe — they call her Babe, her name is Laura; and Tekla — Albert Hagberg came from Sweden, and gave her a Swedish name; and then Muriel — she was Miss Alaska in 1953 in Fairbanks and one of the top finalists in the Miss Universe contest; and then there was Einer Hagberg, my youngest boy.

And then when I was a child, we kids, never had measles. We didn't have chicken pox. We didn't have any whooping cough — no children's diseases because we traveled by dog team. And it takes a long time.

When my children were growing up in Haycock, 60 miles from Candle, they caught every disease that children have. Because the airplanes brought it in. And I caught every child's disease with them. And it was hard. Especially the mumps and the measles. Ah, it was tough. We were all sick. And we had to keep our windows darkened. And the children's dad had to take care of us. It was just like a little hospital. (Laughs.)

Before the Second War, I was hauling mail by dog team. I had the contract from Alaska Airlines. That was back in 1939-40. And I had to get that mail. The airplane was leaving Nome. And I'd get the mail down to Dime Landing. They couldn't land up in Haycock. The landing field was covered with snow. And so they had to land down on the river.

And I told the kids, I said, "Now I'm going to deliver the mail because the plane is leaving Nome. And I have to get down there. I'm going on skis." I had to ski seven miles with the First Class mail on my back. And I told the kids, "If I don't get back tonight ..."

I told them what to do ... My oldest son — 13 years old — he took care of the family. They helped me. They knew how to work, did everything around the home. They'd bake cookies. And they made root beer. And they did everything, take care of the house when I'm gone.

So I skied. There were three big hills I had to climb. And the last hill, when I got to the top ... I stuck my ski pole into the snow and rested. And I heard a wolf barking at me, down in the gully, to the right of me. It was pitch dark.

Oh, I just hightailed it down that hill as fast as I could. When I got down to the bottom of that hill, I felt like that wolf was ready to bite me! (Laughs.) And I fell down. And the house was just right near. I got to the house. So I got there and it was pitch dark, not a moon, no star, and I got down there.

But then, during the War, a sergeant came up there named Muktuk Marston. They were forming the Alaska Territorial Guards. And Governor Gruening was there. He said, "Give her a gun." To me.

So Muktuk Marston handed me a 30.06 from World War I. That's what we all had. And we had to practice shooting, lying down and on our knees and standing. Targets, all along. And I won the contest. Forty-nine out of fifty was my score. And the reason I didn't get the perfect score: I shot at that one target twice.

Because I hauled mail by dog team, Governor Gruening said, "Give her a gun." And the Japanese were all around us up there. We had blackouts. We didn't dare have the blinds. We had to have black curtains. Not a speck of light was to show. And that's what the whole town there in Haycock had to do.

When I came here to Fairbanks, Governor Hickel was the governor then, and Muktuk Marston and General (Conrad S. "Nick") Necrason gave me a medal. There 'tis.

And I watched for those airplanes. I was scared because traveling on the snow, they could see my dog team. I was scared and I was always so glad when I neared that bridge. If I could get down underneath there. (Laughs.) That was funny. I wouldn't have time for nothing.

We moved to Fairbanks in 1943. And we were gold mining. But gold mining had sort of subsided since the war. Everything kind of went down. We moved to Fairbanks and had a hard time finding a home there during the war. There were soldiers looking for places to live.

And that's when they were trans-porting these airplanes from the States to Russia. They were coming in forma-tion ... They'd stop in Fairbanks. The Russians were just thick there in Fair-banks. They'd stop off at Nome and then right on to Russia with all the airplanes.

Then when I moved to Fairbanks from Haycock by airplane, I finally found an old house — a two-story house. We finally got the place all cleaned out. And I fumigated it. And used disinfectant and everything else on the whole inside. And then I wallpapered the whole house and got linoleum and got that taken care of. And got the doors fixed and cleaned up everything. That's when we started trying to live. (Laughs.) With six kids it wasn't too easy.

But we finally got settled. Then I got a job, after I got the kids all in school. I finally went around doing housework for all these good, nice homes ... I did housework for others, which kept me going for the kids' pin money, too. Go to the movies or take care of some of their needs.

Then I got a job at Universal Foods out at Ladd Field at that time ... I was a waitress for Universal Foods. And they were going to have a contest amongst all the waitresses. A popularity contest. And they asked me to run in that. I said, "No." I said, "I have six children." I said, "I have no time to run in any contests."

But I was voted in. Well, since I got that many votes, I thought I would run then. And I won the contest. It was a landslide. And I won the trip around the United States and money. And I thought, "Well, I'll just take the money." And I thought I would do that, and then I'd wait for my husband to come in the fall, when he's through gold mining up in Haycock.

And when he did come, he says, "You're going! I want you to go. And I want you to visit my family and my sister back in New York." And I said, "Well, I'm scared to travel. I've never traveled before in my life. I've never left the kids in my life."

And he says, "I want you to go. It's your trip. You deserve it." And I said, "Well, okay." And I said, "I want to travel by train. Because I want to see the country and see what it's like in the States."

And I traveled by train. And I got to New York. And they were right there to meet me — his sister and her husband. And they took me all over New York and seen all the different sights ... They kept me for Christmas and New Year's. They did not want me to leave.

And I tried several times to go and make reservations to go on to Florida. Because it was all paid for. And so I was just getting ready after New Year's to go. And then just before I left I got a telegram: "Dad is ill. Hurry home."

So I thought, "My goodness. He wasn't sick when I left." So I started back. I couldn't finish the trip. I got to Chicago, and we toured the whole city of Chicago and seen all the sights.

And we ended up at Welcome Traveler's Radio Program. Tommy Bartlett's program.

And I was in line. And when I got to the door this lady says, "Oh, where are you from?" I said, "I'm from Fairbanks, Alaska." She said, "Oh, will you wait here a minute, please?" And I said, "Sure."

And I had my fancy fur parkee on and the whole line up of people behind me. And I wondered, "Why did she do that to me?" The door was closed. And I stopped and was thinking. And she said, "Okay, you can come in." And they were busy getting a table for Alaska. They had a table for every state of the Union. And they were busy getting a table for Alaska.

Whoever came from that state sat at that table. They had none for Alaska, so they put me up on the grandstand where they played music. There was another table there with two women from Holland. And I was so glad that I wasn't the only one sitting up there and everybody staring at me. (Laughs.)

They thought Alaska was a foreign country. And they argued with me, and said that, "No, you're wrong there about belonging to the United States." I told them that, "Yeah, we were." (Laughs.) They just couldn't believe that Alaska belonged to them.

Tommy Bartlett himself came over to my table. And he asked me all kinds of questions and I told him that my husband was a gold miner. And I had six children. And I won a trip around

241

the United States. And I got a telegram that my husband was ill, and now I'm on my way back. I couldn't finish my trip.

And then he said, "You come with me. This is no place for you." And I thought, "My goodness, now where's he going to put me?"

He got me up on the stage — a nationwide hookup, microphones all over. And I got up there and they were having more fun talking about Alaska. And I'd answer every one of the questions they asked, even about Dan McGrew.

And I was winning all kinds of gifts on the program. Every time I'd answer a question, I'd get a gift. Pencils and gold pens and sweater sets for the girls. Wrist watches for all the kids. Gold wrist watches. And I won a lot of items. And finally they said, "Here is a bathroom set for your husband when he gets well." And slippers and all kinds of nice things for him. And I said, "Oh, that's nice."

Finally, they said, "Another thing we're going to do for you: We're going to make a telephone call to Fairbanks so you can speak to your husband." And I said, "Noooo!" And they said, "Oh, yes."

I was so happy. So finally they waited, and I waited. And they asked me to come over to where they were all sitting. A lot of people all around the big table. And I went there and we were talking and laughing and having more fun. They were still asking all about Alaska.

And finally they said, "We contacted Fairbanks. And we talked to the doctor. And he said your husband passed away yesterday."

After I was so happy, answering questions all about Alaska, and they told me that, I could not move. I couldn't think. I couldn't move. And I was trying to tell him that he was not telling me the truth. I couldn't even say that. I couldn't talk. I wanted to tell him that he was lying. But I didn't like to say that word.

So, finally, they gave me a beautiful room on the top floor of this big building they were in. I said, "No. I don't want to go to bed. I'm fine." I said, "I gotta go home to my six children. And I gotta go."

And so they got me on the train. They had reservations. I cried all the way across the United States. Stayed in my room. I couldn't eat. I couldn't see people or nothing. They had already made reservations for me on Pan American. And they sent me flowers. And just everything — did everything for me, this radio station.

And then I got to Fairbanks. It was the first week of January after New Year's. It was 65 below, pitch dark, four o'clock in the morning we got into Fairbanks. The cabdriver took me home. I went in there — everything was frozen. No kids. Nobody home. All the neighbors, friends, took the kids and took care of them for me.

And this cab driver, he knew my oldest boy. He said, "Come with me.

C'mon, get out of here." I just went berserk. I went into the bedroom. I thought, "Maybe he's still there." You know, I was goofy.

He took me up to where the kids were. But they were all sound asleep. I wasn't about to wake them up in the morning.

So I said, "I'm going back down to the house. I gotta heat it up. I gotta take care of things and clean it up." So I went back down there. And I chopped some kindling. We were burning coal and wood at that time. And it was pitch dark. But I got some kindling. And I got the fire started and warmed things up and let on like everything was the same as before. You know — warm.

And the kids, they came home. I said, "C'mon, I'm gunna get you kids some breakfast and we'll get things started." From then on we tried to do the best we could.

Finally, the funeral was over. And then finally they got to school and tried to get into a routine. That was in '47.

I had to think of a way, too, to make a living when he passed on. With six kids I had to do something. So I designed a parkee. And I made parkees, and that's how I raised my family. I'm still making parkees, but here in October, 1984, I sold my business to my granddaughter and her husband. And I'm trying to retire. But I can't. I don't know what I'd retire to.

But after my husband died — about four or five years later — I got married to Dallas Wright from Coeur D'Alene, Idaho. And the children all thought he was a great guy, and that would have been half the battle, really, that they liked him.

We got married in '52. And so he passed on three years ago. He died of a heart attack. And he was in the hospital six months in Providence Hospital and then in Virginia Mason Hospital.

And right now with all my children being married, I have 31 grandchildren. (Laughs.)

And in another three years I'll be 80 years old! I am waiting for my 26th great-grandchild.

Our Stories, Our Lives contains a collection of personal experiences and traditional stories told by twenty-three Alaska Native elders — Eskimos, Indians and Aleuts — of the Cook Inlet Region.

The series of interviews was conducted and transcribed by A.J. McClanahan, an Alaskan journalist. Dr. Ron Scollon, a linguist from Haines, Alaska, wrote an historical introduction. He is formerly an associate professor at the University of Alaska, Fairbanks.

1/.7